Advertising and Anthropology

Advertising and Anthropology
Ethnographic Practice and Cultural Perspectives

Timothy de Waal Malefyt and Robert J. Morais

London • New York

English edition
First published in 2012 by
Berg
Editorial offices:
50 Bedford Square, London WC1B 3DP, UK
175 Fifth Avenue, New York, NY 10010, USA

Berg is an imprint of Bloomsbury Publishing Plc.

Library of Congress Cataloging-in-Publication Data

Malefyt, Timothy de Waal.
Advertising and anthropology : ethnographic practice and cultural perspectives /
Timothy de Waal Malefyt, Robert J. Morais. — English edition.
pages cm
Includes bibliographical references and index.
ISBN 978-0-85785-202-1 (pbk.) — ISBN 978-0-85785-201-4 (cloth) —
ISBN 978-0-85785-204-5 (e-book)
1. Advertising—Social aspects. 2. Anthropology.
3. Marketing research. I. Morais, Robert J. II. Title.
HF5821.M26 2012
659.1'042—dc23   2012005581

British Library Cataloguing-in-Publication Data

A catalogue record for this book is available from the British Library.

ISBN 978 0 85785 201 4 (Cloth)
978 0 85785 202 1 (Paper)
e-ISBN 978 0 85785 203 8 (institutional)
978 0 85785 204 5 (individual)

Typeset by Apex CoVantage, LLC, Madison, WI, USA.
Printed in the UK by the MPG Books Group

www.bergpublishers.com

Contents

Acknowledgments

We wish to acknowledge our colleagues and clients who have educated and inspired us throughout our business careers. Many of them agreed to be observed and interviewed; their actions and input informed the essays in this book. In particular, Timothy Malefyt thanks Maryann McCabe as a constant source of illumination who initially introduced him to marketing research at Holen North America (with Steve Barnett, Rita Denny, John Lowe, Vic Russell, and Ilsa Schumacher). Malefyt also thanks Brian Moeran for his constant camaraderie, scholarship, and keen insights; Bo T. Christensen for creative comments; Ciara O'Connell from Campbell Soup Company for her discussion at the 2009 American Anthropological Association Meeting; and William O. Beeman as an inspirer and fellow artist. Malefyt acknowledges, from BBDO, Martyn Straw, Tracy Lovatt, and Sheron Davis, and at Underdog Films, Elaine Epstein. Malefyt also thanks his wife, Monica Pons, and family for bearing through it all, and Louise Lohr Malefyt as a source of inspiration and encouragement. Robert Morais appreciates the sharp eye and mind of his wife, Jane Morais, along with her encouragement, and the profound influence of his children, Daniel and Betsy, on his worldview. We also want to mention the kind staff of the Park Café in New York, who permitted us to linger over lunchtime Greek salads while we discussed the content and structure of this book.

We want to express our thanks to the reviewers of our book proposal and the draft manuscript for their suggestions. We are especially grateful to many staff at Berg and their partners who helped bring this book to publication: Kathryn Earle, Anna Wright, Noa Vazquez, Ian Buck, Sophie Hodgson, Tiffany Misko, Adam Yeldham, and Michael Solomons.

Occasionally, we identify the brands we have worked on and clients we have served; in several instances, we elect to describe our examples more broadly in categorical terms. Our decisions were based on whether there was a need to preserve client confidentiality.

Some of the essays that appear in *Advertising and Anthropology* were adapted from work previously published or presented at conferences. All of the following works were revised significantly before appearing in this collection.

Advertising Meetings and Client Relationships: Robert J. Morais (2007), "Conflict and Confluence in Advertising Meetings," *Human Organization*, 66/2: 150–59.

Rituals of Creativity in Advertising Agencies: Timothy de Waal Malefyt and Robert J. Morais (2010), "Creativity, Brands, and the Ritual Process: Confrontation and Resolution in Advertising Agencies," *Culture and Organization*, 16/4: 333–47.

Fieldwork in Advertising Research: Timothy de Waal Malefyt (2009), Paper presented at the American Anthropological Meetings in New Orleans, Louisiana, November.

Advertising Emotions: Timothy de Waal Malefyt (2007), "From Rational Calculation to Sensual Experience; The Marketing of Emotions in Advertising," in H. Wulff (ed.), *The Emotions: A Cultural Reader*, Oxford, UK: Berg.

Creativity, Person, and Place: Timothy de Waal Malefyt (2011), Paper presented at Creative Evaluative Practices Workshop Program, Copenhagen, Denmark, September.

Advertising, Automobiles, and the Branding of Luxury: Maryann McCabe and Timothy de Waal Malefyt (2010), "Brands, Interactivity, and Contested Fields: Exploring Production and Consumption in Cadillac and Infiniti Automobile Advertising Campaigns," *Human Organization*, 69/3: 252–62.

Business Anthropology Beyond Ethnography: Robert J. Morais (2010), "Anthropologists and Business: Through the Looking Glass," *SfAA News*, 21/3: 5–8.

Hybrid Research Methodologies and Business Success: Robert J. Morais and Timothy de Waal Malefyt (2010), "How Anthropologists Can Succeed in Business: Mediating Multiple Worlds of Inquiry," *International Journal of Business Anthropology*, 1/1: 45–56.

Preface

Advertising Anthropologists: The Case for Observant Participation

Once upon a time, advertising was an insignificant trade. For the most part, ordinary people either were unconscious of or ignored advertising because it played no part in their everyday lives. The explosive growth of the advertising industry that accompanied the equally marked development of capitalism during the twentieth century, however, did two things in particular. On the one hand, it made people aware of the numerous new products that were coming onto the market while reminding them of the continued existence of old ones. On the other, it led to cries of "Foul!" Advertisements *made* us buy things that we didn't want or need. They not only persuaded; they also *insinuated* in all sorts of ways—that we had bad breath, that our clothes weren't clean enough, that we had "BO." Advertising promised to help us re-attain that state of grace from which, perforce, we had first been removed in disgrace.

Although social criticisms of advertising have been around more or less since the day the industry came into being, less attention has been paid to *how* people in the industry go about their jobs, what it is they do, or try to do, why they do so, and who precisely is responsible for which part of all the work that goes into the creation of an advertising campaign. This is what *Advertising and Anthropology: Ethnographic Practice and Cultural Perspectives* is all about.

For many decades, the scholarly study of advertising was confined, so far as I am aware, to one authoritative business history: Ralph Hower's masterly and detailed archival account of the rise and expansion of the U.S. advertising agency, N. J. Ayer & Sons, from 1869 to the date of the book's publication, 1939. There was not much of scholarly significance before the appearance, in 1951, of *The Mechanical Bride* ([1951] 1967). In this book, Marshall McLuhan analyzed examples of newsprint and advertising to show how they were intended to get inside "the collective public mind" and, in so doing, create "the folklore of industrial man."

This seems to have initiated a number of other works of social commentary, more and less well known: Vance Packard's *The Hidden Persuaders* (1957) is still the lodestone, perhaps, for those convinced that advertisers and marketers are out to hook us into consumption practices and, ultimately, to "package our souls"—a stance seemingly apparent in E. S. Turner's *The Shocking History of Advertising* (1953), which he starts with the sentence: "Advertising is the whip which hustles humanity up the road to the Better Mousetrap." A few years later, however, saw the first serious examination of the advertising industry since Ralph Hower's business history: Martin Mayer's (1957) *Madison Avenue U.S.A.*, which, the author later relates, was simultaneously hailed as "the most damaging attack ever on the advertising industry" and "the most effective defense of the industry ever written."

The importance of *Madison Avenue U.S.A.* was that it gave the first public prominence to four advertising men, in particular: Bill Bernbach, Norman B. Rossiter, David Ogilvy, and Rosser Reeves. Its success no doubt encouraged Ogilvy to write his *Confessions of an Advertising Man* (1963), which in itself encouraged the republication of a handful of other titles by well-known members of the advertising industry: for example, Claude C. Hopkins's *My Life in Advertising and Scientific Advertising* (1966, first published in 1923 and 1927, respectively), and James Webb Young's *The Diary of an Ad Man* (first published in 1946) and *How to Become an Advertising Man* (1963). Another work in this vein was *A Tribute to Leo Burnett* (1971), consisting of memoranda, speeches, and aphorisms made by Leo Burnett during his life and put together by his colleagues after the great man's death.

Such books may be seen to some degree as advertisements for the advertising profession itself (and occasionally—notably David Ogilvy's *Confessions of an Advertising Man*—as self-promotion for the author and his agency). Others that followed were less obviously self-promotional and sought to amuse as well as instruct: Peter Mayle's *Up the Agency* (1990), for example, or Randall Rothenberg's *Where the Suckers Moon* (1994). But such titles were never quite detached enough, or probed deep enough, to satisfy those who wanted to know what *really* went on in the trade.

Maybe this was why, from the 1970s onward in particular, scholars—including historians such as Jackson Lears and Pamela Walker Laird—began to take the advertising industry and its products more seriously. In 1972, the writer and critic John Berger compared representations in advertising with those in art in his BBC television series and accompanying book, *Ways of Seeing*. This was followed by the first of a number of overtly structuralist and/or semiotic analyses of advertising as a "system of signs," which sought to examine the nature and implications of their "underlying structure": Varda Langholz Leymore's *Hidden Myth* (1975). This book was followed by Judith Williamson's *Decoding Advertisements* (1978), which analyzed a number of ideologies and meanings incorporated in products of the advertising industry. Although not overtly following this line of thinking, Erving Goffman's *Gender Advertisements* (1979) showed how the visual images of men and women in ads constituted ritualized gender displays, which themselves "iconically" reflected "fundamental features of the social structure." Also less strident in its approach than some of the work coming out of cultural studies was Roland Marchand's *Advertising the American Dream* (1985), a detailed and thoughtful analysis of trends in the style of U.S. advertisements from 1920 to 1940.

In *Advertising: The Uneasy Persuasion* (1984), Michael Schudson adopted a sociological approach to the advertising industry and "its dubious impact on American society," although his work was not nuanced by detailed observation and fieldwork.

It was here that the discipline of anthropology finally made its mark. This time the impetus came from the United Kingdom, and the focus of its research was neither U.S. nor British advertising but that found in other parts of the world. In 1990, Brian Moeran spent twelve months conducting participant-observation fieldwork in a large advertising agency in Tokyo—research that he later published as a monograph. *A Japanese Advertising Agency* (1996) provided the first detailed sociological account of how people in the advertising business go about their work, of the different kinds of work (accounts, marketing, creative, media buying, and so on) in which agency employees are engaged, and of how the industry as a whole is structured into competing institutions of advertising companies, agencies, and media organizations. This pioneering work was later supplemented by a second book, *Ethnography at Work* (2006), which showed how a single case study of preparations for an advertising campaign could then be theorized in six different, complementary ways.

A Japanese Advertising Agency marked the beginning of a number of excursions by anthropologists into the study of advertising in different parts of the world. For example, while carrying out fieldwork in Trinidad in connection with his research for *Capitalism: An Ethnographic Approach* (1997), Danny Miller wrote about the local advertising industry on that island. It was followed by Steve Kemper's monograph on the Sri Lankan advertising industry, *Buying and Believing* (2001). In *Shoveling Smoke* (2003), William Mazzarella took the India advertising business as the basis for his ethnographic study of globalizing consumerism. Malefyt and Moeran (2003) brought many of these and related studies together in their edited volume, *Advertising Cultures*.

Which brings us to *Advertising and Anthropology: Ethnographic Practice and Cultural Perspectives*. This book clearly picks up on earlier studies conducted by anthropologists, but it is distinctly different in one very important way. Whereas anthropologists such as Kemper, Mazzarella, Miller, Moeran, and others derived their research from more or less thorough, more or less limited, fieldwork in or around one or more agencies, Timothy Malefyt has been working full-time in advertising agencies for over fifteen years while Bob Morais has been in advertising and marketing research for even longer. In other words, although trained as anthropologists, both authors are more than participant observers. The very nature of their work in the advertising industry has transformed them into observant participants. It is observant participation that gives their work a distinctive edge; observant participation that proves just how wrong a provincial governor in the United States can be when he dismisses anthropology from his state's university education.[1]

Observant participation means *doing*, rather than simply recording, what goes on. With a combined experience of four decades of work in the advertising business, Malefyt and Morais *know* what it is to manage clients and projects according to budgets and deadlines. They *know* the differences between large agencies and small; between account management, strategic planning, creative work, and marketing research; between products and brands. Having worked for a wide variety of clients in the automobile industry, digital communication, financial services, foods and beverages, health and beauty, hotels and hospitality, household cleaning, pharmaceuticals, and technology, they *know* their trade. They are the intelligent, skilled practitioners of whom scholarship has such desperate need. As advertising men, they perform the job at hand in the interest of building their clients' brands. As anthropologists, they are able to step back and observe the world in which they work. How often do we find this in other fields of business?

So, what does this book teach us? It teaches us about what goes on in the day-to-day life of advertising agencies (rather than in some *Mad Men* pastiche thereof). We learn about what happens when agency personnel meet with clients, about how they achieve their mutual objectives through subtle verbal and nonverbal behavioral cues during the course of delicate negotiations. We learn about creative work and how it is imbued with ritual that mediates the tensions between stability and change, between the client's brand and advertising agencies' endless quest for innovation. We learn, too, that creative people often adopt the ways of anthropologists in their search for "transitional spaces," where conflicting or paradoxical tensions can be transformed into creative (or scholarly) insights.

Then there is the role of marketing and the current shift toward experiential or sensory marketing rather than reliance on selling brands on the basis of cognitive or rational attributes. Marketing people now prefer more sensory and emotionally based methods, because it helps them interact with their consumers and, at the same time, learn more about how consumers think about their brands and use them in their everyday lives. Of course, ethical considerations come into play here, as elsewhere, and the authors discuss the ideological divide within the discipline of anthropology about whether anthropologists should, or should not, work in the world of commerce. But, rather than adopt a customary (and easy) standpoint that places the anthropology critic *out*side the advertising industry (a standpoint echoed in the approach of those who criticize finished *advertisements* without taking into account the working processes of *advertising*), the authors make use of their personal experiences with clients, agency personnel, and consumer research to provide an *in*side view of ethical tensions.

This discussion leads to the methods adopted by anthropologists and some ad agency personnel who try out—albeit limited forms of—what might be termed "business ethnography." Ad agency personnel are *not* lone fieldworkers, of the kind we have learned to love and hate in anthropology. They work together with others—notably with their clients, who sometimes join anthropologists to observe, comment on, and interact in the ethnographic process. Fieldwork in corporate settings, therefore, often includes multiple interactions and interpretations by others and is usually set within the currents of cultural issues. As a result, fieldwork in ad agencies is a highly political and economic as well as social enterprise. In navigating multiple viewpoints and ends, agency and client *co-produce* the finished work.

Such contested and negotiated meanings are part and parcel of the products advertised and not just of people participating. In a chapter on two luxury car ad campaigns, the authors tease out the dialectic between, on the one hand, producers trying to read their consumers and, on the other, consumers assessing the imagery communicated by producers. The issue here is how material culture is lived experience. Yet lived experience lies at the heart of success in business, too. Malefyt and Morais argue that marketing research and strategic planning in advertising offer viable and financially attractive career options for anthropologists, because many businesses today seek deep understandings of consumer lifestyles and brand usage and believe that anthropologists can provide such understandings.

All the same, if they do choose to go into the advertising world, anthropologists must embrace additional theory and methods from other social and behavioral sciences. The authors argue that psychology is particularly important here, because business executives tend to believe in a psychological rather than sociocultural approach to human agency that views consumers as atomized individuals. Although anthropologists may strenuously object to such an approach on the grounds that we are all creatures of the societies and cultures in which we live, they need to learn the language and culture of their corporate clients—in the same way that they would do when conducting fieldwork in a more traditional setting.

So there you have it: a thought-provoking book that tackles business practices, ethical considerations, disciplinary tensions, theoretical issues, and methodologies all at once. Hold your breath, therefore, and plunge in! This book is designed to help you swim, not sink, in the twinned worlds of advertising and anthropology.

Brian Moeran
Copenhagen

Part I
Introduction

Anthropologists In and Out of Advertising

This book is written by anthropologists for anthropologists and others who are interested in advertising and related industries such as marketing, marketing research, and design. We hope that our experience, views, and recommendations will be of value to those who work or plan to work in these kinds of enterprises and contribute to anthropologists' study of organizational culture, consumption practices, marketing to consumers, and the production of creativity in corporate settings. We write as anthropologist-cum-business practitioners who have spent substantial time working within advertising agencies. For a combined forty years, we have been employed by advertising agencies large and small in such disciplines as account management, strategic planning, and marketing research. We have collaborated with a wide array of agency professionals: account executives, account planners, creative executives, media planners and buyers, producers, digital specialists, product, package and Web designers, marketing research firms, and financial managers. Our clients have included brand manufacturers in a broad range of categories, including automotive, digital communications, financial services, foods and beverages, health and beauty aids, hotel and hospitality, household cleaning products, pharmaceutical devices and medicines, industrial products, and technology. As of this writing, Timothy Malefyt leads an in-agency ethnographic unit that collaborates with creative executives, account managers, and account planners on client brands and new business pitches across the BBDO worldwide network. He has been in this role for nine years and previously held account planner positions in two other advertising agencies for six years. Robert Morais spent twenty-five years employed by advertising agencies engaged in account management, account planning, and advertising research. Currently, and for six years, he has been a principal at Weinman Schnee Morais, a marketing research firm that works with advertising agencies and marketing corporations.

When we first embarked on our business careers, we were integrated into our companies as business employees, not anthropologists. We were hired to be account managers (Morais) and account planners (Malefyt) and were trained by our agencies to master the requirements of our jobs. We were educated in the fundamentals of advertising account management and strategic planning; we learned how to be market researchers, data analysts, focus group moderators, brainstorming facilitators, soothsayers, communications planners, strategic thinkers, and writers of the blueprint for advertisement development, the creative brief. We gained the ability to work intimately with colleagues and clients, often mediating across conflicting departments, disciplines, personalities, and objectives. We were taught to respect and include our clients' and colleagues' points of view in our thinking, especially when their views contrasted with our own. We grasped early on that we should look toward the goal of representing consumers' beliefs and practices about brands while inspiring and building teamwork among our colleagues and clients. Throughout our professional lives in advertising, we have experienced the intensity, thoughtfulness, and hard work entailed in developing an advertising agency's strategic and creative products. These efforts include preparation for meetings internally and with clients, multiple discussions and plans of action with teams before and after meetings, the exhaustion of long nights and weekends working on a new business pitch, the responsibilities for brand analysis based upon consumer attitudinal and behavioral data, media planning, and sometimes contentious relationships with our clients, the demanding corporate executives who manage a brand and hire our firms. We have felt the emotional ups and downs of winning and losing accounts, and we have generated strong friendships with our colleagues. Over many years of immersion in what might be called extended fieldwork, we have become advertising professionals in addition to anthropologists. Our everyday business employment requires us to focus sharply on our clients' brands and the business of our companies, which informs an analysis of the inner workings of advertising agencies. We contribute our best strategic thinking, manage staff and client relationships, and operate within tight deadlines and budgets. Our day-to-day mission is very different from that of cultural anthropologists in academia, where professors often occupy siloed domains of expertise and power. However, like academics, we have often lost ourselves in the demands of our work and navigated the politics of cooperation and competition.

Through all of this, we have a developed an experientially based understanding of how the advertising business works and the process by which disciplines and hierarchies come together to increase clients' brand sales and grow an agency's client roster. This phenomenon of having "gone native" is what now allows us to analyze our advertising agency experience in a unique way and write about agencies from an insider's vantage point. For the past several years, we have stepped back and studied the advertising industry as anthropologists, and we have continued to be involved as advertising and marketing research professionals. Through our on-the-job experiences and by systematic observation and interviews with colleagues and clients, our analysis of our work lives has comingled with our day-to-day responsibilities. We are more than participant observers; we are, in a variation on John Sherry's term, *observant participants* (Sherry 2003: xii). This collection includes updates on work that we published previously as well as new essays. This volume, then, constitutes our report to date from the field. One purpose in writing from the native's point of view is to amend Reinharz's contention that "there are few published accounts of [going native] since those who have gone native cease to publish" (1988: 168).

The experience of having gone native or "pure participation" (Dewalt and Dewalt 2000: 263) can be analyzed in the current academic context of self-reflexive participant observation in fieldwork. Reflexivity involves the challenge of first confronting and then sorting out one's own experience in a situation in contrast to that of the other. Typically, the task of the anthropologist in fieldwork is to work with informants to access the interplay between self-reflection and immediacy by constructing grounds for mutual experience (Rabinow 1977: 38–39). This dialectic between self and other is what lies "at the heart of reflexivity that defines anthropological knowledge" (Behar 1996: 82). Indeed, when one is fully immersed in the fieldwork experience and, more precisely, the lives observed, the knowledge gained is not mere data collection; it provides a sense of the self *as the other*. This is what Polanyi (1958) calls tacit knowledge and is developed in and through the self, both to inform the interpretation and to incite the production of knowledge as something that is lived and experienced. In studying the Yolmo ways of healing, anthropologist Robert Desjarlais (1992), as described in Dewalt and Dewalt (2000: 264), trained to become an apprentice shaman. Beyond observing Yolmo culture, Desjarlais found it necessary to learn how to move and experience his body as a Yolmo shaman. He notes that, as he gained cultural knowledge, learning how the Yolmo sip tea, catching the meaning of jokes, and participating fully in their everyday lives, his interactions shaped his "understanding of local values, patterns of actions, ways of being, moving, feeling" (Desjarlais 1992: 26). This degree of pure participation goes beyond just producing knowledge of another's way of life. It is personal knowledge that is embodied as daily living and is experienced in sensing, feeling, and thinking. As James Clifford writes, the ethnographer who fails to fully experience the world of the observed through participant observation finds it more difficult to critically examine research assumptions and beliefs and even themselves in relation to those they study (Clifford 1997: 91).

We have fully experienced the world of advertising in Clifford's sense. Moreover, our dedication to both our jobs and to anthropological observation has produced a duality in our professional lives. We are at once business professionals and anthropologists who study the business profession. Our views as business professionals and anthropologists who present and publish academically are not mutually exclusive. Extending on our response to Reinharz (1988: 168) above, we hope that professionals in business and academia, often cast at odds with each other, find greater integration and collaboration. We have accomplished this objective in our careers. Malefyt is a part-time professor and presents at academic conferences; Morais guest lectures at universities and participates in academic conferences. Both of us publish scholarly books and write articles for peer-reviewed journals. Working in a corporate setting and contributing to the academic community is not an either/or proposition. We urge those engaged in the field of business anthropology to join us in forging connections between the academic and practicing domains if they are not yet doing so.

We also have opportunities to reflect on our findings from a broader cultural, social, ethical, and economic perspective than is available in academic settings alone. Whereas most academic anthropologists choose a subfield, a people, a focus on some aspect of culture and spend years developing thoughts around a single fieldwork episode or revisiting a familiar location, we are exposed to myriad situations, ideas, thoughts, locations, cultural and personnel issues. On any given day, a new client can be won. During the course of a day, we can be working on projects for an orange juice brand, an industrial lubricant, and a dental product. Each of these categories presents a different set of clients and consumers and marketing challenges as well as call for distinct analytical and conceptual frameworks to address business opportunities. Working across brand categories and consumer experiences has necessitated that we take a broad view of our projects and see them as part of a network of connected cultural systems. When, for example, we observe creativity expressed by mothers facing the daily decision of what to prepare for the family dinner, we note interconnections with ways they depend on their cell phones, Internet and mobile devices to keep track of family wishes, changes in individuals' schedules, last-minute recipe searches, and so forth. While the brand categories in this scenario are distinct—a food company and a telecommunications company—this confluence of experiences is precisely why an anthropological perspective that cuts across manufacturers' categories is advantageous in business. Anthropological approaches to consumers' lives take a holistic approach that incorporates the range of behaviors that people are involved in on a daily basis. This intersecting of lives, resources, and technology is only one illustration of research projects that link our thinking with the larger landscape of consumer experience, category fluidity, and cultural interconnectivity. This process also demands that we engage a range of intellectual approaches within anthropology (structural, functional, psychological, cognitive, symbolic, semiotic, practice theory, historical, etc.) and from outside of anthropology, in disciplines such as personality and social psychology, linguistics, literature, and philosophy. We also incorporate observations and insights from popular consumer culture. All this enables us to understand consumers more fully and serve our clients' objectives in addition to making contributions to scholarship.

Throughout this book, we consider advertising from experience "near" and experience "far" viewpoints (Geertz [1983] 2000). We examine how advertising agencies produce creative work from both an internal organizational and consumer research perspective. The extensive literature from a cultural studies perspective examines advertising as a producer of symbols and form of social discourse, which circulates broadly in the public realm. Advertisements have been labeled an empire of signs (Baudrillard 1994; Lash and Urry 1994), a discourse of persuasion (Jhally 1987), a public ideology (O'Barr 1994), a circulation of ideological "texts" for public consumption (Williamson 1978), "social tableaus" of society for immigrants (Marchand 1985), and a system of symbols (Sherry 1987). Advertising messages compete in "sign wars" (Goldman and Papson 1996: 2), reinvent cultural difference through commodity image production (Mazzarella 2003b), and have been described as an "absolute simulation . . . the superficial transparency of everything" (Baudrillard 1994: 87). This scholarship draws attention to the ways signs and symbols are produced and circulated in society.

The essays that follow are from a different perspective. We join a growing number of anthropologists and other social scientists who analyze advertising culture and its practices from within agencies and among its people (Couvson 2009; Malefyt and Moeran 2003; Moeran 1996, 2005, 2006, 2009, 2010; Zwick and Cayla 2011). Brian Moeran, in particular, in his groundbreaking 1996 advertising agency ethnography, provides one of the first in-depth and thorough accounts of advertising from within a Japanese advertising agency. Other scholars and anthropologists have also described personal roles in industries related to and including advertising (Baba 2006; Cefkin 2009; McCreery 2000; Squires and Byrne 2002; Sunderland and Denny 2007; Wasson 2000; Zukin 2004). Concurrent with the ascent of ethnography in the realm of consumer marketing and research (Malefyt 2009; Sunderland and Denny 2007), the value of anthropology as a discipline is noted by many social scientists and journalists (Ante 2006; Denny 1999; Inglessis 2006; Louis 1985; Miller 1990; Monari 2005; Morais 2009a; Murphy 2005; Sanders 2002; Wasserman 2003; Wellner 2002). McCracken has been particularly vociferous in applying anthropology to business practices (for example, McCracken 2009). Evidence of growing interest in business anthropology includes the appearance of general academic books in the past several years (Jordan 2003; Tian, Lillis, and van Marrenijk 2010). EPIC (Ethnographic Praxis in Industry Conference) focuses on business anthropology, and the Society for Applied Anthropology and the National Association for the Practice of Anthropology have published articles, newsletters, and blogs on marketing and advertising topics. The *International Journal of Business Anthropology* was launched in late 2010, and the *Journal of Business Anthropology* is planned for 2012. There are numerous online communities that discuss business anthropology, many of which engage advertising and marketing issues. LinkedIn, a popular business networking site, includes such groups as Ethnography Forum, Media Anthropology, and the Anthropology Network. Clearly, the trend in business applications of anthropology is growing. Yet, despite all of this activity, there remains a lacuna in the body of literature that includes insider perspectives on the advertising industry from the practitioner's point of view. We are not aware of any other work, other than our own, that reflects an extended career lived as advertising professionals and then described from an anthropological perspective.

Advertising Agencies in the Early Twenty-First Century

Advertising is one component of a marketing mix that includes a wide range of programs, including brand innovation, pricing, packaging, and promotions such as coupons, among other techniques, that are designed to increase consumer purchase of brands. Naomi Klein (2000: 32) writes of the importance of advertising in a new age of branding, where its role has changed "from delivering product news bulletins to building an image around a particular brand-name version of a product" (2000: 6). U.S. manufacturers are committed to advertising as a necessary development of brand image, and they devote substantial time and money to advertising strategy, development, production, and placement. In economic terms, advertising agencies have rebounded from 2008 revenue lows (Kirby and Chesler 2011). After two years of slumping fortunes, the Big Four global advertising agency holding companies— Omnicom, the WPP Group, Interpublic, and Publicis—showed growth with 2010 revenues returning to 2007 levels (Gillette 2010). Total advertising expenditures increased 6.5 percent in 2010 to finish the year at $131.1 billion, according to the Kantar Media Report (2011).

Despite recent financial improvements, advertising agencies face major challenges in the twenty-first century. More than ever before, agencies must demonstrate their value as business partners to their clients. To do so, they are compelled to substantiate the effectiveness of their creative efforts and verify the return on investment of their campaigns. Advertising agencies also fight competitive pressures from marketing consulting firms that threaten to unseat them from their long-held strategic planning role. The greatest issue now facing traditional advertising agencies is technologically driven media fragmentation, encompassing mobile phones and tablets, online video, social media, shopper marketing, site-based media, and product integration in television, films, and online. Advertising agencies recognize that mass media is no longer the foundation of marketing communication and that there is a sea change in client expectations of what agencies can and should deliver. The more adept agencies are reinventing themselves to deliver work that is more technologically adroit and produced better, faster, and less expensively than traditional advertising. As this evolution proceeds, only the fittest advertising agencies will survive.

Agencies and Clients

Many of the essays in this book describe particular practices within advertising as well as our relationships with clients. Despite the old advertising industry joke that "Advertising would be a great business if not for the clients," clients are the essential counterpart to advertising executives. They are the manufacturing professionals who conceive and deliver the marketing plan for a brand, hire advertising agencies, and pay for the agency's strategic and creative services, creative production, and media planning and placement. Advertising agency executives manage relationships with clients in addition to performing duties that are intended to build brand sales. The essays in this volume occasionally refer to advertising as a subset of marketing; marketing professionals' responsibilities include new product development, distribution, sales tracking, consumer promotions, and brand financial management in addition to their role in developing advertising. Our references to advertising and marketing research refer to qualitative and quantitative studies that are designed to gain an understanding of consumers as buyers and to assess their interest in new products and services and the advertisements that attempt to convince people to buy these offerings. Although we have served in a variety of functions in advertising agencies, our jobs today are in the marketing research domain.

Anthropology and Advertising

As in Timothy Malefyt and Brian Moeran's *Advertising Cultures* (2003), we chose to focus on organizational issues rather than aiming to decipher the larger meaning or function of advertising per se, although one chapter, "Advertising, Automobiles, and the Branding of Luxury," does consider the symbolic nature of automotive advertising, and another essay, "Creativity, Person, and Place," offers a theoretical exploration of the workings of creativity.

There are both strong commonalities and substantial differences between anthropologists working in academia and anthropologists employed in the advertising and marketing research industries. *Advertising Cultures* (2003) provides a detailed description of similarities and differences in the volume's introduction, which we will briefly summarize and expand on here. Both academics and business anthropologists attempt to comprehend human behavior and then pass on their understanding to colleagues. Anthropologists in both professions formulate hypotheses about the nature of human interaction and motivations and test their ideas in the field by interviewing and observing "informants" or "consumers." Anthropologists in academia, advertising, and marketing research often seek answers to timeless questions and are frequently inspired by new theories about the nature of human behavior. Anthropologists in academia and business make a living by presenting their findings through detailed interpretations. This occurs whether their interpretive lens is consumers' brand use and its link to advertising messaging or discovering social patterns that compare to other peoples cross-culturally. In a sense, "both advertisers and anthropologists are cultural intermediaries who study others for other others" (Malefyt and Moeran 2003: 13). Both professionals must "pitch" their work in competitive environments in order to be funded. Advertising anthropologists sometimes compete for client work against nonanthropologists who offer variations on ethnographic methodologies (Malefyt 2009); academics submit written proposals for competitive research grants. Both academic and business anthropologists claim an understanding of culture that positions their work as unique and relevant for the client and against their competition. In their striving to understand human nature and win project support, the goals of advertising and academic anthropologists converge.

Where academics and business practitioners diverge is in the specifics of their work and the constituencies and purposes their labor serves. Academics pursue knowledge for many professional and personal reasons: primarily, we believe, to increase knowledge and appreciation of human thought and activity in its myriad forms. Anthropologists employed in advertising and marketing research pursue knowledge, too, but in ways that serve clients whose job it is to sell brands profitably. The academic anthropologist is a generalist who works on her own. She selects a topic of interest, investigates her people, and writes a report (book, paper, or article) for an academic audience. Further, anthropologists in colleges and universities conduct ethnographic research through observations, interviews, and field notes, which are later formulated as narrative documents that provide a testament to their work. In academia, George Marcus notes, "Textualization is the heart of the ethnographic enterprise, both in the field and in the university setting" (Marcus and Fisher 1986: 264). Geertz stressed that culture can be "read" as a text: "Doing ethnography is like trying to read . . . a manuscript" (1973: 10). The *writing* of culture becomes a text and a way of conceiving ethnography through which academics share information and analysis with colleagues. Even when academics gather for face-to-face conferences, they *read* a paper, privileging the text as the primary means of communication between audience and author.

For business anthropologists, reading and writing culture is only one component of a multiphase interactive process within the network of human relationships that comprise advertising development. Anthropologists in business report on respondents' lives and their reactions to brands and then collaborate with colleagues to transpose their findings into strategies, marketing plans, and, eventually, creative work. Anthropologists in advertising work in teams. Far more discussions, interactions, negotiations, and subtle interpersonal skills contribute to the work of transferring ideas in advertising (Malefyt and Moeran 2003: 15). In addition, an advertising agency itself operates within a larger network of interconnected professional relationships. Information is constantly exchanged, revised, and augmented as it circulates among departments within agencies (from account management to account planning to creative to media) and among the collaborative network of satellite companies that source and supplement advertising in media, digital, film, print, and production.

The work created by the advertising anthropologist is, like that created by the academic, textural, but, unlike the academic's work, it flows throughout a network of executives where it is discussed, analyzed, adjusted, and modified; reviewed again; and, with client approval, advanced to a creative product and disseminated to the public. In a sense, texts are transformed and made relevant socially in meetings as the main source of human engagement. For instance, insights from the anthropologist's research are included in a creative brief, the main textual document that informs creative teams. While the creative *brief* is different from the creative *briefing*, which is the meeting where the account planner and/or account manager outline the nature of an advertising problem to a creative team and suggest ways to solve it, they merge in practice and concept. Both the brief and briefing intertwine to work together, with account planners, account managers, and creative executives reshaping the document during the meeting to mold the direction that the advertising will take. As Jon Steel explains, "the boundaries between what is written and what is spoken, in Brief or briefing, themselves blur as ideas constantly evolve and expand" (1998: 141). A major difference between anthropologists working in advertising and their academic counterparts, then, is that the business anthropologist's research is first textualized and then transformed through multiple social and personal interactions for use in advertising development. The transformation of the creative brief through its social life brings to mind Bruno Latour's (1991) observation that technology is social relations congealed in material form; in our case, what advertising people produce materially in the form of briefs, documents, and advertisements are themselves evidence of social relations congealed in material form. As such, human interactions in advertising reveal a main cognitive, social, and practical structure in which strategic and creative ideas created by social interactions are circulated, negotiated, produced, and distributed materially.

The Business Anthropology Imperative

At the 2011 meeting of the American Anthropological Association in Montreal, the halls were streaming with attendees, many of them graduate students in their late twenties looking forward to careers as academic anthropologists. We noted that the vast majority of topics at the sessions were academic rather than applied, with only a few seminars devoted to business anthropology. Acutely aware that the academic job market is tight, we wondered: What is the economic model for placing graduating anthropologists? How will they find gainful employment? From our perspective, academic anthropology functions as a small island in a vast ocean of opportunity for anthropologists. The little island is overpopulated, food and shelter are scarce, and the shores are eroding. The population increases every year, and most of the people who run the island are not motivated to change the status quo. Without the younger population, their roles are less fully justified and their self-interests (teaching less, publishing more) are not well served. Within swimming distance of the academic anthropology island are other lands. They are named for disciplines that appear on the Web site of the National Association for the Practice of Anthropology (http://practicinganthropology.org) and include public health, organizational and community development, social justice, marketing and environmental management, among many others. There are additional fields, too, with names such as management consulting, design, product development, and advertising. Many of these destinations are reachable with swimming instructions from the island. Anthropologists who have left the academic island often find their new home challenging at first, but welcoming and rewarding intellectually as well as monetarily later. Some, like the authors here, remain connected with their place of origin, and both they and their academic colleagues benefit. Residents on the academic island need not be isolated.

Marietta Baba's summary of findings on PhD production and academic employment opportunities in the United States for anthropologists supports the island metaphor. She writes, "The number of anthropology PhD's has increased by nineteen percent over the past decade, while the number of academic positions available to them in the discipline has declined by around fifteen percent over the same period" (2009: 385).[1] Baba's additional comments on this phenomenon merit quoting in detail:

> The academic profession is producing a substantial number of professional anthropologists who have no choice but to practice in extra-academic professional niches. Despite these trends, many faculty members in PhD producing departments continue to prepare their doctoral students for academic roles, though the reality of the professional employment situation appears to be out of synch with the process. (2009: 385)

Observations regarding the overproduction and underemployment of PhDs have also been made outside the confines of academic publications. For example, *The Economist* (Editorial 2010) and *Slate* (Pannapacker 2011) have published articles on the dismal academic job prospects of PhD students and the self-interests of tenured faculty who benefit from low-cost graduate student labor and more time for research and publications. Academic anthropologists, fully cognizant of this state of affairs, are aware of nonacademic jobs for themselves and their students, but the percentage of those who engage in professions outside the academy is relatively small, and only 7 percent are employed in business enterprises (Baba 2009: 385). In advertising and marketing research and related fields such as marketing and design, we have noticed increasing numbers of anthropologists at the doctoral- and master's-degree levels. However, our observation at the 2011 American Anthropological Association meetings suggests that too few PhD-level anthropologists see the attraction of business or are aware of industry opportunities that will afford them careers outside academia. These anxious scholars should consider this: The pressure of conducting business in a global marketplace has created "a permanent state of emergency," according to Nigel Thrift (2000: 674), describing the effects of work life in the early twenty-first century. This situation requires fresh skills, disciplines, and agents to manage the rapid pace of change. Constant innovation, Thrift continues, is a cushion and defense against a more uncertain world, where an advantage of one brand over another is only temporary. The need for innovation, in turn, places greater emphasis on creativity, where executives collaborate and work harder and faster to produce the next big idea. Advertising agencies and their clients seeking big ideas are embracing new ways to access how consumers might be induced to select their brands over those of the competition. This is a major reason the presence of cultural anthropology, especially ethnography, has expanded dramatically in manufacturing companies, advertising agencies, consulting firms, and business enterprises devoted to new product development, marketing research, design, and strategic planning. The growing presence of anthropologists in U.S. businesses demonstrates recognition by industry that anthropologists make a meaningful contribution to corporate goals. Consequently, anthropologists who establish careers in advertising and related fields are discovering a viable and financially attractive option to the frustrating professional path that they face in academia. The math in Baba's analysis indicates that anthropologists must become more receptive to and aggressive in seeking work in industry. In many of our essays, we make it clear that business, particularly marketing and advertising, will continue to be receptive to anthropologists who process the abilities that corporate America so desperately needs.

Our Approach to This Book

The essays that follow describe internal agency and client meetings, competitive pressures, and professional relationships in the context of specific projects on which we have worked. We have not written a comprehensive ethnography of an advertising agency. Rather, we have selected topics that are of interest to us and that we believe will be valuable for anthropologists who seek to comprehend the advertising industry. In Part II, our essays describe the structure, function, and process of advertising agency work and detail how skills in human interaction are as central to success as insights about consumers and the agency's creative work. We also offer our point of view on ethics in advertising and marketing research. Part III illustrates how we work as anthropologists in and with advertising agencies and includes concrete advice for practitioners. In Part IV, we conclude with a discussion about the future of advertising anthropology. Below we will briefly summarize the essays that follow.

Part II: Toward an Understanding of Advertising Agencies

Chapter 2, "Advertising Meetings and Client Relationships," focuses on the meeting between the manufacturer and the advertising agency where advertising ideas are presented, discussed, and selected. Although participants enter these meetings with the common aim of reaching agreement on the ideas reviewed, attendees have additional professional and personal objectives. To achieve their goals, participants must understand unwritten rules, understand subtle verbal and nonverbal behavior, comprehend and navigate the delicate client-agency balance of power, demonstrate negotiation skills, and impress their superiors. This chapter provides a foundational knowledge of advertising structure and suggests that such meetings define the attitudes, behaviors, and symbols of client-agency relationships.

Chapter 3, "Rituals of Creativity in Advertising Agencies," examines how an inherent tension in the structure of advertising agencies drives the production of creativity and is mediated through ritual. We describe innovation and stability for both advertised brands and professional relationships as contrasting and competitive ideologies and everyday practices. We suggest that the brand advertised and the agency's creative collaborations have properties of ritual symbols and that ritual mediates tension inherent in two forces, change and stability, which define the brand and the process of advertising collaboration.

Chapter 4, "Fieldwork in Advertising Research," considers what happens when corporate clients join anthropologists in fieldwork to observe, comment on, and interact during the ethnographic process; how outcomes of fieldwork are influenced by hired consultants who join projects and offer input for client support and brand direction; how multiple and sometimes conflicting views toward consumers and brands are accommodated; and how research objectives reflect consumer trends. This chapter discusses fieldwork in advertising agencies as a highly political, social, and economic negotiation during which executives must navigate multiple viewpoints and goals regarding the coproduction of work.

Chapter 5, "Advertising Emotions," reveals that marketers sell brands less on rational attributes and more on sensory and experiential dimensions that are believed to tap directly into emotional responses from consumers. This shift toward so-called experiential marketing has not only impacted advertising itself, but also has spurred new research processes, including ethnography, along with new models for media planning and placement to create more sensory-based marketing approaches. We argue that marketers prefer sensory and emotionally based methods to motivate consumers because the consumption experience is more intimate, customized, and thought to generate greater brand loyalty.

Chapter 6, "Creativity, Person, and Place," is a philosophical journey into the process by which advertising creatives gather fresh ideas in out-of-the-way places. New thinking is often triggered by odd moments and unusual places, often during "between" spaces that are considered indeterminate. This process of gathering new thoughts by way of between spaces of indeterminacy is also explored as a process utilized by skilled anthropologists in ethnographic interviews and observations with consumers. We discuss the use of these transitional zones as ways for advertising executives to generate creative inspiration for advertising campaigns and for anthropologists to make sense of ambiguities and contradictions in what consumers say to arrive at cultural insights.

Part III: Applying Anthropology in Advertising Agencies

Chapter 7, "Advertising, Automobiles, and the Branding of Luxury," examines how two advertising campaigns for automobiles, Cadillac and Infiniti, either reflected or lacked cultural understanding of a category of consumer experience: what luxury means to consumers in an automobile advertisement. One advertisement captured the cultural meaning of luxury for a car brand precisely, while the other advertisement misunderstood cultural meaning and was rejected by consumers. This chapter shows how material culture (automobiles) engages with cultural concepts (luxury) in a process of negotiation (advertising) with consumers. At the heart of this interactivity lies the negotiated meaning of things in people's lives.

Chapter 8, "Business Anthropology Beyond Ethnography," notes that ethnography has become business anthropologists' unique and, too often, only selling proposition. Despite its value as a marketing research technique, limited time and research budgets mitigate against more frequent adoption of ethnography by marketers. Because many marketers lack an understanding of ethnography or its heuristic applications, they typically select focus group studies instead. This chapter demonstrates how a broad range of anthropologically informed techniques and concepts can be adapted to focus room settings and how this approach benefits advertising and marketing work for anthropologists.

Chapter 9, "Ethics in Advertising," discusses the concept of ethics in advertising and, in particular, the issue of anthropologists' employment in the advertising industry. We contend that an ethical sensitivity among academically focused professionals toward anthropologists in advertising stems from anthropology's historical colonial legacy; anthropologists have long been aware of issues of asymmetrical relations and exploitation by social scientists engaged with native others. We situate our discussion in anthropology's explicit critiques of advertising, commentary on ethics by business anthropologists and other scholars, personal business case histories, and ethics guidelines issued by the American Anthropological Association.

Chapter 10, "Hybrid Research Methodologies and Business Success," discusses the merits of broadening anthropological approaches in advertising and marketing research to include a hybrid methodology that incorporates concepts from other social and behavioral sciences, particularly psychology. Although business executives are aware of the interaction of culture, behavior, and attitudes, they often prefer psychological models of human behavior. This difference in perspective can stoke debates between anthropologists and their clients. We suggest that business anthropologists learn the language and culture of their corporate clients and adopt hybrid research techniques. This will enable them to better connect with their clients' ways of thinking and deliver a deeper understanding of consumers on clients' terms.

Part IV: Conclusion

Chapter 11, "The Future of Advertising Anthropology," outlines several trajectories that business anthropology and advertising might take in the near future and what these directions might mean for practitioners and academics.

* * *

Our aim in these essays is to not only document how advertising agencies function and detail the ways that anthropologists in business study consumers, but also to convey the intellectual rewards of advertising careers for cultural anthropologists.

Careers in advertising and marketing have a special urgency for anthropologists. At the same time, businesses will benefit from anthropologists' expertise and insight. Furthermore, we are advocates for academic programs in the humanities and social sciences that offer more collaboration with corporate enterprises to advance mutual consilience. This volume reflects our belief in building bridges across many realms that will advance anthropology in advertising and business.

Part II
Toward an Understanding
of Advertising Agencies

–2–

Advertising Meetings and Client Relationships

This chapter focuses on the meetings between the brand manufacturer (client) and the advertising agency, where advertising ideas are presented, discussed, and selected. These meetings constitute a central event around which agency life is focused, and they contain the defining attitudes, behaviors, and symbols of the client-agency relationship. In describing the roles of the meeting attendees and their contrasting objectives, strategies, and tactics, we will provide foundational knowledge for much of what we discuss throughout this book.

To place advertising meetings in context, we should consider that advertising is a highly competitive industry in the United States; agency firings and account reassignments are common. As Malefyt (2003: 139, 142–43) points out, a consequence of this volatility is that "the process of ad production . . . is one directed . . . not so much at the brand, consumer or even rival agencies, but towards the client." This behavior reflects Michell and Sanders's (1995) finding that advertising development processes and interpersonal relationships have more influence on agency loyalty than the perceived quality of the creative work. Other studies have examined the roles of agency executives who create advertising (Hirschman 1989; Young 2000) and interaction across disciplines within agencies and with clients (Kover 1995; Kover and Goldberg 1995). Moeran (1996: 79–87) concentrates on events surrounding a presentation in which an agency is competing to win an account (also see Johnson 2006). Miller's (1997: 182–94) ethnography on the development of an advertising campaign in Trinidad could apply to virtually any advertising agency in the United States, and to the process that we discuss here.

The Meeting Defined

The meeting as a focus of anthropological inquiry does not have a rich tradition; the most extensive attention paid to meetings by an anthropologist is Schwartzman's (1989) study on meetings in a mental health organization. Her definition of a meeting is a useful starting point. For Schwartzman (1989: 7), a meeting is:

> A communicative event involving three or more people who agree to assemble for a purpose ostensibly related to the functioning of an organization or group, for example, to

exchange ideas or opinions, to solve a problem, to make a decision, or negotiate an agreement, to develop policy and procedures, to formalize recommendations . . . a meeting is characterized by talk that is episodic in nature.

Because advertising creative meetings occur in a designated place (the agency's or client's conference room) for a discrete period of time (normally sixty to ninety minutes), they can be viewed analytically as frames (Goffman 1974; Moeran 2005: 43–57). Moeran's (2005: 63–79) discussion of frames in a business context is useful for understanding creative meetings not only as a frame within agency life but also as the key frame for interpreting and understanding agency-client relationships.

Advertising Creative Meeting Participants

In client creative meetings, agency attendees include account managers and creative executives. Many advertising agencies involve account planners in these meetings, and planners often play a key role in advertising creative development. Client-side creative meeting participants are the marketing employees of the manufacturing company that has hired the agency. Clients are the gatekeepers for creative work; they must be convinced that the ideas they review merit exposure to consumers.

Advertising agency account managers represent the agency to the client, communicate client needs to the agency, and help ensure that agency departments get the creative work and other client assignments done on strategy, on time, and on budget. The account manager's job is often a difficult balancing act. During the course of creative development, the account manager will, on different occasions, stand with the agency, between the agency and its clients, and with the clients. Account managers deliver the initial client assignments and direction for the assignment to agency creative teams, contribute to the creative brief, provide their sense of how well the drafted creative work delivers on client needs, and suggest areas in which the creative product should be revised or replaced before client presentations. Account managers represent the position of the agency on their work, but they must be flexible enough to know when a stance must be altered to answer client demands. Conceptually, account managers are concerned with keeping the brand in line with client expectations and maintaining steadiness in agency-client relationships as well as delivering a strong creative product to their clients. Operationally, account managers fill a multiplicity of roles and functions. They are salespeople who are expected to convince (sell) the client to accept (buy) creative ideas. They are traffic managers who cajole their colleagues to keep the agency's work flowing. They are relationship builders who establish trust with all of the individuals with whom they interact professionally. They are diplomats who smooth ruffled feathers on their agency team and with clients. Good account managers are perspicacious and articulate, personable and savvy. They are smart business executives, proactive managers, problem solvers, astute social psychologists, smooth networkers, natural leaders, and persuasive communicators. Account managers are more similar to their clients than any other agency staffer. As one client said, they "dress and speak like us; they are more like us [than creative people]." This perception—and reality—often results in conflict for account managers in their interactions with creative executives as well as other agency colleagues, as we will detail in the next chapter.

Advertising agency creative executives are organized into dyadic copywriter–art director teams that develop advertising ideas. A creative director with experience in writing or art direction supervises creative teams. Creative directors are venerated within the industry, and they often receive the highest salaries among agency personnel. Referred to collectively in the industry as "creatives," these imaginative executives work from the creative brief agreed upon by the agency-client team to conceive and design what is referred to as "the work" for the agency. They differ in temperament and personal style from their MBA-trained clients and from their more pragmatically oriented account manager partners; their separateness from the ordinary adds to their status. Creative executives feel a sense of ownership about both their creative process and their creative product. They spend weeks inventing narratives, meticulously designing graphics, and carefully choosing words. They have pride in their craft and passion for their ideas. When revisions are suggested, creatives often resist because they feel the purity of their work will be defiled and their efforts compromised. For this reason, creatives often find it painful to listen to critical comments from account managers and clients. At the same time, they depend upon account managers to provide clear direction for their work. Moreover, creatives value strategically perceptive, creatively astute account managers who help them make their work better. Creatives also know that account managers who are wired to their clients smooth the passage of their ideas toward client acceptance. In creative meetings, the creative director is the selling partner of the account team but argues from a creative rather than a business perspective, which is the function of account managers.

Account planners are charged with advertising strategic development. Their responsibilities include the design and management of consumer research through focus groups, ethnographies, and surveys; writing creative briefs; testing creative ideas; measuring advertising effectiveness in the market; and tracking of advertising campaigns. The essence of the planner's role is to inform and guide the creative process by being the expert on the consumer and the consumer's relationship with brands (Rainey 1997: 1). Pressure on agencies to act as complete idea generators for clients' brands has elevated the role of account planners in commissioning consumer and brand research into a type of creative work. Not all advertising agencies have account planners on staff; when they do not, the planner's role is handled by an account manager.

While clients are the primary audience in advertising creative meetings, there is also interaction, and not always agreement, among members within the agency and client teams. Hirschman (1989), citing Turow (1984: 21), characterizes clients as patrons of the agency (Hirschman 1989: 42–43) and then describes the roles of several participants in the creative development process. Miller (1997) remarks on the tension between account managers and creatives in Trinidad and notes that creatives are "artists" and account managers are responsible for clients' "commercial concern" (Miller 1997: 188). As Brian Moeran notes, "That 'humdrum' account and 'creative' copy and art personnel do not always get along is a well-remarked fact in the advertising industry" (2006: 81). Even within creative teams, Young (2000) found that copywriters and art directors have different feelings about creative development. Across agency and client lines, within agencies, and, to a lesser extent, within client teams, contrasting responsibilities and attitudes have a major impact on the conduct and outcome of advertising creative meetings.

Goals: Mutual and Otherwise

Agency and client executives enter creative meetings to reach agreement on the work and advance the most promising creative ideas to the next step in the development process. Clients hope to manage a smooth process within specified time and production cost parameters. They also strive to showcase their professional skills to management. Clients are acutely aware that their comments during creative meetings are heard not only by the agency but also by their superiors, and clients believe that looking smart to both the agency and their superiors is critical. As one client said, "If you say what your boss agrees with and he says he agrees, the agency (as well as your boss) thinks you are smart." Agency executives share the desire to move the development process forward seamlessly. They know that the better the clients appear to their own management, the more loyal these clients will be to the agency. Agency staffers enter the meeting with a strong desire to sell specific creative work that makes the agency team, and specific individuals within the agency team, look insightful and inventive.

The agency also has an agency-building agenda; imaginative creative work can help win new business. Additionally, creative work is often pushed by individuals who want to build their personal portfolio of work to win industry awards and as an asset for future jobs. Most importantly, agencies must leave the meeting having preserved, and ideally enhanced, their relationship with the client. A smooth development process, high creative test scores, and positive business results are important. Exhibiting leadership and creativity, managing the meeting, accepting the final decision with grace, attaining camaraderie, and getting it (i.e., understanding client personality and culture, listening carefully to client comments, knowing client preferences) all contribute to the larger objective of a stronger agency-client bond and retention of the account. The hierarchy of goals in creative meetings depicted in Table 2.1 is based on observations and discussions with agency account managers and creatives and client marketing managers.

Table 2.1   Hierarchy of Agency and Client Goals

Agency Goals	Client Goals
Preserve the relationship	Look smart and capable
Enhance perception of the agency and self	Exhibit leadership and control over meeting
Sell creative work the agency can showcase	Manage project development on a timely basis
Sell creative work in fewest number of presentation rounds	Help develop creative work that management is comfortable with
Get high advertising test scores	Get high advertising test scores
Grow brand sales	Grow brand sales

Before the Meeting

The creative development process may be initiated because brand sales are softening, the current advertising is reaching consumer exposure wear out, a launch of a new product is planned, the agency has won a new account, or a client simply wants new creative work. The client or agency crafts a creative brief that will serve as the strategic blueprint for creative development. Account managers build a timetable for development, presentation, testing, and production of the creative work. They review the brief with the creative team and provide creatives with intelligence regarding the client's intellectual and temperamental terrain.

Creatives are given two to three weeks to develop ideas. Guided by the brief, they develop concepts across a continuum of boldness. They will challenge their clients' comfort levels and they will present ideas they are fairly sure the client will find acceptable. Conservative ideas carry special risks. As one creative director said, "I always give them something I know will sell, but I have to be careful because everything you put on the table is for sale." Account managers, eager to please the client, request safe work and negotiate with creative directors about which work to present to a client. If a creative director insists on presenting a storyboard that the account manager believes is marginally related to the strategy or edgy, the account manager asks the creative team to present an execution that is closer strategically or more conservative executionally. Often the creative team and account manager strike a deal to offer both approaches. The body of work is reviewed first by the creative director, then with the account management team, and finally with agency management. Several rounds of internal agency meetings occur before creative work is presented to the client.

For illustrative purposes, we will describe meetings that will culminate in a television commercial. There is no standard number of television storyboards that are presented in a creative meeting, but a battery of five to eight ideas is typical. Agencies group storyboards into categories based on executional styles—for example, realistic, slice-of-life situations that are problem or solution oriented; celebrity presenters; demonstrations with competitive comparisons; an image-driven idea; or a humorous situation. Sorting of creative work is also done according to variations on the strategy that emphasize particular understandings about the target consumer. For example, several advertisements for an over-the-counter wart remover might be written to a "removes warts in one step" consumer promise while varying thematically. One underscores the time that mothers save avoiding a visit to the doctor; another focuses on consumer trust of the brand; and still another connects with the embarrassment that people feel when they have warts. Sorting storyboards provides an opportunity for the agency to explain its thinking and demonstrate that no stone has been left unturned in the pursuit of creative ideas. Clients find categorization helpful for organizing and evaluating ideas.

When the work is reviewed in the agency's offices, or even while en route to the client's office, the agency team decides which storyboards to recommend. Many marketers field one or more rounds of advertising testing and usually only three to four storyboards will advance to testing; the remainder of the creative work presented is killed in the meeting. Some clients ask that the agency propose a single storyboard for production, which makes the agency recommendation process more difficult. During the internal agency meeting, an account manager may argue for a storyboard that compares a brand directly with a competitor because he or she believes that a senior client desires this approach. An art director–copywriter team may press for an idea that they want to produce for their own portfolios. The creative director may think his or her idea is the most persuasive or so imaginative that it will help the agency win new business. The decision regarding the agency recommendation is usually made jointly by the creative director and the most senior account manager. There will be a top choice, followed by two to three other options.

Meetings with existing clients rarely involve formal rehearsals. The sequence of the storyboard presentation is discussed before the meeting, and account managers prepare their setups. Senior account managers may telephone their client counterparts to sell them on the general quality of the work beforehand. When clients contemplate an upcoming creative meeting, they hope, as one client said, "that the agency has found the holy grail, that these guys will tell you how to sell a brand in a way that you have never seen." Agency professionals enter creative meetings with some trepidation. They understand the strategy, the consumer, and the client, but client response to creative work is unpredictable. Agency anxiety derives not only from the looming assessment of their work but also from the clients' impending judgment of the people who created it.

The Meeting

The men and women who enter the conference room for a creative meeting exchange cordial remarks about family members or weekend activities to ease tension. Senior clients sit near the center of the table, directly across from the agency presenters, and client subordinates take seats on the same side of the table as their bosses. Agency presenters occupy the center positions, directly across from the clients. More senior advertising agency executives often sit to the extreme right or left of center. The meeting, often referred to as a copy meeting, begins formally when an account manager delivers the setup, outlining the meeting objective, which is to review the advertising. The account manager then outlines the anticipated plan for the new creative work. This could include replacing weak advertising, refreshing a successful campaign, or exploring advertising that may succeed current advertising after testing among consumers. The outcome of the meeting is expressed: "When we are in agreement about the strongest approaches, we will conduct focus groups, then field quantitative testing, then place the advertising in a test market, and, if the market test is successful, we will air the new creative nationally." After completing the meeting objectives, an account manager or account planner reads the creative brief. The brief commonly includes:

- Objective of the advertising
- Target market segment to whom the advertising must appeal
- Insights about the target consumer usually based on research
- Positioning or selling proposition for the brand that sets it apart from competition
- Promise that the advertising must make to the consumer
- Support for the promise that provides a reason to believe the promise made
- Tonality of the advertising
- Mandatories, or items that must be included in the advertising

The setup for the meeting conveys that the agency understands the business context, reminds attendees of the strategic blueprint on which the creative work is based, and sets up client expectations by framing the creative work. After the setup is completed, the creative director explains how the creative team undertook the assignment and explored a wide range of approaches. Creative teams responsible for each idea then expose their ideas to the client. Presenters begin with an explanation of the thinking that took the team from the creative brief to the creative execution. For example, a commercial for a nutritional brand might be inspired by an insight that people over age fifty want to stay healthy to continue to do the things they have always enjoyed. Creatives often use client buzzwords. As one associate creative director said, "When you use their language . . . phrases like 'good recall device' . . . it puts them at ease." The art director describes each storyboard frame, and then the copywriter reads the copy. Storyboards are presented one by one in this manner until all of them are exposed. As the storyboards are presented, clients jot down notes based on a mental checklist that makes evaluation of creative work more systematic. Client criteria for each storyboard typically include:

- Gut reaction
- Consistent with objectives?

- On strategy?
- Connect with the target consumer?
- Clear?
- Distinctive to and ownable for the brand?
- Cut through the clutter of other advertisements?
- Competitive?
- Reflect the character of the brand?
- Extendable to a long-term campaign?
- Supportable scientifically and/or legally?

After all of the creative work has been presented, the creative director or a senior account manager summarizes the ideas, groups them into categories, and discusses the storyboards the agency feels have the greatest merit. Agencies never disparage any of the work they present. Although most clients use the agency recommendation as guidance for their own evaluation, some clients ignore it. In either case, an agency recommendation provides perspective on the relative strength of the ideas and gives clients time to reflect on the work they have been shown. The advertising agency team has lived with the creative work from inception through several rounds of discussion. As one account manager said, "The agency is intimate with the work. The client is not."

After the agency recommendation has been made, clients offer their reactions to the work. Junior client executives usually speak first, followed by coworkers in ascending rank. Junior staffers voice thoughts that correspond to their mental checklist. Senior clients provide more expansive remarks on the fit of the advertising with overall brand business objectives, but even company presidents might comment on a turn of phrase or a product demonstration. During this appraisal, at least one client will express appreciation for the range of thinking and the effort that the agency has expended. This statement is intended to set a positive tone for the ensuing critical comments. Agency professionals know it is mere civility. Some clients prefer to reflect on the creative work, listen to a colleague's comments, and speak only if they have something significant to add, but junior and midlevel clients feel pressure to make cogent remarks. As one client noted, "If you have nothing to contribute, you don't belong in the meeting." A client's career development goals are well served by displaying a grasp of creative concepts and an ability to identify the ideas that have the most potential to grow a brand.

When viewing an array of creative ideas, clients who are unimpressed will rarely say, "None of this works; go back to the drawing board." Instead, they declare, "This is an interesting range of ideas," which is code for "I don't like anything you have shown me." Even when clients reject a storyboard, they may select a phrase or graphic that they encourage the agency to include in the next round of creative development. When clients are responding unfavorably, the hearts of creatives sink, but agency professionals know they must respond to the critique. Not every client comment is addressed. Agencies pay the most attention to, as one client phrased it, "the biggest paycheck." Another client said, "Pencils are raised when the senior VP talks." Comments by junior client executives are heard, but acted upon only if the most senior client present concurs. When all of the clients have responded, the agency expresses its appreciation for their remarks without appearing sycophantic, answers questions that the client has raised, and challenges criticisms tactfully. The agency recommendation is defended with a balance of conviction and conciliation; the agency must convey that it has a well-reasoned point of view while making it clear that it is receptive to the clients' viewpoint. Agencies differ in how resolute they will be in their defense of creative work. An agency that recommends storyboards A, B, and C over D, E, and F may be told by the senior client that only E is acceptable and another round of creative development is required. Some agencies acquiesce immediately or, in agency parlance, "roll over." Other agencies push back until they have convinced the client to accept their argument or they have exhausted all hope that the client can be dissuaded from their own position.

Experienced account managers know the difference between what clients say and what they mean. When a client asks, "Why did you choose that particular graphic?" it is code for "I dislike the graphic." The question format avoids direct conflict. The agency must decide to fight for the idea and explain why it chose it or offer to consider alternatives. Account managers, generally more conciliatory than creatives, feel that, as one account manager said, "Creatives would be better off listening and ferreting out the real issues" rather than leaping to the defense of their work.

Senior agency executives feel pressure to sell their work to clients. They may believe in the quality of the creative, but they also want to avoid endless rounds of redevelopment. In client meetings, account managers take the lead in selling an idea; in addition to their persuasive skills and knowledge of the client's temperament and culture, their personal relationship with a client can help win the agency's case (cf. Moeran 1996: 39–68). As they listen to client comments, agency executives consider the source and formulate their response. Does this client want to look smart in front of the boss? Is that client afraid of championing an idea that is outside the threshold of corporate risk? Does he not understand the idea? Does she not like it? If a client states that an image campaign is too ethereal and contends that a slice-of-life approach would be stronger, and the account manager or creative director knows that this comment is driven by a desire to increase sales quickly with comfortable (low-risk) creative work, the account manager might say, "An image campaign is what our brand needs. If we go this way, we'll be more competitive than ever." Experienced account managers know to stop selling when clients express that they are closed to further discussion. Moreover, the agency must withdraw gracefully. The client must not be made to feel like a bully; if clients sense that the agency team is beaten down, they may request another team within the agency or, worse, consider a new agency. As one creative director phrased it, "A good general knows when to retreat and still retain dignity. You need to be looking to the next meeting, how you will come out in a good position to do better next time." One senior account manager estimated that "You can push clients ten to twenty percent from where they are, but you will never move them more than fifty percent." When agencies push too hard, frustrated clients may dismiss them because they feel the agency does not understand what they want.

After client executives make critical comments, they provide direction to the agency for the next round of creative development. A client will ask that copy be clarified or a product demonstration be simplified. Clear direction is critical. When a client says, "I just don't think that tagline works," the agency is not certain what will please the client. When a client says, "I'd like to see a tagline that expresses our brand's superiority over the competition," the agency can craft copy that will be more acceptable in the next round of creative work.

When all of the comments and responses have been voiced, an agency account manager summarizes the agreements reached and the actions that will be taken following the meeting ("next steps") along with a timetable for accomplishing them. The happiest outcome for agency and client is to advance the process to focus group assessment or production. A requirement by the client for new creative work or substantial revisions stalls progress. When the former result is achieved, participants congratulate one another and say, "Good meeting." Meetings that close without progress are disappointing, but euphemistic phrases such as "Productive meeting" or "We're moving ahead" help mitigate disappointment. Even a "good meeting" may not be good for everyone. Creatives might feel the most conservative work was sold or individual participants may fear they performed poorly during the session. A meeting succeeds on all fronts when the agency and client concur that the best work was chosen, clients feel they have been listened to, and the agency feels that it, too, has been heard. Everyone smiles and departs knowing that they did their job well. A good meeting means that the agency-client relationship has been preserved and very likely strengthened. When a meeting fails to achieve its stated objectives, agency account managers know that they must telephone their client and reassure them that the next round of work will be better.

After the Meeting

Minutes after a creative meeting adjourns and the client and agency teams separate, postmortems begin. Clients usually move on quickly to their next task, although there may be a brief conversation about their delight or disappointment in the agency's work. The agency team gathers and engages in a more extensive assessment of the meeting, often replaying specific client comments and agency responses. Many account managers feel that an unsatisfactory creative meeting undermines their credibility with the client, who may wonder if, as one account manager said, "I have communicated to the creative team what is in the client's head." Creatives must overcome personal demoralization when clients have requested significant changes in their work. As a creative director said, "The advertising will get worse with changes and changes and rewrites and rewrites." One copywriter noted that sometimes "you come back after a meeting and blow off steam. You can't just sit down and start over again until you have done that." After sufficient discussion, account managers review the actions required for the next step in the creative process with the agency team.

Understanding Creative Meetings: Structure, Sentiment, and Meeting Management

Despite options such as telephone conference calls and videoconferencing, in-person, face-to-face advertising creative meetings occur because they allow direct interaction that connects people emotionally as well as intellectually. For agency professionals, creative meetings are ideal venues to sell creative work and enhance client relationships, enabling agencies to better gauge reactions, negotiate with clients, and showcase themselves professionally. For clients, the conference room setting is a superior opportunity for personal performance and professional camaraderie. In face-to-face creative meetings, clients can also demonstrate vividly the power and control they have over their agencies.

Status and Role

When senior agency executives select flanker positions to the far left or right of the center of the conference table, they do so to stress their separateness from other agency staff and to occupy a perch from which to offer commentary during the creative meeting. Their distance from the fray carries other symbolism; it is a vantage point from which they can make the big-picture statements that demonstrate a mastery of the full business context of the creative work. Seating is also important for agency managers to assess and respond to client reactions, including nonverbal reactions to the work. Senior agency executives usually place themselves within the direct sight line of senior clients. The sequence and content of client commentary reflect the status and role of the speaker (see Schwartzman 1989: 291–93 on social position and speaking sequences in meetings). The lower the status, the earlier one speaks and the more circumspect the comments. Higher-status clients offer their thoughts after lower-level managers, giving them the dual advantage of having heard what their colleagues said and additional time to reflect on the creative work.

Rules of Engagement

The agency team is a kind of secret society (Goffman 1959: 104) with unwritten rules of engagement in the presence of those outside the society (Meerwarth, Briody, and Kulkarni 2005). Internally, as Hirschman (1989: 51) observes, "conflict, mutual distrust and power struggles are inherent in the advertising process," but, as Kover and Goldberg (1995: 55) note, the agency must show a "united front" to the client. One of the more egregious meeting sins occurs when an agency representative deviates from the previously agreed upon agency position during a creative meeting. Advertising agency executives who take the risk of improvising a fresh point of view are well advised to do so only then they have the experience and client-sense to express an idea that will advance the interest of the agency. Otherwise, the consequences can be severe. Reprimands of subordinates who diverge from the agency's recommendation are common; cautionary tales tell of employees who transgressed being fired on the return airplane flight after a client meeting. Clients are under less pressure to express a uniform point of view, but most client cultures encourage consensus and clients know that moving creative work forward requires agreement on the direction they provide to the agency.

Reading the Room

Just before a creative meeting many years ago, a well-known advertising executive was asked by one of his agency associates what he recommended. His reply: "Read the room." His meaning: assess client reactions as ideas are presented and adjust the agency recommendation to match the ideas that the client will accept. During creative meetings, agency executives do not watch their colleagues present; they watch their clients. They scan faces for confusion, comprehension, and delight. They study eyes and body language. They pay attention to how many notes clients are taking, and they watch for client reactions to specific graphics and copy. When the agency summarizes the body of work, when clients comment, when the agency responds and the client counters, agency executives read the room. This process of reading the room helps the agency control creative meetings. When a client is perceived as unreceptive to an agency recommendation, an agency executive formulates a defense that shows cognizance of the client's discomfort: "The idea in this board is totally new in this category. It will startle the consumer, and it will cut through the clutter of competitive advertising. This approach may make us a bit uncomfortable, but it is precisely the kind of advertising the brand needs right now to succeed." If the agency executive senses that the favored board is being judged extremely poorly and even a strong argument will not persuade the client, the executive will cast a glance at colleagues and soften the agency recommendation: "The idea in this board is totally new in this category. It will startle the consumer, and it will cut through the category clutter of competitive advertising. But, because it is so cutting edge, we should test it among consumers to see if we have gone too far."

One agency creative director described how he visualizes a conference room swaying as arguments veer side to side. He prepares his arguments and chooses a position based on where the room lands. He may agree or disagree with the prevailing client point of view, but he will choose his statements carefully to ensure that the meeting does not become contentious. The process of reading the room, like comprehending the difference between a wink and a blink (Geertz 1973: 6–7), requires deep contextual understanding. Senior agency executives, especially account managers, must know the psychology of the participants, the true quality and strength of the creative work, the corporate cultures, and the relationships of the meeting attendees. The power and accuracy of an agency executive's intuition, of knowing by seeing and listening, is critical.

Defending the Work

Clients may criticize creative work because they believe it is off strategy, it fails their checklist of acceptable advertising, or it is inconsistent with "what we know works." A major issue for creative executives is how to best protect the integrity of their idea when clients feel, as an associate creative director said, that "challenging their beliefs is like challenging their religion." Kover and Goldberg (1995: 56–59) describe several strategies that copywriters use to argue for their work, all of which are also applied by art directors and account managers. These tactics include selling ideas with passion; a frontal attack; presenting work that is likely to sell; a risky proposition; as noted earlier; offering the appearance of acceptance, then doing what they wish, which may be effective with small revisions but is not viable when the issue is whether an idea should even be produced; and, finally, the "aleatory game," which entails hoping for the best outcome. Experienced account managers lower rising temperatures in contentious creative meetings by intervening with phases such as, "That's a good thought. We'll consider that." Agency colleagues and clients depend upon account managers to control meetings; account managers know that an adroit defense of creative work and the ability to defuse difficult situations is a measure of their value.

Although clients often claim they want breakthrough advertising, many clients are nervous that edgy creative work will violate the character of their brand, unless the brand character is, by definition, edgy. Moreover, creatives feel that clients often don't get it when particularly inventive executions are presented, a reaction that Schudson (1984: 81) terms "aesthetic insensitivity." This lack of comprehension sometimes traces to a creative idea that, when presented in storyboard form, does not fully convey the idea in that form. In these cases, agency executives ask clients to either use their imaginations or take a leap of faith that the idea described will be impactful and compelling for consumers. Clients' lack of understanding of a creative idea is demonstrated by the common client practice of expressing a wish that selected copy or graphics used in one storyboard also be used in other storyboards. Similarly, when a client feels that an execution has too much humor, the client may ask the agency to dial it back. As one creative said, "When they change the board, they pull out the one thread that holds it together." Clients' desire for a recitation of a brand's features, attributes, and benefits can snuff out a creative idea. As a creative director said, "The idea gets whittled away by the client's checklist." Clients believe that they own the creative work. When they want changes, the agency knows that it should, after discussion, agree to make them. Creatives feel that they, as the inventors of the idea, own it (Hirschman 1989; Kover and Goldberg 1995; Young 2000), which adds tension to creative meetings. As Kover (1995: 604) writes, "Copy writers have a 'reputation' in the folklore of the advertising business. They are charged with defending their work and its integrity against any charge, no matter how small." Kover's explanation for this behavior is that "Copy writers do not merely present advertising, they present *themselves*" (Kover 1995: 604, emphasis in original). He notes that copywriters speak about their work as if it is "a piece carved from their private being" (Kover 1995: 604), and Kover and Goldberg (1995: 53) remark on the resentment that creatives feel when clients alter their work (for a discussion on creatives' identity in advertising agencies, see Hackley and Kover 2007).

How aggressively creatives and account managers defend creative work is contingent upon agency and client cultures. Many clients see challenges to their criticisms as evidence of agency conviction, and they respond positively as long as the defense is respectful and cordial. Seeing an agency acquiesce when a storyboard is critiqued suggests that the agency has little heart for the work, and the client may wonder why the agency presented it. When the agency fights too long and hard, clients become annoyed. Clients also know when agency executives claim, "I agree with everything you have said," they are about to disagree and prolong a discussion. In such situations, clients anticipate that after the meeting they will have a conversation with a senior account manager who will fix it. If the account manager cannot deliver what the client wants, that manager risks replacement by an account manager who will. When the choice is between fighting the good fight for the creative work and protecting the agency-client relationship, the latter is the necessary course. Agency executives understand that advertising may be at the intersection of commerce and art, but commerce is the main drag, and clients control the road.

Agreements

Agreements are the actions that will be taken to revise, test, or produce creative work after a meeting. The word *agreement* has an egalitarian and conciliatory connotation; it also implies that the client and agency concur on what needs to be done. However, *to agree* does not always mean to be *in agreement*. The review of agreements in creative meetings is, in fact, a recitation of client directives. The word *agreement* fuels the illusion that the client and agency are peers, and it smooths over disagreements that may have occurred during the meetings, but there is no mistake that the clients are in charge.

Impression Management and Impressing Management

Presentations by agencies in creative meetings are performances according to Goffman's definition: "all the activity of a given participant on a given occasion which serves to influence in any way the other participants" (Goffman 1959: 15) and are "social dramas" (Turner 1974, 1988; cf. Moeran 2006: 60–77 for a similar perspective). As a creative director said, "The spotlight is on you. You have the chance to convince someone that something you have created is worth the world seeing." A central tenet of Goffman's analysis, impression management, is evident throughout creative meetings. Agencies attempt to impress clients with an understanding of the client's business, their devotion to the brand, and their passion for the creative work. An expression of passion can persuade clients that creative work is worthy of acceptance. As a creative director phrased it, "Passion can be contagious." Clients also aim to impress management. Junior client executives want to demonstrate to their bosses that they are guiding the creative development process effectively and, since they know their judgments are being judged, that they bring their share of insights to the meeting. When creative work is received poorly and no progress is made, a midlevel client can "die inside because it makes my life worse. The process is stalled and I'll get slammed." Junior agency executives want to impress senior staff as well, and all of the agency presenters must impress their clients.

Rites of Passage

Creative meetings are a rite of passage as defined by Van Gennep ([1909] 1960; cf. Moeran 1996: 94). Creative work is separated from its development while in storyboard form; selected ideas are transformed during the meeting by suggested revisions and then returned to the development process for consumer assessment or airing. Creative meetings are the liminal period (Van Gennep [1909] 1960: 21), "betwixt and between" (Malefyt 2003: 145; Turner 1964), during which the transformation occurs, a process we will address in the next chapter.[1]

The successful transition of a storyboard from preclient exposure to initiation as a client-approved board is hailed with as much jubilation as other rites of passage throughout the world. Meeting participants are transformed as well. It is not only the storyboard that is evaluated in creative meetings, it is also the people who created or contributed to the work. Extending the argument from Geertz (1973) that cocks symbolize men and from Kover (1995) that storyboards represent copywriters, all of the advertising agency and client executives who display their imagination, intellect, experience, and professionalism in a creative meeting are as exposed and judged as the advertising ideas. In this sense, approval or disapproval of a body of work and the achievement of goals in creative meetings is not just business. It is personal.

* * *

Advertising creative meetings are, as Schwartzman notes of all meetings, "sense makers" that help participants "define, represent, and also reproduce social entities and relationships" (Schwartzman 1989: 39), and they function as "social and cultural validators" that enhance a sense of community and identity within an organization (Schwartzman 1989: 41). Moeran observed this phenomenon in a Japanese advertising agency, when he noted that meetings are "frames in which participants made sense of their organization and their actions taken therein" (Moeran 2005: 14). Sensemaking modes in creative meetings include the comprehension of verbal codes that mollify tense situations, the reading of verbal and nonverbal behavior, the understanding of the subtle machinations surrounding the client-agency balance of power, and the craft of negotiation. Miller (1997), writing about an agency in Trinidad, agrees with Moeran, writing about an agency in Japan, that presentations "define and maintain the advertising community as a whole" (Moeran 1993: 88). Schwartzman contends that meetings are organization life "writ small" (Schwartzman 1989: 39). Similarly, advertising creative meetings contain the essence of agency-client relationships: conflicting objectives, displays of status, opportunities to show supreme insight, to control without appearing controlling, to demonstrate passion without being combative, to persuade without browbeating, and to accept without embracing. Agencies work hard to sustain creative integrity, but preservation of the agency-client relationship is paramount, for without the relationship, there is no advertising assignment and no creative meeting to attend.

Despite the conflicts in creative meetings, the confluence of professional and personal objectives makes these meetings a powerful mechanism of action in the advertising industry. They function because they provide a venue for commercial ideas to be challenged and made stronger and for participants to achieve goals that secure their positions and advance their careers. In creative development, the agency's desire for art shaped by the demands of commerce meets the clients' need for commerce clothed in seductive art. During creative meetings, the often dazzling fusion of business goals and creativity and of divergent organizational, attitudinal, and temperamental styles, converge. Some advertising agency executives say, "It's all about the work." Others view their business cynically, as the management of agency-client relationships. Both are correct. The work of the agency is the creative product and the creative meeting itself.

Rituals of Creativity in Advertising Agencies

Advertising agencies labor hard and fast to innovate and be creative. They must regularly produce creative products in the form of advertisements and other branded ideas for their clients. Moreover, the new creative work must be different from the work that it replaces within a current campaign and stand in contrast to the advertisements of competitors. Advertising agencies produce no standardized product—each ad is a "one-of-a-kind set of ideas" (Moeran 2006: 80). This requirement places extreme pressure on agencies to continually dream up fresh ideas. To do so, they depend on internal mechanisms that satisfy the demands of clients, respond to the competitive marketplace, and garner industry attention so they can win awards. We argue in this chapter that rituals around the production of creativity are a central means by which advertising agencies are able to do the work they do.

Creativity is the mainstay of advertising agency output. Creativity occurs as a group dynamic when agency executives—particularly account managers, account planners, and creatives—gather to plan and create ads. Research on creativity, from a psychological perspective, shows that it is embedded in social groups and that creative products emerge from collaborative networks (Farrell 2001; John-Steiner 2000; Paulus and Nijstad 2003; Sawyer 2003, 2006). Yet, even though the importance of group collaboration is recognized, there is little understanding of the mechanisms whereby creative products emerge from group interaction (Sawyer and DeZutter 2009: 81). Furthermore, while much has been documented on the creativity of advertisements, their circulation in society, and their effect on culture (Marchand 1985; Mazzarella 2003b; Moeran 1996; Miller 1997; O'Barr 1994; Williamson 1978), few anthropologists have explored the creative process within advertising agencies (Malefyt 2006; Malefyt and Moeran 2003; Moeran 1996, 2005, 2006, 2009). Here, we explore creative development in advertising agencies as a group dynamic that is facilitated by a ritual process. We contend that through rituals that center on a key symbol, the brand, creativity in advertising agencies is managed, controlled, and channeled.

Rituals, Symbols, and Advertising Agency Creativity

To understand how rituals and their key symbols shape the production of creativity in advertising agencies, we situate the roles and functions of various agency people in the idea of "social drama" as defined by Victor Turner (1974, 1988). Turner's concept of social drama illustrates how certain principles of an organization and its values, such as producing creativity, operate through schisms and reconciliations (1988: 37). Social dramas, Turner suggests, are cultural performances that convert the "raw material" of society into a new order. They are frameworks in which rituals are enacted and transform social and natural reality so that a group can move forward as well as look back and affirm itself. In an advertising agency, social dramas are regularized occurrences that rely on key symbols and rituals as mechanisms to mediate, transform, and produce the necessary symbolic and normative change for creativity to occur as an agency product.

Creativity, Brand, and the Need for Ritual

To understand the internal dynamics in which agency personnel produce creative work, we must first distinguish brands from products. The term brand broadly applies to goods, services, and even executives in the fields of marketing, advertising, sales, promotions, public relations, and design among others. Brands conjure up images of an objectified product or service that can be bought, sold, traded, aspired to, and so on by consumers. Brands offer something extra to the consumer, a perceived "added value" (Davidson 1992), which advertising promotes through the circulation of images and associations. Kotler contends that almost everything can be a brand. "A brand is any label that carries meaning and associations" (Kotler 2003: 8). Brands are also different from products in how they embody cultural contradictions. Brands, paradoxically, thrive in a contrastive world of similarity and difference. As products proliferate in a particular competitive market, their benefits and features compared with other products tend to blur. For example, all soft drink colas as similar products to some degree offer sweet taste, caffeine, and carbonation and provide a burst of energy. Brands, however, operate in the nontangible realm, where differences among similar products are brought out through contrastive symbols and ideologies. Coke, the soft drink cola, is advertised as "the real thing" in opposition to Pepsi, which is advertised as "the choice of the new generation." As James Twitchell (2004) writes, brands thrive in surplus conditions because they achieve value relative to other brands. Michael Callon and others define a brand by a combination of characteristics that establish its singularity. Brand singularity assumes value in relation to others. Defining a brand means positioning it in a space of other brands, in a system of differences and similarities, and of distinct yet connected categories (Callon, Meadel, and Rabeharosoa 2002). Advertising campaigns purposely build off this similar-but-different tension, as advertising highlights the singular qualities of one brand relative to a field of competitors. Advertising agencies must be aware of rival campaigns, new fads, and trends and consumers' complex relationship to brands, because market changes can quickly alter a brand's perceived value. This creates a field of ambiguity, potential, and change for consumers' relationship with brands. It also makes for a symbolic totem around which rituals that construct advertising in an ad agency revolve.

Brands embody another set of contradictions. They shift between subject and object, between a focus that keeps them as an enduring aspect of sameness and as a beacon of change. Inherent in brands is a dynamic of change and continuity. To constantly differentiate their position from rivals, brands must always innovate their communications with consumers in the marketplace. Even traditional brand management teams continually refresh advertising campaigns to be current in the consumers' minds (new songs, slogans, package redesigns), because change, at least positive change, creates value (Appadurai 1996). Coke continues with new songs; Pepsi redesigns its logo. Yet brands also need to retain their essence of sameness, continuity, and familiarity. Launching "New Coke" in the 1980s was a disaster because it alienated loyalists. The company quickly reverted back to its familiar formula to reassure customers that they could buy the Coke they loved. Brand innovation of a familiar subject occurs as a result of constant realignment and fresh advertising campaigns relative to marketplace changes and is central to advertising agency work in and of itself.

These paradoxical properties make the brand a highly charged, ambiguous, and, therefore, ideal symbol for ritual use (Douglas 1966; Turner 1969). Turner discussed highly charged cultural phenomena as ambiguous, multivocalic, unifying, and in need of strict ritual to guide and contain them. Brands, in this light, can be seen as ritual symbols. Ritual symbols, according to Turner (1969) and Kertzer (1988), have three main characteristics. They *condense* a range of meanings and unify them into a cohesive emotional whole; they are *multivocalic* because they express many points of view at the same time; they are *ambiguous* because they shift and adapt to suit purposes. A brand has all of these symbolic characteristics, just as it functions as an everyday product for consumer consumption. In particular, a brand's ambiguity—as an overarching symbol that is also a malleable product—allows individuals and groups to use social practices to gain authority and legitimate control over it. In this sense, brands achieve value as a ritual symbol in agency work through their ambiguous mutability, which can be used to shape representations of reality.[1] Supporting the need for ritual, the stewards of the brand—manufacturers and advertising agency executives—have different perspectives on its meaning because of the brand's unity, multivocality, and ambiguity.

Advertising agencies are the authoritative cultural force charged with transforming ordinary objects (products) into elevated symbolic vehicles (brands) for which consumers are willing to pay more. In this role, agencies are a site of cultural production (Bourdieu 1993) that reorders external cultural transformations (brand advertisements) through internal enactments of social dramas (rituals) that unite, contest, and reconfigure the brand in familiar yet novel ways. Through consumer research, intradepartmental negotiations, and creative work, actors in advertising agencies mediate stability and direct change through the brand, which, in Turner's terms, is a ritual symbol, around which the social drama of stability and change is enacted. The representational and paradoxical meaning of the brand is especially apparent in the context of advertising agencies when the brand is the subject of advertising development. The brand has an essential enduring character that must be sustained because substantial change for a brand risks alienating loyal brand users. Yet to compete in an ever-changing marketplace, the brand must also frequently be reinvented and refreshed. Creativity around the brand is thus ambiguous and contentious; it needs ritual action to make it happen. Adding to the complexity is the agency innovation process, during which creatives stress change and account managers work to secure the stability of client relations. These products and practices require a mediating structure, which we locate in the ritual process.

Innovation, Collaboration, and Ritual

The innovation generated by advertising agencies is manifested in novel strategic ideas, original research, and imaginative advertising campaigns that win agencies clients and attract consumers to brands. Multiple agency departments collaborate with copywriters, art directors, account planners, account managers, and others contributing to the process. This mode of production has been of interest to anthropologists recently (Malefyt 2009; Malefyt and Moeran 2003; Moeran 1996, 2005, 2006, 2009). In the previous chapter, we described it briefly as a rite of passage, but advertising agency collaboration has not been examined fully within a ritual framework.

Ritual has been studied by anthropologists for over a century to elucidate the process and meaning of life stages, belief systems, political movements, social conflict and resolution, and identity (Douglas 1966; Durkheim [1915] 1965; Kertzer 1988; Turner 1964, 1969; Van Gennep [1909] 1960). Innovation and collaboration in advertising have rarely been treated jointly, especially as they together form the core of interaction and difference that exemplify a ritual process. Moeran has offered a detailed discussion of advertising development as a social drama but did not focus on ritual per se (Moeran 2006: 65–69; see Goffman 1959 for a related discussion on impression management). Ritual offers a construct for analyzing the multiple roles and transformations that define advertising agency contestation, collaboration, and creative innovation. Rituals are also a mechanism by which operating tensions within the agency and symbolic cultural tensions of the brand are resolved. Douglas (1966) affirms that rituals are enacted to resolve cultural tensions. Rituals reformulate experience and create a sense of control, a new order out of disorder. Disorder by implication offers unlimited and indefinite patterning, a possibility to reorder in a new way (Douglas 1966: 95). But disorder is dangerous. In advertising agencies, tempers often flare and people resign or are fired. This is why a process of transforming disorder into new order is needed to mediate danger and unleash potential ideas for new and breakthrough creative work. Ritual also organizes the roles of people involved toward a particular end, occurs within a set time frame, with a set of performers, and requires an audience, a special place, and occasion of performance (Turner 1988: 23). These elements constitute the observable functional aspects of the ritual and evoke the symbolic dynamics of social drama in which advertising agency innovation occurs.

The process of brand innovation in the agency can be viewed as ritual rite of passage consisting of the three phases identified by Van Gennep ([1909] 1960: 21). At various stages of advertising innovation, the process *separates* members and their work, places them in a *liminal* (often sequestered) location where they and their work undergo transformations, and, finally, they and their work are *reintegrated* into their workplace at a changed, often higher status. In chapter 6, "Creativity, Person, and Place," we discuss how creatives separate themselves from work in transitional places to gather creative muse. Here, we examine the interdepartmental agency dynamics that mediate creativity. Specifically, the ritual phases begin with a client assignment that requests that new work must break with advertising that represents the brand in the present (separation). New advertising, needed to propel brand sales, must be a departure that is sufficiently innovative in message and storyline to be judged by the client first, then by the target consumer, as something fresh and persuasive. The next phase includes research, strategy development, and the generation of the creative product, as well as the collaboration these processes entail (transformation). The final phase is client acceptance and public launch of the advertising campaign (integration). Following Van Gennep ([1909] 1960: 182), death and rebirth is symbolized in this passage; the current brand advertising dies and a new advertising campaign is reborn.

We locate the mediating (transforming) work of ritual in the tension of two collaborative yet often conflicting agency perspectives and efforts: the account team and the creative team. The account team knows the client's corporate culture and they work to maintain the agency-client bond. At the same time, the account team supports the agency's creative work and sells it to the client. The creative team sees their work as a way to express their talents and innovative thinking. They source and align with consumer values and popular trends. Some creatives even imagine dialogues with consumers to arrive at and validate their campaign ideas (Kover 1995). Creatives often desire that their ideas gain traction so that they and the brand gain consumer and professional recognition.

During the creative revolution in the 1960s, the difference between creative and account sides of agency life began to become even more distinctive. Creatives were encouraged to be anticlient in their creative pursuits—acting out quirky behavior, wearing long hair and casual clothing, and subject to emotional outbursts (in Moeran 2006). Meanwhile, account managers (the "suits") aligned with the client desires for more rigorous scientific testing of creative work and measuring commercials against media weight, often against the wishes of creative teams. Indeed, as Moeran explains, "it is this inherent potential conflict between accounts and advertisements, money and ideas, producers and consumers, account managers and copywriters and art directors that inspires and constrains the ideas and practices of creativity in all advertising industries throughout the world" (Moeran 2006: 83). In this way, behavioral, attitudinal, and philosophical differences evolved to differentiate agency dynamics into opposing yet complementary forces that require resolution.[2]

Advertisements as well as advertising executives operate on multiple levels of contradictions in an ever-changing symbolic world of tensions. The collective work of an agency mediates and gives value to brand contradictions, as the brand itself serves as the source by which agency personnel express, and then resolve, their tensions to move forward with the agency's tasks. The brand—the subject of the agency's relationship with clients and the external consumer world and the object of internal creative efforts for success—needs ritual to mediate contradictions and to reconcile this tension into entities that are productive to innovative creative work and client security. In this way, advertising agency dynamics are an ideal modern location in which to study rituals of creativity, since agencies are a site where ordinary products are transformed into elevated brands and teams work to resolve tensions that lead to a creative product.

Account Managers and Creatives as Collaborators

A booklet from the American Association of Advertising Agencies suggests that the first golden rule of agency-client relationships is "It's not 'us' and 'them,' it's 'we'" (Grant 2002: 18). However, even when the "us" is in alignment, the "we" is problematic given the sometimes divergent goals of clients and agencies. Account managers, as collaborators with their creative executive cohorts and business partners with their clients, are beholden to both of these parties. They struggle with their complex role and the perception of them by colleagues and clients. Are they champions or compromisers, collaborators or traitors, stewards or sellouts, allies or the opposition, advocates or adversaries, one of us or one of them? Ultimately, account managers see the needs of their clients as paramount because protecting the agency-client relationship means protecting their agency—and their jobs. Given the interaction of these two sides—the account side wanting client (and metaphorically brand) stability and the creative side desiring to distinguish itself with iconoclastic work—the ritual process mediates the tensions to bring the work to completion. In fact, without mediation, there might be unresolved tensions, resulting in no movement for change or creativity to occur. The internal agency and agency-client interactions during creative development constitute a social drama in which rituals thrive (Turner 1974, 1988) and as described by Moeran (2006: 65–69). Conflict and resolution, the central characteristics of social drama, bring to prominence the fundamental characteristics of society (Turner 1974: 35) and advertising agency life. Discussion, negotiation, dysfunction, disharmony, and reconciliation is the process by which the ads we watch on television, read in print, hear on the radio, and see on the Internet are produced, circulated, and consumed in society.

Advertising Development and the Liminal Period

Collaboration and contestation among agency account managers, account planners, and creatives occurs throughout the entire advertising development process, but the liminal phase is of special interest as a space for the management of stability and innovation. We follow Turner (1964, 1969) in defining the liminal period as transitional and transformational, as a threshold over which, in an advertising agency, the creative work must pass. (The liminal period is often described as a sacred space, but it is as much a space where scenes of play and experimentation occur as it is for solemnity and rules [Turner 1988: 25].) The liminal phase places things in their subjunctive mode, where social flow bends back on itself, the what-if phase of possibilities, suppositions, desires, and hypotheses.

In advertising agency practice, as in other domains that join art and commerce, such as fashion, film, and music, there are several discrete ritual occasions and liminal periods that mark the agency's collaborative efforts on innovation. After a client assignment, there is a discovery period during which, through research, the agency seeks a different perspective on the brand from a consumer point of view. The research explores assumed meanings that the client and agency share and seeks out new insights that ignite fresh ways to represent the brand strategically and creatively. The research is synthesized in a creative brief. Creative development work is a further separation from the brief. Creative executives re-express the strategy in formats (storyboards for television, computer-generated art for print, scripts for radio) that they anticipate will have client and consumer appeal. Their work is reviewed by agency account managers and account planners before it is presented to the agency's client. The additional phases that follow include meetings on creative work with clients and the production of creative ideas for public exposure. Each of these phases also contains liminal periods. Moreover, these ritual events are performances that require a high degree of collaboration to function effectively (Beeman 2007: 276). Account managers support account planners when they brief creative teams on research and strategy and support creatives in client creative presentations because these agency performers need assistance to direct their respective audiences to attend to their research insight or the big idea. Account planners inform account managers of their insights and depend upon their influence in briefings if creatives offer resistance. When the agency presents new advertising ideas to the client, creatives often need the backing of astute account managers if the client doesn't get it.

Consumer Research and Insight Formulation

The work in generating a new view of the brand that will feed creative development typically begins with qualitative consumer research. Agency account planners are charged with this effort in which they, along with specialist research vendors, seek to discover a fresh perspective or previously unseen behavior among consumers or uncover a brand assumption that can then be expressed as a new message about the brand. The research design must be innovative to bring original thinking that leads to new creative ideas. The challenge of this effort is that the research must find insights that are compelling, spark creative ideas from creatives, appeal to consumers, and do not alienate clients. Often, account planners work with account managers to best temper and integrate the new learning into forms that can be accepted and workable for the creative team. In one assignment, the branded version of a feminine hygiene product that centered on the advertised idea of protection was found not to resonate with women who used this product. Rather, women in the interviews focused on the natural construction of the cotton features of the brand, which they said made them feel more comforted and cared for than other brands. Because this insight was different from the current brand positioning of protection, some form of mediation was needed to best integrate the research finding into the agency's creative process. A creative brief, written to the new insight, needed to mediate the old and the new advertising approaches. In this case, the idea of protection was integrated with the idea of comfort and naturalness to be mediated in a creative expression of "natural comfort that you can trust." This insight helped evolve the brand position of protection and would lead to new creative efforts stressing natural comfort and care as the lead brand benefit. From a branded perspective, the insight was similar to rivals in the category of feminine hygiene products—some form of protection is conveyed in all advertising. Yet the insight was different from rivals in stressing the natural comfort of cotton features in order to differentiate the brand. During this liminal period, agency planners and account managers collaborated closely to resolve conceptual and interpersonal tensions and arrive at a creative brief that would inspire creatives. The brief was presented jointly by planners and account managers to the client to ensure the corporation's buy-in of the integration of two different approaches: the old (e.g., protection) and the new (e.g., naturalness).

The Internal Agency Creative Review

We can also apply a ritual analysis to the process of account management–creative collaboration when the two parties meet to discuss work the creatives have drafted for a client meeting. During these internal agency sessions, account managers provide input, eliminate ideas, and suggest new areas to develop. They want the ideas to be innovative, but their primary concern is maintaining stability with their client. Account managers do not want creative ideas to introduce too much change, but enough to demonstrate a departure from current advertising while sustaining the brand's essence. The internal agency sessions, then, constitute a liminal phase, serving as a threshold over which the new body of agency work must pass. During the transition, creatives and account managers collaborate to transform the work so that it can move forward. Creatives enter this phase with ideas they feel are strong, but account managers often disagree. The internal agency review follows a ritualized process, evident behaviorally and linguistically. Creative teams present their ideas in draft form, and account managers comment on each execution. Account managers might observe that some work is off-strategy, critiques might be offered on storylines that the account manager feels will not be seen as relatable by the target consumer or will likely be disliked by clients, or opine that certain phrases and narratives simply don't work. An account manager may urge creatives to design clearer product demonstrations or add more mentions that a new product form is a breakthrough. If the account manager feels that the body of work does not cover a full range of ideas, additional work is requested. Throughout this exchange, creatives are loath to revise their work. They defend their thinking, based on the belief that their insights are sound, their imagination is robust, and their skills are unassailable (Kover and Goldberg 1995). Creatives believe account manager meddling will defile the purity of their creations. Account managers do not share this veneration and remain agnostic until clients approve the work. This conflict also speaks to creatives' mistrust of account managers' commitment to their working partnership. Whereas account managers see their role as collaborators, creatives often view them as adversaries or client appeasers.

Account managers understand they have a delicate task during this social drama. They begin by lauding the overall effort and then comment gingerly on each execution. Suggestions are phrased carefully so as to not offend and to underscore collaboration: "Let's be sure this storyboard expresses the consumer benefit clearly." To ensure creatives do not perceive account managers as the source of criticism for subpar work, judgments are shifted to consumers: "We need to have more brand identification in this work because the testing we did recently told us consumers have trouble remembering the brand name." To convey that there should be an account management–creative partnership in managing risk to the agency in the agency-client relationship, an account manager will say: "This is such a breakthrough execution, and I love it. I just wonder if we should tone it down a bit so the client is not scared to air it." During the talk about which work to revise or eliminate, and which work needs to be further developed, negotiations ensue, and battles rage. By the end of the review process, some work remains intact; other work is revised; new work is planned. All parties agree on the objectives and timing, the next internal meeting is arranged, and the process begins again until everyone concurs that the work is ready for passage to client review. If negotiation reaches an impasse, the highest-ranking agency executive selects the work that will move ahead and determines which of the changes will be made.

During the internal review process, as creatives, account managers, and account planners grapple with the balance between brand continuity and advertising innovation, they consider: How malleable is the brand character? How innovative can a new creative execution be before it deviates too far from the brand's essence? Will an idea the agency presents be considered by the client as so radical that the client perceives that the agency does not grasp the brand's essence, and will that perception jeopardize the agency-client relationship? Will consumers accept this new image of the brand? Is highly innovative advertising, even if accepted by the client, worth the risk that consumer sales may suffer, and the agency is fired by the client? Creatives are acutely aware that they must generate imaginative work that retains the brand's essence but departs from ideas that have previously represented the brand in the marketplace. Additionally, they know that their innovations will validate the agency's value to the client. They also understand that if their thinking strays too far from the brand's essence, account managers will attenuate or kill some highly progressive ideas. Account managers, more concerned than creatives with what is right for the brand strategically and executionally, also focus on what will fly within their client's culture. For them, the stability of the agency-client bond outweighs pressure placed upon them by creatives to push hard for bold innovations that stretch the boundaries of a brand's essence or the comfort level of their clients. Even when account managers claim they will fight for innovation, creatives know that their cohorts are likely to roll at the first sign of client disapproval.

This liminal phase of collaboration is a highly charged drama where tensions surface and metaphor reigns (Fernandez 1986: xi–xii). Creatives protect the purity of their ideas because their product represents them as individuals, their alignment with consumer trends, and their current career status and future career progression. Account managers worry about the impact of innovation on the brand's essence and the agency-client bond, so they reduce risk. The brand advertising, then, is a metaphor for the advertising agency's overall collaborative process, of working through roles, ideas, and professional ambitions (cf. Fernandez 1986: 20–22). Creatives, as representatives of ingenuity and advocates of change, are protagonists of risk but also of potential reward for the agency. Account managers, as representatives and the protectors of their agency, product, and clients, are collaborators in this drama, but they know that their primary function is to manage risk for the agency.

The Ritual Framework for Agency Innovation and Collaboration

The ritual process in creative development is more than a symbolic reflection of social operations. The cultural acts of conflict and collaboration in the liminal phase are, in and of themselves, agents of innovative change. They are the drawing board on which creative actors sketch out "designs for living" (Turner 1988: 24). As a ritual process, advertising work necessitates the efforts and collaboration of distinct and often contrary departments and individuals, wherein actors are organized, assigned different roles, and divided in time. Various roles are allocated to agents for the collaborative transformation of the creative work into something innovative. In addition, the ambiguity, multiplicity of meaning, and condensability of a brand give the brand its power and value for innovative change. From the perspective of collaboration, the brand's qualities allow it to be treated as a key symbol that is used in a ritual process and modified by agency executives. The brand is a social force reflective of permanence and change, similarity and difference as it brings together actors from the strategic, creative, agency management, client, and, ultimately, consumer domains, all engaged in the continuous negotiation of brand meaning.

Every social world has a primary frame of interaction or drama in which that world is legitimized and sustained (Moeran 2005; Turner 1988). In the world of advertising, the brand becomes a ritualized framework in the social drama that sustains and gives legitimacy to the actions of advertising agency executives. The brand is not an objectified thing or symbol for individuals as commonly treated by marketers and agencies, but rather represents a dynamic space or frame for strategic interactions (Moeran 2005). Action to change the brand occurs in the agency, even as executives work to protect and maintain the integrity of the brand. The brand is a paradox in its own right and a metaphor for the drama that defines agency relationships. Neither the brand nor the relationships are static. The brand and its agents are in movement and both represent a space of possibilities where ritual transformations occur. As an expression of social interaction and an outcome of ritual transformation, the brand acquires social value and acceptance, which allows all these interactions between the actors to be legitimate.

* * *

Ritual is frequently regarded in scholarship in only those aspects of social life and social action that appear exotic in relation to what we consider normal; anthropological approaches have often distanced ritual from ordinary experiences (Hughes-Freeland 1998: 1). To place ritual in relation to the operations of everyday business, as we have done in this essay, is to recognize the value of anthropological analysis in mainstream applications. We have identified and analyzed ritual in a way that does not traditionally look like ritual. We have shown that ritual can appear ordinary (as it can also appear exotic), but in either form, ritual is critical to understand as a structure and process that channels social behavior toward purposeful ends. While meetings and presentations are common occurrences and part of daily life in an advertising agency, the brand is held with sacred reverence and regarded with ritual etiquette when advertising is developed. The paradox of the brand and its relation to the advertising agency reveals how formal structures and specific social roles within agencies are given purpose and direction to guide and reinvent a sacred symbol through conflict and resolution. This process furthers our understanding of how social action and performance can assume a collaborative function in creative production. This chapter also affirms the view that creative generation in terms of cultural production does not occur in a vacuum as in isolation by the sole artist. Rather, creativity occurs as a product of social relations and interactions in a field of strategic possibilities (Bourdieu 1993: 34). Bourdieu explains in other artistic fields the active roles of advertising creative and account teams are, in a sense, defined in relation to each other's position within a system. From these positions and even from negative relationships, the roles of individuals and teams within advertising agencies receive distinctive value from positions relative to each other and to the brand that define a "space of possibles" (1993: 30). Out of these positions, the rituals performed to mediate similarities and differences and stability and change operate within a field of production to make advertisements. This insight affords an understanding as to why and how advertising agencies maintain clear roles. What may seem ordinary in business becomes critical to the functioning of agency health and life.

–4–

Fieldwork in Advertising Research

What happens to the anthropological process when corporate clients come along in fieldwork to observe, comment on, and interact in ethnographic research? How are outcomes of fieldwork influenced by hired consultants who join projects and give their input for client support and brand direction? How are multiple and sometimes conflicting views toward consumers and brand objectives mediated with popular trends and social movements? These questions, rarely vetted by the lone anthropologist in traditional ethnographic fieldwork, are part and parcel of the experience of corporate ethnography in advertising and marketing research. While traditional fieldwork is concerned with self-reflective, single-authored representations of native others (Clifford 1988; Clifford and Marcus 1986), corporate fieldwork often incorporates multiple perspectives of others, deals with social currents of the time, and still respects the anthropological adage of "representing the social reality of others" (Van Maanen 1988: ix). In fact, as we will discuss, rather than presenting issues, these circumstances can be opportunities for anthropologists to guide and direct corporate ideologies and consumer practices in positive ways. Anthropologists in corporations can favorably influence often-conflicting marketing perspectives of clients and consultants by redirecting more limiting views of consumers toward broader cultural understandings.

In this chapter we discuss the pragmatics of conducting ethnographic fieldwork in corporate settings where anthropologists are involved in negotiating the outcomes of fieldwork. This concept of mediating multiple agents, such as clients, consultants, and informed consumers, is examined here during the course of fieldwork as an example of what we do as cultural experts in our organizations: coalesce broader cultural perspectives—in this case, the health and wellness movement—with specific ethnographic assignments from clients. Responding to McCracken's call for greater integration of cultural leadership in corporations (McCracken 2009), we see great value in anthropologists conducting research that blends current cultural trends with specific client goals in ethnography. We also discuss this process in chapter 10, "Hybrid Research Methodologies and Business Success," because we view it as a critical advantage to what corporate anthropologists can offer advertising and marketing enterprises. While we present a specific case study here, this situation is typical of work in advertising and marketing research today. We show how anthropologists can help mediate client objectives, consumer perspectives, and the goals of hired consultants to better inform corporations about consumers' attitudes and beliefs toward health and wellness and improve the marketing of a food product.

Mediating fieldwork is presented here as a critical first step in mobilizing individuals who bring different perspectives to bear on a research project. Their different interests and perspectives form a complex network of working relations that the corporate anthropologist must work with to inform a common goal before, during, and after research. Exploratory consumer research, conducted in ethnography but also in focus groups and via other qualitative research, is typically the first stage in an extended marketing or advertising plan. As a result of fieldwork collaboration, an objectified vision of the consumer is produced, represented in an insight report and video film, which is then used to develop brand advertising, help in product innovation, or aid in formulating strategic direction for the brand under question. What is notable here is that the process of mediating social relations in fieldwork is transformed into the production of knowledge (Bourdieu 1993) in the form of a report or film, which then circulates back into advertising agency creative briefings and/or client marketing strategy to produce further work and guide future ideas, including advertisements and media plans. The anthropologist employed in advertising is thus challenged to direct this process at the earliest stage of production. This process of initiating cultural production can work positively in two ways: on the one hand, interactions among corporate executives, advertising agency anthropologists, and a hired consultancy show how particular agendas can be integrated toward a more cultural and holistic understanding of consumers and produce more relevant branding ideas and ways of communicating to consumers. On the other hand, modern reflexive practices of engaging consumers through ethnography increasingly include corporate representatives, such as clients and consultants who join in fieldwork to observe and talk firsthand with consumers. As companies seek to develop closer consumer relationships for product improvements, anthropologists in advertising agencies and market research firms have greater influence in shaping corporate discourses and marketing practices toward more accurate consumer representations. Thus, the value of corporate anthropologists in directing and mediating sites of cultural production through the immediacy of fieldwork is a vital first step toward furthering productions of knowledge practices in advertising agencies. Anthropologists possess greater impact in shaping corporate marketing plans by working alongside clients *within* advertising agencies than they do working *externally*. We suggest that anthropologists have substantial responsibility in shaping corporate ideologies and consumption agendas toward purposeful ends.

The Rise of Reflexive Awareness

Popular trends and theoretical orientations occasionally coincide, as they do for this project. Reflexivity as a theoretical concept is implicit in the fieldwork of early anthropological founders such as Malinowski, revealing why he was doing what he was doing and reflected in his published work (Malinowski 1989). Reflexivity also became popular in academic circles in the 1980s as more anthropologists sought greater awareness in how they constructed their native subject in "writing culture" (Clifford 1988; Clifford and Marcus 1986; Marcus and Fisher 1986). Academics today are aware of reflexivity as a social movement that links power, ethics, and new forms of social action and exchange among individuals and organizations. Modern life can be characterized as more reflexive in that consumers and organizations are increasingly set free from existing social structures to be more self-monitoring of their actions and the actions of others. Through rapid forms of communication that relay information quickly and foster instant images of the local and global, individuals increasingly monitor themselves, their actions, and their relations with others, directly and continuously (Amin and Thrift 2004; Beck, Giddens, and Lash 1994; Giddens 1990, 1991; Lash and Urry 1994; Thrift 2000).

The reflexivity movement is evident in the increased awareness of social interconnection among people and processes that exists on a global scale, where the day-to-day life of individuals and corporations is influenced by expansive choices and international reactions. Local activities such as shopping for food and selecting products in the market, for example, are affected by remote events (e.g., global distribution of food, drought of crops in other lands, price fluctuations due to changes in transportation costs). Importantly for companies, the growing advocacy of an informed public reveals how the reflexivity movement increasingly questions current manufacturing practices and food delivery systems. People are more concerned with monitoring food practices, such as the acquisition and distribution of food materials, humane treatment of animals, and the proper manufacturing of consumer goods. Increased reflexivity has led to the rise of social movements against mass manufacturing and more support for practices such as buying local produce in farmers' markets, more organic and natural foods, humanely raised livestock, and the reduction of chemically processed foods. For instance, the slow food movement arose to combat the growing propensity for mindlessly eating fast food. It is also a movement about slowing down in general and raising social awareness and consumer activism to keep traditional food ways intact from control of multinational agribusiness (Hamilton 2009). Wellness is another such reflexive disposition that converges with other cultural movements, such as concern over global warming, diet and obesity, fair trade, energy consumption, and fair labor practices. These movements spread rapidly by social networking on the Internet and politicize support for better food practices from manufacturers. Anthropologists attuned to these cultural movements can better inform corporate agendas about improving marketing practices to be in line with consumer trends.

The reflexivity movement today is also turned inward toward companies to involve more corporate "self-conscious reassessment" (Marcus 1998: 7). New reflexive ideologies and practices expose how corporate managers are rethinking their habits of thought in the midst of great social and economic change. Corporate adoption of more reflexive practices registers not only internally with new modes of organizational "soft" practices (i.e., increased public relations efforts and corporate philanthropy) but also new means for understanding other subjects of value—namely, the consumer (Fisher and Downey 2006; Marcus 1998). Marketers are moving toward more engaging interactions with consumers to foster interactive styles of communication that model dialogue (Lury 2004: 44). The rise of the brand, in particular, is used as a tool to foster greater interaction with consumers,[1] and is witnessed in the exponential growth of the Internet through Facebook, consumer blogs, and Twitter (Anderson and McClard 2008). As manufacturers become more in tune with consumers, social systems, trends, global and local practices, and choices people make in their lives, anthropologists play a role today as internal mediators and advocates to companies, integrating cultural awareness into more direct consumer dialogues that shape more informed marketing practices.

Direct involvement of clients with consumers and cultural trends, such as the health and wellness movement, can be better accomplished by involving them firsthand in ethnographic research. Ethnography is increasingly perceived by corporations to be more innovative than traditional focus groups for more deeply probing consumer attitudes, behavior, and lifestyles (Zukin 2004: 110). The rapid growth of ethnography by most Fortune 100 corporations attests to this rise (Malefyt 2009). We address the issue of consumer research in more detail in chapter 8, "Business Anthropology Beyond Ethnography," where we consider alternatives to ethnography for anthropologists engaged in qualitative research. Contrary to popular belief, facts in consumer research are not self-evident but require that cultural meaning is at times interpreted, coalesced, and made visible for corporate clients (Sunderland and Denny 2007). This is where the mediating work of the anthropologists begins. Hired brand consultants and corporate clients often have set agendas for ethnography that focus on what is important for the brand, strategy, and/or marketing plan rather than the consumer. This way of conducting research extracts the consumer from the setting (McCracken 2009). As corporations enlist their executives to join ethnographic fieldwork, anthropologists must intervene and act as guides in the process. The results can improve understanding of consumer motivation and behavior and contribute to better communications and product development. We believe that anthropologists should use ethnography and other forms of qualitative inquiry as more than just a method of conducting research. Anthropologists can incorporate understandings of the lived experience of culture in consumers' lives—both in fads and trends and in deep-seated beliefs—in their broader analysis of consumers. This analysis can better inform and mediate the client's observations of the research itself, whether it is in the form of ethnography, focus groups, or other approaches. Informing clients of cultural trends and popular movements along with research-based analysis of consumers helps clients perceive what they might not notice and inspire discussions with clients and consultants later in the process to produce better systems of knowledge in corporations. We present an example of this process in an ethnographic encounter with a corporate food client.

Beginning the Project

In the fall of 2008, Malefyt and an anthropological colleague, Maryann McCabe, conducted twelve ethnographic interviews on behalf of a corporate food client of BBDO. The research was carried out in three U.S. markets: Portland, Oregon; Ann Arbor, Michigan; and suburban Philadelphia, Pennsylvania. All respondents were recruited for demonstrating moderate to strong healthy eating habits and lifestyles. Half were recruited as loyalists, and none rejected the brand under study, Healthy Brand (a pseudonym). A diverse range of men and women were recruited from a mix of professional and working classes as well as retired and semiretired occupations. Each interview was led by Malefyt or McCabe, a corporate representative, a hired brand consultancy, and a professional videographer who filmed the interactions with consumers.

From the corporation's point of view, the research was intended to gain a deeper understanding of specific attitudes, motivations, and behaviors of consumers in relation to marketing Healthy Brand. Our assigned task as anthropologists was to observe behaviors around food practices and discuss with consumers their attitudes toward health and nutrition. Research specifically sought to understand consumers' ideas and practices around healthful foods and particularly to uncover their attitudes and use of canned food. Given the food company's public commitment to reduce sodium across all its product lines as a health measure, insights around perceived health benefits of the product were important. The advertising agency had been communicating to consumers a low-sodium benefit for Healthy Brand for many years. The food company wanted to know if this message still resonated or was losing its point of difference within the food company's larger portfolio of products. Additionally, the corporate brand team wanted to evolve Healthy Brand to be less about the reduction of negatives (i.e., lower sodium, fat, and cholesterol) and more about promoting a positive health message. The challenge for us as anthropologists was to integrate these functional objectives about the client's brand with larger insights about cultural movements on health and wellness and inform the client on how they shaped values and beliefs toward their product.

Coalescing Objectives

When we were first given the assignment, we met at the client's corporate office to discuss the research objectives, our plan of execution, and the type of respondents we wanted to interview. Typical of corporate research, we began our ethnographic project from plans laid out by work from previous consumer research the company had conducted. The objectives for this particular project were driven by the hired branding consultancy's goal of making Healthy Brand more top-of-mind as a health food choice for consumers. The consultancy was interested in marketing individual concepts about health, and they came to the project with a specific set of health concepts to test in the field. Their goal was to develop and refine a series of brand positioning statements for Healthy Brand food. This involved testing consumer reactions to specific benefits on health foods in a series of separate and distinct concepts. Each concept would then feed into the consultancy's brand strategy for the food corporation. The food client supported this agenda, wanting to better understand how to position its Healthy Brand line of foods within the larger breadth of its product portfolio.

We wanted to integrate these particular objectives from both client and consultant with larger cultural ideologies of health and wellness and how such notions intersected and flowed with everyday practices of food, eating, and socialization. We used ethnographic fieldwork to meld specific functional objectives of the client and consultancy with larger cultural understandings about food movements and wellness trends. As anthropologists working inside corporations and alongside clients, we felt that we could develop a perspective that integrated these objectives into a cohesive whole for current and future Healthy Brand communications and marketing campaigns.

Incorporating Consumer Models in Research

One of the challenges for anthropologists working in corporate America is dealing with corporate models of consumers. The client had presegmented consumers for our study into two consumer categories by virtue of surveyed consumer attitudes and behaviors toward health, their desire for quality, and their concern for convenience in meal preparation. Their focus was on two segments of food consumers: one segment proactively lived a healthy lifestyle and the other pursued healthier eating as a *reaction* to emergent health problems. A major objective of the research from the client's perspective was to better understand behaviors and motivations in these two segments of consumers. The food corporation had determined that the reactive segment, what they termed "Wellness Reactionists," had been a core target of Healthy Brand for decades. This segment tended to consist of older consumers who had changed their diet based on doctors' orders and who, in a sense, had come to healthy eating via a health problem or the lack of good health. "Striving Body Imagers," the proactive segment targeted by the food corporation, tended to be described as younger and more focused on body image (i.e., diet and weight loss) than on staying healthy as they aged.

Adding to this challenge, hired consultants often infuse their marketing agendas into existing corporate models. For the consultant, the two segments—Wellness Reactionists and Striving Body Imagers—each presented a different approach to health and, therefore, a different marketing opportunity for Healthy Brand food. The consultant referred to recent survey data on these two segments showing them as viable targets for marketing different messages, which also suggested that the targets would pay more for products and brands that supported these efforts. From these data, the consultant wanted research to prove how Healthy Brand would appeal to each segment in a different way with different brand benefits and thus provide a greater range of marketing possibilities and selling opportunities for the brand.

Corporate anthropologists frequently must interpret and incorporate consumer segmentation studies into their work. A segmented approach, like the one here, is based on a marketing perception that individuals make consumption decisions based on particular needs and wants that vary by types of people and their profiles. The problem for anthropologists is that this view assumes consumers make habitual choices based on fixed identities and common circumstances. A segmentation model appeals to an individualistic and singular orientation toward the world. The choices that such individuals make are taken largely apart from the broader social influences and shared cultural values of consumers. Another difficulty that anthropologists see in a segmented view is that the notion of consumer types largely depends on self-reported behavior, which is contingent upon perceptions from within that person's world of familiar people, habits, and routines. Someone may see herself as more healthful in cooking foods, for instance, and be affirmed by her husband when framed against her family background of eating fast food. Her decision to cook meals at home more often may signal to herself and others a more healthful effort toward self-sufficiency and independence. Thus, self-reported behavior must be analyzed within the larger domains of cultural influence.

Rather than see consumers as individual types, an anthropological approach to diet and healthy eating notes that what is considered healthy in the United States varies greatly. Anthropologists might inquire of respondents what in society influences them to choose certain foods or go on or off a diet or eat foods considered more or less healthy. This focus redirects questions and analysis to the cultural influences that affect individuals in terms of social trends and fads and deep-seated beliefs as well as under various changing circumstances in their lives. Nevertheless, anthropologists working in corporate America must incorporate frameworks and language of segmentation models and particular marketing agendas and translate them into cultural perspectives that clients understand and find useful (see chapter 10, "Hybrid Research Methodologies and Business Success," for an example of blended approaches).

Bringing Clients into the Field

In each of the markets that Malefyt and McCabe interviewed respondents, a client from the food corporation and a member of the consultancy team accompanied them. During interviews with respondents, Malefyt would deviate from the discussion guide. Rather than adhering strictly to preset questions as formulated by the consultant, Malefyt followed consumers' own dispositions and responses toward health and wellness that occurred naturally. When opened up in this manner, interviewees discussed the importance of wellness differently than they would likely have from directed questions about health. Wellness was described as more than just good health. It was characterized as an acquired philosophy that embodied daily practices and outlooks on life. Rather than drill people on health facts, as the consultant wanted, Malefyt noted how proud people felt talking about their wellness routines, how socially aware they were on environmental concerns, and how knowledgeable they were about the nutritional benefits of healthy eating. Most people we interviewed actively chose foods grown by local farmers or grew their own produce, joined food co-ops, and participated in neighborhood community gardens and other forms of social activism. Consumer responses showed a high level of concern for recycling, minimizing their carbon footprint, and speaking out against waste, as well as choosing food products that contained few or no preservatives. In all of this, respondents showed a level of reflexive responsiveness to wellness trends by ordering and reordering their priorities and ways of consumption, not in terms of health facts, as the consultant wanted, but in monitoring their social world and social relations within their world relative to food.

Malefyt directed further conversations on health into social and personal philosophies toward living life. Respondents referred to their bodies as representing "starting places" or "foundations" for wellness. They described wellness through lived experiences with food, an embodied knowledge that emanated from their selves to other domains: social, cognitive, spiritual outlook. Respondents expressed the idea that mind, body, and spirit were all integrated. As a woman in her fifties mentioned, "When your body is well, you feel good emotionally, and this goes outward to positively affect your relations with others, as well as being in tune with a higher spiritual dimension." A man mentioned that, for him, "wellness is physical, mental, and spiritual. The three parts are all linked so closely together for me that you can't be 'well' in one without influencing the other. This is how I become more aware of my body."

Malefyt's conversations then turned to body messages as projected by popular media. This revealed an almost antimarketing view toward wellness, which surprised the attending consultant and client. The consultant wanted to query respondents on aspirational images of health. The consultant believed that consumers used a particular product to achieve greater health and desired a perfect body as an outcome. Malefyt began questioning respondents in this way but received resistance from respondents. One man expressed irritation against the marketed Hollywood image for men. He stated, "I am anti body-type. Men are told they have to look like a V, with six-pack abs. People aren't like that. People are like us. Let's work hard and be healthy in a manageable way."

To encourage respondents to reflect more on health, Malefyt transitioned the discussion away from appearance and looking good to what awareness of their body meant. As respondents became more introspective, they began to speak about being in tune with themselves and of accepting who they were. These responses ran contrary to the corporation and consultant's initial plan to communicate better health through marketing a "better you." Yet by probing on more holistic attitudes toward wellness, spirituality, and food as commensality, respondents described a certain satisfaction with who they were currently.

Indeed, when Malefyt deviated from specific questions about evaluating oneself through health, food, and brand choices and instead spoke to respondents about their social lives, people spoke of the larger social and political decisions that impacted their food choices. They spoke of buying more local produce to keep farmers in business and not wanting to buy food that was transported across vast distances. Some consumers showed that they were harvesting their own crops in small community gardens because it was "good exercise for me." Another respondent spoke about the sense of responsibility she felt for taking care of her health in conjunction with "things you do as you age." She stated that, "If you are reasonable about your health, the larger effect is not to impact the hospital system." This notion of reducing one's footprint, she said, assumes more personal responsibility, so that in "being aware," one becomes a "better consumer." "If I make it my responsibility, then it doesn't become your responsibility; I set an example."

As anthropologists, these and similar comments brought attention to the importance of situating future corporate marketing plans for food, wellness, and health in a larger cultural context of reflexive responsibility and the wellness movement. With the trend of companies acting more socially responsible, desiring greater dialogue with consumers, and showing a greater degree of transparency, Malefyt and McCabe felt that they could sway the client and consultant to modify their initial thoughts and marketing plans after the research to incorporate more of these reflective learnings.

Getting to Agreement

Enlisting the client and consultant to join fieldwork may appear as a first step toward reaching greater corporate dialogue with consumers. Nevertheless, what began as an attempt to raise awareness of consumers' desire for healthier foods from a more holistic perspective was interpreted independently by the corporation and the consultant. Each came away with ideas of what they heard consumers say, resulting in a different direction for their marketing plans. The food client and the consultant assumed their own interpretation of fieldwork that worked toward their agendas and marketing purposes.

The food corporation was impressed with consumer awareness and practices around health labels. The level of stated consumer awareness of ingredients in canned and packaged foods suggested to the client that product labels were more important to consumers than previously thought. As respondents discussed and the client heard, the importance of fresh ingredients, sea salt, and lack of preservatives were all described as active markers of healthy products. Developing newer labels that informed people of ingredients struck a chord of opportunity for the client. The food corporation at this time was also developing richer pictorial imagery on its product labels, both in the context of images of food on the can and in the grocery store, where a serving dispenser rack was being restructured. The research affirmed for the client that vibrant images as well as descriptions of healthful ingredients were important for consumers, indicating fresh foods and nutrition in the food brand. The use of such images on products and store racks and new nutritional labels would signal visually to consumers that the company was listening to their needs and represent a new image of health from the company. In other words, the client incorporated from the interviews the most tangible dimensions from discussions, such as descriptions of ingredients and images on cans, to affirm what he wanted to hear from respondents. When put into practice, these markers would signal greater awareness of people's needs and increased dialogue with consumers.

The consultancy also gathered from the ethnographies the idea of greater consumer awareness but took it in another direction. They interpreted from the interviews a latent consumer desire for particular responses to physical health concerns. The consultant was eager to particularize ideas of health by dividing consumers' reactions to concepts into component parts. Marketing messages would respond to health benefits in functional terms. For instance, heart health, weight management, energy, vitality, and purity were specific concepts that the consultant asked us to probe for relevance relative to consumer notions of food, diet, and overall health. Distinct benefits for health would align with specific marketing needs of the two consumer segments and create two or more possible campaigns. The consultant's perceptions of the ethnographic interviews followed and supported his preconceived plans to market the client's product along two approaches.

As anthropologists, we presented to the client and consultant a more holistic and cultural view of the consumers. We connected what we observed and heard with the ways healthy-oriented people described and practiced wellness in their lives. Wellness was not a contained collection of facts or stated goals that people aspired toward, such as getting to a certain weight. It was rather a collective set of dispositions that oriented consumers to think and act in certain ways, beneficial not only toward the self but also to others. Wellness reflected an awareness of self in connection to others that assumed a sense of personal responsibility to act more diligently toward the environment, be attentive to the impact on one's surroundings, and make decisions concerning what goes in one's body, how one feels, and what one puts out for exercise—all toward a goal of living life with a heightened state of awareness. This ethical disposition was not only about food; it also encompassed a wider sense of appreciation that continually adjusted to the contingencies of the day, week, season, and overall aging process in reflective ways.

In the ensuing discussions with the client and consultant, Malefyt and McCabe's interpretation of wellness lacked measurable end points and presented unspecific goals and so became a point of contention with the hired consultancy. We described wellness not in terms of satisfying a particular need state of consumers but rather as a disposition, an orientation, and a sense of continual movement in life. We saw the importance of wellness in relationships, in attitudes and practices, and in greater personal agency, often against marketing efforts. Yet, by the consultancy's standards, these explanations were too vague and indeterminate. We had also challenged the consultants' emphasis on marketing specific areas of health by consumer types, such as heart health and weight management. We stated that it was neither of these concepts in particular, or any other of the specific concepts, such as energy, vitality, or purity, because, in a sense, it was all of these. Rather than argue that one area of people's health was more important than another, we stated that a singular focus, such as heart health or purity, had more of a negative impact on health ideas, because for consumers this stressed the alienation of one part of their body from the whole and had an antiwellness message for consumers. Focusing on the heart apart from one's life, for instance, placed heart problems too sharply in relief and influenced respondents to think less about their overall well-being. A holistic way of thinking about wellness, we argued, operates antithetically to singular ideas of health and instead orients people's beliefs and practices to the subject of living well and enjoying their lives.

We argued for a marketing plan that was integrative of wellness trends and for how food connected people socially in their lives. We thought it best to situate the food brand as a means to greater health rather than as an end in itself. The canned food was not an end meal in itself but was often blended with other healthful ingredients in recipes. People cooked with it, used it with their recipes, and often added other vegetables, stirred in fresh herbs, or served it with homemade bread. We further suggested that this food could metaphorically become an extension for connections with others, as a means to enhance relations with family members or friends. We thought Healthy Brand could better identify with consumers and tap into a larger wellness trend by asserting itself less as a distinct branded entity and more as an integrated part of people's lifestyle. We also suggested that wellness was a consumer framework for judging qualities of products and brands within an orientation reflective of the self. The consumers we spoke to were less swayed by individualized product messages and more concerned with using a food product to enhance connections with others in their lives. The ethnographic film created by the videographer reflected this insight and showed the lived experience of wellness as a series of connections in people's lives and as an active and continuously changing disposition for choice, not as a static marker of brand loyalty. We concluded that the food corporation needed to show relevance and greater awareness of wellness, not just health, in its product lines and communications in order for consumers to make the connection to their own lives.

As a result of this discussion, and as an outcome of this project, differences were reconciled. Our emphasis on engaging the larger cultural idea of wellness helped the client realize it could craft a new marketing campaign that was much broader than merely positioning Healthy Brand food as a heart-healthy option that the brand consultancy proposed. Indeed, when we reiterated in our consumer film and in the final document the consumer view of wellness in terms of balance, spirituality, and connection, the singular positioning statements tested by the brand consultancy were deemed too limiting. Bringing clients and consultants along in fieldwork was not enough, since insights are not self-evident. Our analysis and further discussions with the client, in which, through film and presentation, we integrated the idea of wellness with what respondents said individually, helped the food corporation understand differences between ideas of health as they had instilled in their corporation and wellness as conceived and practiced by consumers. Notions of health as previously marketed to consumers from within the corporation were mostly associated with negatives. Health was a cautionary term marketed with approbations of dos and don'ts. Yet after this research report and film was presented to several corporate teams, the company assumed a revised notion about wellness that circulated throughout the organization. The food corporation decided to apply our research learning to Country Origins Brand (a pseudonym), a new, more healthful product being launched that was made entirely of healthy and fresh ingredients with minimal processing, salt, and additives. Intermingling cultural trends with the immediacy and directness of ethnographic research helped steer a new marketing direction and create new knowledge practices within the company. This reveals the value of anthropologists in and along corporate work to help integrate broader, more holistic considerations of consumers into internal knowledge practices and marketing campaigns.

Reflexive Selves and Reflexive Corporations

Anthropologists working in advertising agencies and marketing research firms can and should influence corporate ideologies and perceptions of consumers by encouraging ethnographic fieldwork that directly engages corporate managers in sites of consumer practices and fields of production. The fieldwork experience enlists corporate clients in the process of observing and interacting with users of its own brands. When the anthropologist conjoins what is observed in local contexts with larger cultural trends, clients become more informed participant observers, are involved more subjectively in the conversations, and may arrive at new levels of awareness about their brand with consumers. This mode of mediation with clients through guided ethnography can inform better ways to manufacture and market a wide range of brands. In this regard, the task and responsibility of anthropologists working in advertising and marketing research is not only to create more compelling messages for its clients' brands but also to maintain and build strong relations between corporate clients and consumers. Whether the anthropologists or consultants win the day, better-informed clients in corporations make better products for consumers. More interaction, contestation, and integration of ideas offer more ways to influence one another's perspective. This results in more positive outcomes for all. As Ulrich Beck optimistically states, "More reflection, more experts, more science, more public sphere, more self-awareness and self criticism can open up new and better possibilities for action in a world out of joint" (Beck 1994: 177).

–5–

Advertising Emotions

Advertisers have discerned that in a crowded marketplace with many similar products, the best way to reach consumers is by fostering emotional attachments to things. Things are not mere objects, but as products and brands they have social lives (Appadurai 1986), biographies (Kopytoff 1986), personalities (Aaker 1996), and identities (Kapferer 2004) through which consumers develop strong emotional attachments. By marketing directly to people's emotions, advertisers hope to bypass reason, which might cause people to otherwise pause and reconsider a purchase. Advertisers have also discovered that through developing sensory-oriented experiences with products and brands, they can engage an individual's emotions more directly, immediately, and personally.

This chapter discusses a current advertising trend and new marketing model that reflect a major shift in the way advertisers market to consumers. The classic advertising approach no longer follows a mass-market model of consumer decision making, which was based on rational choice, public discourse, and highly textual modes of communication. Rather, advertising practices now follow a sensory-emotive model that attempts to engage consumers personally through multisensory experiences with brands. While creating emotionally compelling advertisements has existed implicitly for some time, this new analysis explores the use of explicit sensory-based approaches that attempt to tap directly into consumers' emotions. This change demonstrates how advertisers increasingly conceptualize and practice advertising as a mode of customized interaction with consumers on a personal level.

The shift toward sensory-based emotional advertising follows a sea change in the marketplace. Old mass-market models of consumer decision making no longer operate because advertising media have become more individualized. The modern digital world presents a multiplication of media contexts. Through the Internet, digital technology, and the proliferation of mobile devices, advertisers are now able to customize messages to a specific person at any given moment, thus greatly expanding marketers' reach and frequency of messaging. The rise in individual digital devices has also made mass media such as television more personal as well, according to recent network spending results. Social media, such as Facebook, Twitter, and YouTube, stimulate an interest in watching television, and viewers share their comments about what they watch with family and friends online in real time. This synergy, or what is called the "multiplier effect," has increased network spending on

TV, and it coverts a traditional mass media advertiser into a modern personalized means of reaching people. In 2010 the networks added $500 million to $700 million in advertising spending, and in 2012 spending is projected to increase $600 million to $800 million more (Elliott 2011).

In addition, advertising spending budgets that once were solely directed to one-way mass modes of TV, radio, and print have broadened to embrace a range of personally engaging modes of marketing. New interactive media includes the Internet, in-store displays, public relations marketing, experiential marketing, direct mail, trade promotions, product placement, event sponsorships, and viral marketing. Advertisements now link a mass TV campaign to an individual's style of usage. Nike, for example, can personalize its TV messages through online interaction and coordinate with a local events promotion so that individuals can track their runs, visualize their progress, and purchase premium running shoes (Gillette 2010). The range in new media has turned controlled, one-way messages for mass audiences into ongoing one-on-one dialogues with customers (Sacks 2010).

Despite these vast changes in the consumer landscape, the literature on advertising has not sufficiently addressed new media and related marketing approaches. A cultural studies perspective typically regards advertising through traditional one-way mass marketing and views advertisements in terms of their discursive nature and sign value, not for their emotive or sensory engagement. From Williamson's (1978) textual analysis of advertising's structures and Jhally's (1987) and Marchand's (1985) "decoding" of advertising's social messages, advertising has been labeled an empire of signs, a discourse of persuasion, and a system of symbols, among other terms. These classic works regard advertising production as a culture industry that circulates mass images to the consumer marketplace and creates social discourses for advertisements that are read and analyzed from a distant viewpoint (Baudrillard 1994; Goldman and Papson 1996; Lash and Urry 1994; Perry 1998). More recent critiques of branding and advertising (Arvidsson 2006; Lury 2004; Manning 2010; Manovich 2001; Mazzarella 2003b) continue to treat advertising from generalized producer and consumer interactions and describe interactivity as a vague form of indirect negotiated meaning between marketers and consumers. Brand advertising, for example, is outlined ethereally in terms of "floating signifiers" or through "self-referential signs" (Beebe 2004: 626). These mainly semiotic critiques continue to stress brand advertising's sign value (see Manning 2010) and omit the range of experiential and sensory-oriented approaches.

Lacking in these assessments is any discussion of the interactive ways that marketers now engage consumers and the corresponding ways consumers interpret brand experiences. Beyond the mass advertisement or broadly circulated printed page, what are the effects of marketing approaches that are customized to a user's individual style of consumption? How do sensory-based marketing campaigns evoke deeply felt emotions in consumers? How do advertisers attempt to use various multimedia channels to incorporate back into production the sentiments and personal sensations that consumers experience in consumption? Rather than evaluate advertising as public discourses or texts to be read, we assert that advertisements are increasingly directed to embody personal and privately felt experiences for consumers. Marketers strive for more customized ways to create personal meaning for consumers through branded experiences that appeal to a range in the human sensorium.

We discuss here the advances in advertising and media marketing approaches that target consumers personally through their senses and emotions. Advertisers traditionally relied on targeting consumers' rational decision-making processes through the heavy use of textual content and informational advertising messages. Their once-heightened importance through conventional mass media forms of TV, print, and radio has waned. In their place, direct engagement of consumers through new modes of advertising media are on the rise, tapping into consumers' emotions through their embodied senses, such as smell, touch, taste and richer visual and auditory modes of communication. By engaging consumers directly and personally, marketers are heralding the new reign of emotional marketing approaches. *New York Times* writer Stuart Elliott notes that marketing to emotions has become ever more popular in the advertising industry. Elliott quotes Bruce Hall, a research director of Howard, Merrell & Partners, who states: "You can ask people what they think about an ad, but until you move them on an emotional level, their behavior will not change" (Elliott 2005). Marketing expert Richard Levey affirms that traditional rational marketing approaches have largely failed because "they overestimate the reasoning power of consumers, and ignore the way people actually think and make decisions" (Levey 2004: 22). Dan Hill, president of Sensory Logic, a Minneapolis-based brand consultancy, writes that "consumers feel before they think . . . there has to be a 'gotcha' at the beginning of an ad because interest and relevancy can't wait until the end . . . real persuasion is emotional in nature" (Hill 2007).

The rise of emotional marketing reaffirms the popularity of psychological approaches that celebrate emotions as a means of marketing more deeply and directly to consumers. Reason was once considered trustworthy and emotions were suspect, but now advertisers and social critics are realizing through advances in neuroscience, psychology, and behavioral economics that emotions assign heightened value to things and are the very basis of reason (Brooks 2011). Notably, the study of emotion in culture that began in U.S. anthropology and was highlighted in the work of Ruth Benedict (1934) has now come to be almost fetishized in advertising and marketing today (Malefyt and Moeran 2003: 24).

This shift from marketing mass information that once promoted rational public decision making to marketing personal sensations that now elicits individual emotional desires has an important benefit for advertisers. By avoiding information-based campaigns and by promoting messages that are more private, personal, and individually interpreted, advertisers are less subject to the broad-based scrutiny and public rejection that sometimes hindered campaigns in the past. Advertisers can tailor consumer relations strategically along private lines when they shift marketing messages from the public arena of mass commodities to the personal sphere of embodied experiences.

This effect also delivers greater returns for agency-client relations. Advertisers have discerned that marketing to emotions has solid financial rewards. Since corporate clients increasingly hold their agencies accountable for advertising effectiveness, advertisers have responded by orchestrating marketing campaigns that elicit a greater range in media targeting to maximize their clients' return on investment. By developing a broader range of marketing activities labeled as emotional, sensorial, and experiential, advertisers secure a longer-term investment in their client's consumer and commensurably more work from their corporate client. Using a touch-point case study to exemplify our analysis, we will show that marketers expand the scope of engaging experiences with consumers through a range of engaging multimedia options. This allows advertisers to ultimately increase the strategic value of their contribution to their client's brand. Each interactive modality of the touch-point framework allows advertisers to make more out of the consumer-brand interaction, securing more opportunities for current and future brand work. We can understand the application of such media approaches by first exploring the evolution of consumer decision making, which is predicated on advertisers' basic assumptions of audience makeup, their understanding of human thought and perception, and the best way to appeal to consumers' sense of choice.

From Rational Commodity Images to Branded Emotional Experiences

Marketing is predicated on the idea that people distinguish one product from another by making informed decisions from a range of choices. Choice is based on notions of value and difference that define a world of goods (Douglas and Isherwood 1979). Choice also expresses a valued sense of freedom that defines U.S. society (Beeman 1986). Valuing goods by apparent contrasts and differences is how Levi-Strauss alleged "primitive cultures" classified and understood their world (Moeran 1996). Below, we trace the movement of choice in U.S. advertising: from marketing choice by providing rational information to a general public to marketing choice by offering emotional-sensory experiences to specific individuals.

For most of the twentieth century, U.S. advertisers appealed to the notion of consumer choice through rational selection, assuming U.S. audiences to be largely undifferentiated. Early advertising images were conspicuously absent of ethnic, gender, or socioeconomic differences that defined U.S. society. Images, instead, reflected the self-restrained dominant order of white Protestant men (O'Barr 1994). O'Barr observes that advertising "has tended throughout the twentieth century to treat the American public as a colorless, English-speaking mass audience of rather uniform tastes, preferences and sensibilities" (1994: ix). Noted historian Daniel

Boorstin reiterates the view that early U.S. advertising was a "declaration of equality," one that assumes a mass market and "thrives on tastes that are completely average" (1965: 88–89). Embedded in these early advertising messages was the presiding notion of an orderly society of uniform tastes, where homogenized consumers shared a more or less a similar disposition for selecting products.

In the 1960s, advertising legend David Ogilvy evidenced the rational approach to choice with advertisements that were copy heavy and singularly focused on information. He inveterately maintained that effective ads should let facts speak for themselves and declared, "If your advertising is going to be successful, if it is going to stand out from the clutter, you must be objective about the benefits of your product" ([1983] 1985: 109). He plainly stated that more facts were better:

> The consumer isn't a moron; she is your wife. You insult her intelligence if you assume that a mere slogan and a few vapid adjectives will persuade her to buy anything. She wants *all the information* you can give her. (Ogilvy 1963: 96, emphasis added)

Following his factual emphasis, products of better quality should rationally stand out from competitors by virtue of their visual apparentness. This line of reasoning may also explain Ogilvy's predilection for print advertising in which sensorial information is singularly visible. A rational orientation favors enticing consumers through visual modalities of advertising. Furthermore, this justification for privileging textual information in advertising is situated in perceptions of a classic Western sensory hierarchy, where vision and audition are ranked at the height of rationality and reason.

According to David Howes (2005a), Western culture customarily associates the discursive and visual realm of the human sensorium with rational thinking and planning aspects of culture and civilization. Plato and Aristotle ranked vision and audition, respectively, as the higher senses of rational perception and cognitive planning. Conversely, tactile, taste, and smell were the lower senses relegated to the realm of unruly base emotions (Synnott 1991: 62). Such associations assume that physical feelings and sensations of the body link directly to human emotions and lie in contrast to higher-order thought and reason, which are viewed as purely mental phenomena (Lutz 1988). This ranking of vision and audition over the other senses is privileged in Western culture, not only through everyday images and language of things seen or heard but also as practiced and experienced as something tacitly lived in society (Howes 2005a: 3–5). Kathryn Linn Geurts (2002) suggests that not all sensory systems in cultures stress the same order. While Western children are taught to relate to the world visually through detached object relations, African children, for example, learn to connect with their world through all of their senses, including a sixth sense of balance. Differences in sensory order, she writes, are socially informative, since they are "profoundly involved with a society's epistemology, the development of its cultural identity and its forms of being-in-the-world" (2002: 3).

Because cultural systems inculcate a worldview through a particular sensory order, advertising also can be viewed as a system that supports a cultural framework that ranks certain sensory orders over others in appealing to consumers. Advertisers tacitly rank and prioritize sensory-based marketing approaches to align with shifting social views of what they believe are influential consumer dispositions for choice. This approach to consumer thinking and feeling, and the corresponding line of sensory ranking, informs a hierarchy of advertising communication that reflects a particular view of society. Earlier advertisements were indeed information heavy in textual presentation, as evidenced by Ogilvy's statement above. A once-dominant white male orientation toward society favored highly visual and auditory modes of advertising that presented product information in ordered formats. This approach conformed to established notions of a uniform society—one that was imagined as civil, orderly, and dominantly white.

Customized Marketing: Targeting Emotions in Consumer Experience

In today's marketplace, the overwhelming proliferation of products and diverse audiences has overturned marketers' earlier ideas of marketing based on fewer choices, social uniformity, and consumer rationality. Marketing to emotions today is thought to bypass issues of diversity and unite consumers at a basic biological level, cutting through the clutter of multiple competing products and avoiding public skepticism that brought criticism from past marketing approaches. Marc Gobe, author of *Emotional Branding*, claims that consumers are introduced to over three thousand new brands each year and so cannot distinguish between one cola and another, one sneaker and its competitor, or the many different kinds of jeans, coffees, or gas stations. Amid this ocean of offerings, "the emotional connection is what makes that all-important, essential difference" (Gobe 2001: xxvi). Marketers have turned to sensations in the body as a way to reach consumers individually and unite them emotionally.

Marketing directly to an individual's emotions rather than to a mass audience supports another widely held Western belief: emotions lie at the heart of the true self. Emotions are thought to not only identify the private self in opposition to public reason and rational intellect, but also "emotion is held as a sole essential aspect of the individual, the seat of the true and glorified self" (Lutz 1988: 56). Lutz details how thoughts and feelings of the heart are commonly seen as the true seat of the individual, while things of the head are regarded as the more superficial, socially influenced aspects of the self (1988: 68). Marketing expert Dan Hill supports this assumption when he advises his clients to pursue "the (emotive) hearts and (sensory) bones" of their consumers rather than listen to what people might rationalize in their heads (Hill 2003: 134; also see Morais 2009b). Another marketing expert, Scott Robinette, sums up the essential value of marketing to emotions:

Experiences that trigger the senses entertain, though the effects fade as new stimuli arrive. Experiences that engage the mind inform and satisfy, but their impact diminishes as thoughts move on to something else. The most compelling experiences though are emotionally affective—they may pause at the sensory and rational levels. But they eventually touch the heart and linger there. (Robinette, Brand, and Lenz 2001: 76)

These passages associate the realm of emotions with the metaphorical domain of the inside. Marketing to inner qualities assumes that the true essence of consumer motivation and brand loyalty lie deep within all individuals. By addressing consumers at the deepest biological level, marketers believe they evade the social, gender, and ethnic distinctions that divide audiences and that they can appeal to the biological commonalities or assumed universal needs that define all humans (Feit 2007). Politically, this perception allows marketers to direct their message to an inner human domain, apart from public discourses, social differences, and popular scrutiny. By selling consumers personal experiences for what is felt, advertisers are assured that if what counts for public advertising can be challenged, what counts for the way people feel about it privately cannot.

Marketers now stress the importance of selling to all the senses. Ford automobiles focus on the sound of their doors closing; Singapore Airlines has patented its "warm towel" smell; Crayola crayons are known as authentic for their distinctive scent. Howes points out through these examples that marketers are now charging messages with sensations in every media modality, thereby attempting to blitz or otherwise bypass reason by means of emotions. The proliferation of sensory-engaging marketing approaches has launched what he calls "the progressive privatization of sensation" (Howes 2005b: 287–88). This move toward marketing directly to emotions produces brands that are more personally meaningful to consumers, because it shifts the focus of brand messages away from a public realm of visual and discursive scrutiny to the private realm of brand experiences in feelings, tastes, and personal responses.

Appealing to emotions through experience was first heralded as a new marketing approach in *The Experience Economy* (Pine and Gilmore 1999) and *Experiential Marketing* (Schmitt 1999). These works detail the way progressive companies move beyond mass branding approaches that treat products as commodities to more engaging approaches that stage brands as personal experiences and felt sensations. Disney, Starbucks, and Harley-Davidson are examples of successful brands that create emotionally engaging and sensory-stimulating experiences for consumers. Harley-Davidson riders are known for their emotional attachment to the brand, which ostensibly unites riders across socioeconomic statuses. As evidence, its "tribal" members brandish tattoos, wear distinctive Harley clothing, and belong to one of over 1,200 Harley Owners Group (HOG) chapters that hold rallies nationwide. Six hundred and fifty thousand Harley customers of all backgrounds "regularly ride together, bond together and speak passionately about their Harleys, thus strengthening their brand commitment" (McMurtry 2004). Starbucks is another experiential brand that, beyond serving coffee, offers an environment abundant in rich textures, colors, aromas, taste treats, and music and induces a respite from a busy world. Trend expert Virginia Postrel writes that "Starbucks is to the age of sensory aesthetics what McDonalds was to the age of convenience or Ford was to the age of mass production" (Postrel 2003: 20). Consumers return loyalty to brands that engage them in emotionally satisfying experiences. In 2007 a reported 20 percent of Starbuck's loyal consumers averaged sixteen visits a month, fueled by their passion for coffee experiences (Price 2007). Emotions are thus targeted through sensations to direct consumer preferences and brand consideration. As Gerald Zaltman, former Harvard business professor and founder of the widely-used Zaltman Metaphor Elicitation Technique (ZMET), summarizes, "a Nestle crunch bar has immediate sensory benefits such as taste, texture, and sound. But these benefits also evoke powerful emotional benefits, such as fond memories of childhood and feelings of security" (2003: 19).

In the following case study, Malefyt traces an advertising agency's and client's discussion on consumers' experience and ensuing marketing strategies for home-delivered pizza. The discussion reveals how advertisers target various emotional states and experiences of consumers who order and consume a brand of home-delivered pizza. The pursuit of consumers' emotions through experience leads to an idealization, even a fetishization of consumers through a sensory-emotive platform. In addition, the marketing methods advertisers use among themselves and share with their corporate clients facilitate greater affinity between agency and client through a mutual shared understanding of their subject.[1] As such, the emotional marketing of the consumer-brand experience offers an expanded framework upon which marketers engage consumers personally through multiple levels of contact. It also generates distinct marketing opportunities for the advertising agency to strengthen relations with its corporate client.

Case Study: Marketing Pizza for Home Delivery

When strategizing marketing plans for home-delivered pizza, advertisers use a systematic process to map out consumer-brand interactions along the lines of experience and emotions. A recent framework to emerge for marketing experiential approaches is the touch-point model. A touch-point framework classifies and orders the most salient consumer-brand interactions in terms of particular experiences consumers have with brands in the trajectory of a consumption experience.[2] The touch-point model demonstrates the ways marketers interpret consumer experience and emotions for purposes of shaping customized media and marketing messages. Each touch point represents a strategic opportunity for marketers to explore and develop a consumer-brand relationship along sensory and emotional constructs. In the process, consumer experiences and emotional needs form the basis for developing a broad marketing mix of brand messages, product placement, and other marketing initiatives.

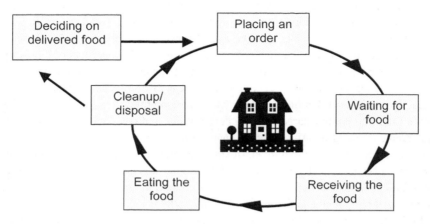

Figure 5.1 Touch-point chart.

Advertisers of Fresh Pizza Express (a pseudonym) used the touch-point model to expand on a general consumer profile: the average U.S. mother, aged thirty-five, with three or more people living at home, supported by an annual household income of $52,000, and ordering home-delivered food 1.6 times per month.[3] While a rational, information-based approach to marketing home-delivered pizza might limit itself to this demographic profile, an experiential model was used to customize a marketing approach based on specific conditions that were emotionally differentiating for consumers.

From previous market research on mothers who routinely decided on family dinners, the advertising agency account planning and account management teams arrived at a consumer problem involving the issue of choice. Women of working- and middle-class family households routinely confronted a "dinner dilemma" in which they had to decide what to serve their family for dinner that evening. Framing this typical episode as a problem offered fast-food manufacturers, such as Fresh Pizza Express, an emotional crisis they could address strategically. The target mother in "crisis" was then segmented into two distinct emotional predispositions that informed a unique set of need states, which marketers could attend to: mothers were either hurried (i.e., motivated by pressures of the day and preferred a quick, inexpensive dinner solution), or they were prepared (i.e., influenced by a thought-out, prepared occasion and desired an enjoyable, relaxed family dinner experience). Consumer need states may derive from actual consumer experience, but typically they are exaggerated into different entities, producing distinct opportunities for marketers (Mazzarella 2003a: 62). Here, segmenting consumers into two need states had practical implications for the advertising agency's marketing plans. Rather than accept consumer choice as mediated by rational thought, which could be reduced to fewer marketing options, an emotional need state approach explored a fuller range of potential consumer behaviors that increased the array of marketing possibilities. The experiential aspects of consumption helped direct and broaden the marketing opportunities as it offered increased dimensions for understanding consumers' relationships to brands. Each consumer segment presumed an emotional disposition and particular relationship with the brand, which necessitated a distinct media plan for the advertising agency to execute. Each touch-point scenario compelled the advertiser to manage the consumer-brand experience along media lines that involved greater roles from the various advertising agency departments and services. Thus, from the consumer touch points of deciding on delivered food, placing an order, waiting for food, receiving the food, and eating the food to clean up and disposal of materials, each consumer-brand interaction presented an opportunity for the advertising agency to increase its strategic value and hence its economic capital (Bourdieu 1993) by linking a consumer emotion to a particular marketing method and media approach.

Hurried mothers were ostensibly motivated by pressure from daily demands. Their emotional need state was concerned with minimizing dinner preparation time and food costs. These mothers desired a family meal delivered promptly, inexpensively, and in a manner that would immediately satisfy the family. The pizza brand's service dimension would fulfill this emotional state. Conversely, prepared mothers intended for a more relaxed dinner occasion with their families and so invoked an emotional state that anticipated a more festive mood and different marketing opportunities, such as watching a rented movie or inviting friends over. Thus, the experiential dimensions of consumer-brand interactions produced two distinct emotional consumer profiles from which further marketing and media initiatives were developed.

The advertising agency proceeded through each of the touch-point dimensions to discuss with the client the different ways in which these two consumer segments could be marketed. On the dimension of deciding to order pizza, an agency account supervisor stated that hurried mothers were predisposed to feeding their families quickly and affordably, with little thought of seeking group consensus. Expedited prepackaged offers and whole meal specials would appeal to these mothers over inventoried items. An agency media planner suggested reaching hurried mothers by airing specials on radio during prime drive-time occasions, such as late afternoon weekdays when mothers typically drove their cars home or picked up children from school. Branded placement of meal deals would correspond to out-of-home locations, such as on billboards, banners, and stand-ups near family destinations and associations, and specifically in locations of Little League parks, school cafeterias, and Girl Scout or Boy Scout centers. The agency's branding plans would build on the hurried time element and link to local community presence through targeted media placement.

The prepared mothers, conversely, were deemed less pressured by time and value constraints and instead were thought to seek out optimum dinner experiences for their families. The agency discussed marketing dinner experiences to these mothers around a mood of family fun. Since these women were more likely to seek family consensus in deciding on pizza and side dishes, the agency explored ways to promote the brand's variety, specialty. and quality of food offerings. A media executive suggested advertising to prepared mothers though TV spots aired during afternoon programs (soaps), as well as offering them interactive promotional tie-ins with video rental stores, theme park giveaways, and sponsorship programming. This would leverage an emotional framework from consumers of seeking quality family time. Media options thus aligned consumer emotional states with marketed brand values of family fun.

The meeting discussion then turned to consumers' emotional state of ordering meals. Hurried mothers were described as anxious and seeking assurance for quick dinner solutions. The agency account planner discussed women's anxiety as an opportunity to improve phone-in and Internet ordering tactics so that food options would appear immediately available and ease the stress of this consumer segment. The discussion prompted plans for corporate liaisons with the phone company to expedite calls with a speed-dial service to a Fresh Pizza Express order taker. An Internet option was also discussed to facilitate online ordering capabilities that would electronically recall past coupons and orders and automatically generate choices for appropriate deals for returning consumers. Conversely, prepared mothers were described as calmer but seeking to please their family and so were discussed as more open to suggestions for trying additional menu items. The agency stated that dialogue in the form of courteous feedback would help affirm their meal choices. The agency recommended increased training for phone-order receiving staff to be aware of and identify more inquisitive customers, as characteristic of prepared mothers. The receiving staff would then suggest deals to optimize these mothers' anticipated meal experience. Trained staff would recommend to callers new menu items, such as salads, desserts, or candies to complete the fun dinner occasion. The idea was to leverage consumers' consensus-seeking emotional state into purchasing more by offering positive feedback and suggesting additional menu items that aligned brand values with what marketers perceived as the consumer's desire for family togetherness.

The agency and client also discussed the situation of waiting for food, where the hurried mother's emotional state was considered most time sensitive. The agency account planner presented data that showed that consumers use wait time to complete unfinished household chores, such as reading mail or checking their children's schoolwork. An agency Web site developer suggested a way to optimize this consumer wait time by providing online games that could be downloaded to smart phones or accessed on computers to engage the waiting customers. A branded online experience, he mentioned, could not only direct waiting customers to a "Family Games Room" site but also entertain them while they "build a healthy Fresh Pizza Express appetite."

The agency and client discussion then focused on the arrival of delivered food as a key opportunity for greater face-to-face interaction between consumer and brand by way of the delivery person. Research indicated that parents often encourage their child to interact with delivery persons at the door. A marketing opportunity was discussed for training delivery personnel to smile and engage customers, especially if greeted by a child, who was typically observed by watching parents. Research has shown that if children are entertained, parents are more likely to be pleased and engaged as well (Underhill 1999). The marketing team suggested enhancing children's engagement with the brand through seasonal events and a delivery person's uniform: a Santa hat for Christmas, an orange and black vest for Halloween, and "cute bunny ears" for Easter. This approach was bound to leave positive impressions and improve the customer's experience. Another marketing opportunity centered on using a fast-swipe machine at the door for automatic debit payments to ensure speed and convenience for hurried mothers, while a delivered TV guide with tear-out brand promotions featuring "Fresh Pizza Express—What's on TV tonight," would offer casual family TV viewing recommendations for prepared mothers. Each marketing approach was designed to emphasize a strategic option according to the particular emotional state of the consumer in that situation.

The conversation between agency and client then focused on the different ways that the target consumers' would consume the delivered food. This constituted a heightened opportunity for marketers to link an emotional situation of each target consumer with the sensory properties of the brand. Family eating locations were discussed. Hurried mothers were discussed as beginning to relax as food arrival fulfilled their need to expedite the family dinner. Hurried mothers were also considered more likely to consume the meal at the kitchen counter or dinner table. This presented a chance to reinforce future food-ordering decisions that centered on the kitchen location. Coupons and magnets could be included in the pizza box to provide refrigerator reminders for these women that their next pizza purchases were readily available. This tactic evidenced semiotic markers, for which the brand Fresh Pizza Express could assist anxious mothers to ease into their homes. Conversely, prepared mothers were discussed as desiring to reconnect with their families through shared behaviors so that eating locations might include other collective social activities such as watching TV, playing family games, or outdoor backyard activities, such as eating on patio tables.

To enhance the eating experience for the prepared mother segment, the agency recommended adding branded disposable patio tablecloths or emphasizing family interactions with inexpensive games that could be included with orders. A product design executive from the agency suggested offering branded accoutrements of blended spices, hot pepper, seasoned salt, and dipping sauces or introducing a dessert option to further expand the entire meal experience. An agency account executive suggested developing dessert options with an ice cream and cookie manufacturer so that the customer's pizza-eating experience could be extended in branded ways and increase corporate revenues.

The final discussion concerned the disposal of residual packaging items, such as the pizza delivery box and napkins. The agency's packaging design manager stated that branded messages to consumers could enhance the cleanup experience of the occasion. The two emotional states of the target women required different ways of handling this action. Hurried mothers were deemed more practical and expedient and so desired to move on to other tasks. Fresh Pizza Express could respond to hurried mothers by offering them branded options for leftover food storage. Fold-in boxes or perforated storage options on pizza boxes could extend the brand experience into the refrigerator for storage. Alternatively, for prepared mothers, the pizza delivery box was discussed as more likely to remain on the table longer and so offered a different branded option, such as advertising an inexpensive hologram design imprinted on the pizza box top or inside the opened lid. Box tops were considered ideal branded properties for presenting customers with images that showed a family having fun rather than depicting an image of a logo or plain coupon deals alone. The idea was to depart from the ordinary and engage the consumer with clever, interactive images. Another suggestion was to include branded pizza-scented sticky notes that would remind people through smell of their hunger for Fresh Pizza Express. By including scented reminders and branding images on delivery box tops as well as on table-cloths, trash bags, and wet wipes, Fresh Pizza Express would, as discussed, stay top-of-mind for consumers desiring a home-delivered meal. After the meeting, many of the steps discussed were implemented in future advertising and marketing.

From the above case study, we note how agency divisions interpret, coordinate, and direct a range of consumer emotional states and branded sensory experiences into specific marketing and media opportunities. The identification of and marketing to emotional need states are ultimately designed to correspond to the capabilities and opportunities that advertising agencies and their multiple roles for the client can fulfill. Thus, the emotional experiences of consumers, such as mothers choosing what to order their family for dinner, form a wealth of available cultural material from which an agency and its client construct and produce sensory-rich interactions for consumers in relation to a brand.

* * *

This chapter has argued that the expanding role of consumer choice through various media, brands, and personal sites of consumption has compelled advertisers to utilize a broader sensory range and more interactive media to effectively reach consumers. The case study of the touch-point marketing framework illustrates how consumers' emotional experiences and expectations are objectified, fetishized, and structured into marketable consumer-brand interactions. The process highlights not only the specific sensory orders of Western ideology but also informs a new mode of consumer-advertiser interaction that is increasingly individuated, privatized, and directed away from the public domain of mass communication.

The touch-point approach illustrates the growing importance of consumer sensory-emotive experiences and brand interactions in producing modes of privatized consumption for marketers. Each touch point, as constructed by advertisers and media partners, reaffirms the difference, individuality, and importance of a particular consumer characteristic, as it represents a specific media outlet that yields an expanding set of opportunities for an advertising agency and its partners. Thus, while agencies continuously seek ways to add value for their corporate clients, the raw material provided by new sensory orders and emotional branding on a private consumer level expand the agency's role in the marketing process and mitigate the general public awareness of advertising's pervasive influence. By directing advertisements and media plans to the private and individual sensory levels of consumption, advertising agencies and their media partners not only eschew public rejection that has limited them in the past but also provide further means to advance their corporate agendas in select ways.

This chapter has also argued for revised methods of critical analysis that access new mediated territories of consumer-advertiser engagement and that integrate the politics of sensory orders in the new marketing economy. This critique accounts for the proliferation of sensory-ordered media, which not only dislodge formally dominant forms of mass media and cultural frames of analysis from the privileged positions of visual and auditory hierarchies they once occupied, but revisions the current generalized critique of production and consumption sites toward an increased specificity of what Howes calls the "progressive privatization of sensation" (Howes 2005b: 287).

The effects of the experience economy and the function of marketing within it reveal the multiple ways in which advertising agencies and consumers produce and shape private and individualized means of consumption. Increased media choices and customized products through which people experience consumption generate more opportunities for advertisers to revalue the consumer through innovative media forms. By directing marketing strategies and media tactics through sensory dimensions of consumption, advertising agencies effectively restructure a different kind of marketing reality for consumers. In other words, the more technology invents new modes of personalized consumption—driven by the individualized tastes of consumers (iPads, mobile phones, and so forth)—the more advertising generates marketing opportunities on which to build the self as a private site of consumption. The impact of such new technologies is already transforming a visual reading culture into an audiovisual-kinetic hands-on culture, in as much as the interplay of images, sounds, and graphics become central to our cultural system that supports the self (Schultz and Pilotta 2004: 4). By appealing to individualized consumer tastes through sensory-ordered media, advertisers increasingly craft a privatized consumption space wherein the consumer body is universalized and redesigned as a mediated site of consumer-advertiser interactions. If advertising once held dominance as a public discourse and global system of signs, now these emergent forms of interactive media at the individual level promise advertisers a new realm of consumption in the private sensory experience of the consumer's mind and body.

–6–

Creativity, Person, and Place

Why is it that some localities more than others seem able to loosen strong emotions or kindle inspiring thoughts in people? What is it about certain places and moments in time in which some people are able to draw out brilliant ideas, especially in situations that seem unexpected and unpredictable? The majority of ethnographic studies have focused on fixed and determined places, such as home (Csikszentmihalyi and Rocheberg-Halton 1981; McCracken 2005), work (Goffman 1959; Schwartzman 1989), "third places" (Oldenburg 1989), and nonplaces (Augé 1995). Daily life, however, is also composed of places and moments in time that are transitional, such as riding in a bus on the way home or taking a shower in the morning before leaving for work. Curiously, the emergence of creative thought is often linked with transitional sites rather than fixed and determined places for reasons unknown. This chapter explores the connection between creative thinking and transitional places. We examine the ways in which a sense of "off place and odd moment" encourage a type and quality of creative thinking in people. We are not concerned with attempting to define what creativity is, nor analyze creativity from the internal structures of the mind, since our emphasis is on human situations and circumstances in which creativity arises. In particular, we explore the off places and odd moments in which creative thought seems to regularly emerge for advertising professionals and anthropologists.

Our data are collected from extended work as anthropologists working with creative executives employed in the advertising industry. Advertising creatives are constantly charged with finding new ideas for a brand advertising campaign. We may inquire how they arrive at ideas on a regular basis. In everyday routines, advertising creatives get close to the brand through their work; they are briefed on consumers, they are provided brand information, they attend brand workshops. They often become saturated, even lost in the brand, describing a sense of being too close to it in their everyday work. They become mired down in old thinking, and desire a fresh perspective. So they may take a break, leave the agency, and go somewhere else outside their workplace for new ideas. Nevertheless, just as often, creatives admit that ideas arrive during unexpected moments, such as while strolling in a park, walking a dog, or driving a car. Turner describes these occasions as "interstitial zones" and they are often the grounds for creativity. For Turner, the most creative human spaces occur in such zones of indeterminacy, during nonwork activities of talk, play, and joking that are opposed to earnest workaday routines (in Rosaldo, Lavie, and

–74–

Narayan 1993: 2). Our interest is not in *what* advertising creatives are doing when ideas arrive as much as it is in the between places that oppose work *when* creative thoughts arrive.

Similar to advertising creatives, corporate anthropologists often receive creative ideas in odd places and during odd times, such as when doing fieldwork with consumers. Their work involves encounters with others in localized sites that are themselves transitional and indeterminate, at least from the perspective of the anthropologist visiting the home of a consumer. The anthropologist's temporary presence in a consumer's life brings a degree of unfamiliarity to the interview situation, disrupting his or her normal routine and inciting a fresh perspective from the respondent in describing an otherwise familiar routine. Anthropologists make the *familiar strange* by their presence and questioning. Here, we explore how the anthropologist's method of participant observation evokes a space for creative thought in its indeterminacy because it operates from two distinct and contradictory domains of experience. As both observer and participant, fieldwork involves subjective attachment to the time, place, and experience of the interview, while it requires objective detachment from the situation. This paradox of involvement and detachment generates insights from a transitional sense of moving back and forth between emplacement and displacement in the fieldwork situation itself. Thus, the anthropologist's own predicament in the ethnographic context affords sharper perception of indeterminate situations and contradictory messages from consumers.

In this chapter, we look at emplacement in transitional places as embodying a resource that advertising creatives and anthropologists avail for gaining new perspectives on their work. For both, creative inspiration emerges out of movement into transitional places, where embodied perceptions interact contextually with temporary situations. Creative imagination occurs for creative executives when they open themselves to new thoughts in odd places and unusual times, and for anthropologists when they open themselves to the between and look for linkages in disparate domains of consumer experience where none apparently exist. The characteristic between-ness of these sites and their opposition to dwelled-in places such as home or work, provide a dynamic quality of duality in experience and awareness that can elicit creative thought for the observer-self in that situation.

One caveat before we proceed. Even as we focus on the observer-self, we acknowledge the notion that creativity as the provenance of the lone individual is problematic. Creativity is not always the result of isolated acts from lone individuals but often is a collaborative effort among people and a continual dynamic achieved over time (Hallam and Ingold 2007; Liep 2001; Moeran and Strandgaard Pedersen 2011; Sawyer 2007). We concur that creativity is not always generated by the lone individual but rather from places and situations that have their effect on individuals. We build on the idea that as knowledge is embedded in objects (Latour 1987) and in bodily practices (Polanyi 1958), it can also be embedded in certain places. Gaining fresh insight from one's placement in certain contexts occurs because our sense of place is not neutral; rather, it generates a dynamic experience that interacts with thought (Basso 1996; Casey 1996; Feld 1982, 1996). Architects and designers note the connection between space, human behavior, and creativity: tighter enclosed dwellings improve human performance in detail-oriented tasks, while soaring open spaces inspire lofty thoughts (Anthes 2009). When we allow for the idea that places give back and shape us, influencing our feelings and thoughts, we can look to them as sources of inspiration. Places move our thoughts and emotions, help organize and reorganize ideas, and give new meaning to old thoughts.

Transitional zones possess a creative quality *because* they are transitional—that is, they are not meant to be lived in but rather passed through to some other destination. They oppose and frame places that *are* dwelled in. The concept of dwelling consists in the multiple lived relationships that people maintain with places, and, therefore, it is by virtue of these relationships that such spaces acquire meaning (Basso 1996: 54). Philosopher Gaston Bachelard insists that people require dwelled-in places such as houses in which to dream and imagine, where, he postulates, the house itself can become "a tool for analysis of the human soul" ([1958] 1994: xxxvii). However, for this reason, we can also say that the meaning of transitional spaces by virtue of their disjuncture from permanence, lack of grounded relationships within them, and temporality of passing through them gain significance in relation to fixed places. In fact, the very indeterminate qualities of transient spaces, such that they are not fully objectified (Basso 1996; Heidegger 1977), frame the grounds for creative thought. In other words, transitional zones embody the qualities of impermanence, uncertain personal relations, and temporary situations, which become the conditions for enabling creativity in senses of place.

For advertising creatives and anthropologists, there are fresh perspectives to be gained by stepping away from work routines and into transitional zones, whether for brief moments or longer fieldwork stays. Movement to transitional zones, away from work literally and figuratively, creates a sense of being close to and apart from assigned work, from colleagues on the job, and from routine perspectives and can lead to new reflective thinking. In fact, the temporary situation of transitional zones operates against the stable and dwelled-in nature of fixed places as a means for generating between-ness in which creative ideas flourish. This relationship between boundary, place, and thought is comparable to the way transitional zones are sites of the subjunctive—what if—compared to sites of the indicative—it is so—about which Turner wrote (1988).

This process of movement in mind and body between two contrasting places, of a temporary place in relation to a fixed place, creates a perspective of *duality* that leads to fresh thinking. More broadly, we claim that duality itself affords a state of between that is a necessary condition in the process of being creative. It describes a condition of acknowledging two or more distinct domains, through which juxtaposing senses of place with thought processes and states of being leads to new ideas. Psychologists explain this in terms of two or more concepts intermingling in new ways to arrive at a new idea (Sawyer 2007: 115). Duality is a recurring theme and framework for creativity. It reveals an active state of play "betwixt and between" two opposing poles—in the way ideas, places, and processes intermingle toward creative ends. We will explore this duality of temporality, perception, and movement in place as a means for gathering and reorganizing thoughts in creative ways.

Place, Creativity, and Indeterminacy

Keith Basso (1996), Steven Feld (1982, 1996), Clifford Geertz ([1983] 2000), Renato Rosaldo (1980), and others decry the scant attention paid to our sense of place, one of the most basic dimensions of human experience. Citing philosopher Immanuel Kant, Edward Casey (1996) claims that knowledge begins with experience, and experience is dialectally affected by place. Geertz states in the preface to the 2000 edition of *Local Knowledge* that "Contextualization is the name of the game" (Geertz [1983] 2000: xi). Yet, even as we discuss the importance of place, most people do not acknowledge or are even aware of its effects. Geertz continues that, although "[place] is a dimension of everyone's existence, the intensity of where we are, passes by anonymous and unremarked. It goes without saying" (1996: 259).

Places are worth investigating because they contain certain dynamics that affect the way people think, feel, and experience life. There is no truly knowing or sensing a place from afar or in general (Geertz 1996). Rather, we sense or know a place deeply by being in it. Whenever people step back from the flow of everyday experience and attend self-consciously or unconsciously to place, their relationship to geography is richly lived and deeply felt (Basso 1996: 54). "Places are sensed, senses are placed," writes Feld (1996: 91). Basso calls the reciprocal and dialectic experience of place *interanimation*: "As places animate the ideas and feelings of persons who attend to them, these same ideas and feelings animate the places on which attention has been bestowed, and the movements of this process . . . cannot be known in advance" (1996: 55). The reciprocity of place—the giving and receiving qualities that have an effect on people—can be further discussed in three forms of interactions that influence the emergence of creative thought.

First, our sense of place involves motion. Casey notes that places can be perduring and constant, but they are not inactive and at rest. "Part of the power of place, its very dynamism, is found in its encouragement of motion in its midst, its 'e-motive' (and often explicitly emotional) thrust" (1996: 23). He argues that we can *stay in a place* and be moved bodily by another object such as transportation in a car; *move within a place*, such as physically moving our bodies about in a place as in a room; or *move between places*, which denotes a transition such as in journeys, voyages, and so forth. The idea that places generate motion—emotional, psychic, and embodied— reveals the effect of place in shaping the creative imagination. For instance, noted hip-hop rapper Lupe Fiasco discusses the effect of movement on creative thought for him: "Creativity comes in weird places and in weird ways. Sometimes I find I write better in the car, with just the beat playing and me driving. There's something about the way the thoughts come out when I'm actually in motion" (Fiasco 2011: 60).

The power to gather and rearrange ideas is a second dynamic of place. Casey writes that places gather experiences and histories, languages and thoughts. "Think only of what it means to go back to a place you know, finding it full of memories and expectations, old things and new things, the familiar and the strange, and much more besides. What else is capable of this massively diversified holding action?" (Casey 1996: 24). Even in total stillness, places may seem to speak to us (Basso 1996: 56). In this sense, places can generate new thought as much as release pondered-over thoughts for inspiration. This dynamic is not unlike the psychological concept of incubation, which we articulate here as prompted by circumstances of location.[1] As such, the hold of place gathers and orders things, arranging thoughts, even when things are conflictual. We can imagine how certain places represent regular destinations for receptive individuals when they serve to order and rearrange familiar thoughts with new order or merge well-pondered-over problems in new arrangements (Casey 1996: 24).

Finally, the dynamic of place influences different people differently. The reciprocal process of interanimation affects people in particular ways even for a familiar place, thereby summoning different capabilities for perceiving and sensing place. The same locality may be perceived and apprehended in very different ways according to the intentions of the observer. The situated aims and purposes guide awareness in specific directions and evoke what kind of sentiments and ideas are appropriate. "The professional oceanographer engrossed in a study of wave mechanics will make of a secluded cove something quite different than will a rejected suitor who recalls it as the site of a farewell walk on the beach, and this will be true even if the oceanographer and suitor are one and the same person" (Basso 1996: 89).

However, it is not just a matter of feeling sensation, being moved by place, or gathering thoughts in a place. Even places that are sensed objectively can blur perceptions of reality so that we think and feel differently. Sometimes this leads to confusion and uncertainty over what we experience. As Sartre puts it:

> When knowledge and feeling are oriented toward something real, actually perceived, the thing, like a reflector, returns the light it has received from it . . . the affective state follows that progress of attention, developing with each new discovery of meaning with the result that its development is unpredictable. At each moment perception overflows it and sustains it, and its density and depth come from its being confused with the perceived object. Each quality is so deeply incorporated in the object that it is impossible to distinguish what is felt and what is perceived. (Sartre 1965: 89, in Basso 1996: 55–56)

Thus, acute awareness over thoughts and feelings, ideas and realities due to interaction of place with our existing thoughts from somewhere else can result in states of confusion or indeterminacy in our thinking. Rosaldo (1993) describes this unpredictable effect as the "off-tempo" of everyday life. Indistinct time blurs with place to form "zones of indeterminacy" that foster new perceptions. Such moments of indeterminacy, he notes, are a key quality that "promotes the human capacity for improvisation in response to the unexpected" (1993: 256). We claim these moments in which our sense of place interacts with thoughts from elsewhere, usually about fixed places and most often in transitional places, which creates an awareness of between-ness that is potent for new thought to emerge.

Between-ness and Transitional Spaces

Studies on creativity regularly associate creative thought with qualities of indeterminacy. Paul Stoller describes between-ness as a place for great creativity (2009: 4), Michel de Certeau describes the "art of being in between" as a way to draw unexpected results from everyday situations (1988: 30). For Rosaldo, ambiguity in zones of indeterminacy is key to creativity (Rosaldo 1993), and Csikszentmihalyi (1990a) regards the characteristics of flow as those inexplicable moments of euphoria that we experience at rare intervals. These descriptions regard the unexpected and surprising qualities of creativity in terms of uncertain and unpredictable states and places. They also describe the characteristic between-ness of transitional places.

While transitional places may be stimulating or boring, passed through rapidly or sojourned more leisurely, they are places that are *not* dwelled in. Their temporality provides them with a transitional dynamic for evoking creative ideas. The characteristics of place previously detailed—the ability to incite motion, gather and rearrange thoughts, and affect different people differently—are the qualities that advertising creatives and anthropologists make good use of consciously or inadvertently in availing the indeterminacies of transitional space. For instance, anthropologists Ken Anderson and Rogério de Paula (2006) conducted their most illuminating interviews of the day, unexpectedly, when they spoke with informants during bus and boat rides in a Brazilian town. After a long day of regular prescheduled interviews with informants, they spoke casually and spontaneously with locals on their way home. Anderson and de Paula were alert to the ways that improvised interviews in these situations offered richer opportunities to access the collective thoughts and experiences of locals than planned-out interviews.

We might briefly compare the characteristic between-ness of these sites in the ways that psychologists and anthropologists approach them. From a psychological view, Boden also describes a sense of the between in terms of the "bath, bed and bus" phenomenon (2004: 25). She refers to what creative professionals have been able to tell us about the occurrences of their grand discoveries or works of art in that they were conceived while in the bath, bed, or bus. From psychology, the tendency has been to focus on the mental downtime or incubation period, when a person is not thinking about a problem or is thinking about something else when ideas occur. Moments of indeterminacy appear similar to psychological qualities ascribed to objects in the making (also called preinventive structures). Such objects are ambiguous, novel, have emergent qualities, and so forth, and these qualities also render the objects suitable for interpretation, restructuring, and exploration, which are all creative processes (Finke, Ward, and Smith 1992). In fact, the literature on restructuring indeterminacy has a history in psychology, famously in figure-ground pictures of perception, such as the vase that is also a face, as commented on by Wittgenstein ([1953] 2009).

Nevertheless, while psychological arguments are focused on objects and mental processes, as anthropologists we are concerned with the unexpected moments in human situations when creative qualities emerge. We concur that creativity does not arise out of thin air, ex nihilo (Hausman 1979). Rather, it is generated in specific contexts that are produced by particular circumstances, often in relation to fixed places. Other scholars have written about place, emphasizing a randomness of its "thrown-togetherness" (Massey 2005) or giving primacy to movement rather than to place itself through notions of circumstantial "entanglements" (Ingold 2008). As Ingold puts it, "there would be no places were it not for the comings and goings of human beings and other organisms to and from them, from and to places elsewhere" (Ingold 2008: 1808). Nevertheless, these works overlook the effect that certain transitional places have on individuals and how individuals, in return, appropriate the between-ness of these spaces in purposeful ways. We examine the way ideas arise prompted by aspects of indeterminacy in place itself, whereby we would classify ideas arising from situations of "sleep, bathing, and bus rides" in the same category as transitional zones. In the characteristic ways that creative executives and anthropologists are self-aware at certain moments and ponder thoughts in transitional places relative to work and such that these places are frequently visited, vacationed in, passed through, or field-worked in, they generate sites of the between for new thought. We further examine the purposeful ways that context, perception, and thought in transitional zones conjoin by exploring the emergence of creativity among advertising creatives.

Locating Creativity among Creatives

How and where advertising creatives receive inspiration has been a subject of great interest (Callahan and Stack 2007; Hackley and Kover 2007; Kover 1995). A starting place to explore the creative process is in their everyday work routines. After the creative team has received the brief calling for a new advertising approach, they may explore a few initial concepts but largely reject these for fear of trotting over borrowed ground. They engage discussions, attend meetings, and receive product samples and demonstrations about the brand. Often creative executives become inundated with the brand. Advertising creatives are compelled to set out for fresh ideas, seeking concepts that have not been done before. They may look through older advertisements on the brand, they may brainstorm ideas with others, or they may seek trips or excursions for fresh thinking. However, working in a corporate setting, they are under restricted budgets, busy schedules, and tight time lines.

Myriad constraints are a normal function of the advertising world. Other studies, in fact, show that creativity is inspired by such constraints. Moeran, for instance, describes the working situation of advertising creatives in a Japanese advertising agency, who would rather be subject to constraints and conditions in their work, such as those laid out by schedules, materials, and time lines, than work endlessly "up blind alleys" (Moeran 2009: 5). The parameters set by a client, agency, and creative assignment help frame the necessary conditions in which "ideas can unexpectedly jump out" (Moeran 2006: 88). From our perspective, transitional spaces likewise form the constraints and conditions in which advertising creatives work, since they are apart from but connected to the routines, new assignments, and heavy workloads that frame regularized creative obligations.[2]

While creatives work in the (usually) comfortable office environments of advertising agencies, they often express strong antibureaucratic sentiments toward structured schedules and regimented workloads (Hackley and Kover 2007: 70). They claim to be inspired by going out, working apart from regularized office schedules, often seeking stimulation outside the office. They admit their best ideas are sparked by the aesthetics and happenings of everyday life, away from work, from being open to unexpected ideas, images, sounds, and colors all around them (Callahan and Stack 2007: 272). Sometimes a planned escape leads to new thinking, but just as often ideas come serendipitously in unspecific places and moments. Indeed, many creatives rely on spontaneity and surprise as the means by which ideas arrive (cf. Boden 1990, in Hallam and Ingold 2007: 14). Phil Dusenberry, legendary creative director of BBDO, attests to the uncertainty of creative work. While he advocates the value of a disciplined approach, he also admits that much of the time this doesn't work:

> Insights do not adhere to a strict metronomic beat that begins with research and ends with execution. Insights materialize at any point along the matrix. Sometimes they are the product of elegant research and analysis. But just as often they appear because of a casual remark by the client about what he or she really wants. Or in response to a clumsy execution of an ad that is so lacking in insight that it inspires you to fill in the blank. Or sometimes it's little more than trusting your gut, relying on instinct, feeling moved by a notion and assuming that the rest of the world will be equally moved. (Dusenberry 2005: 19)

Spontaneity and openness to instincts appear to be qualities for creative inspiration in advertising. Other advertising creatives also describe unpredictable moments when creative ideas surface spontaneously or unexpectedly, such as during gym workouts, while out mulling a point, when riding a bike, or walking the dog. Still others describe off places, such as at airports, during morning subway commutes, or in showers getting ready for work (Callahan and Stack 2007: 274–75). Dusenberry recalls that his eureka moment for the General Electric (GE) campaign came unexpectedly during a cab ride on the way to a meeting: "As we honked, bounced, and stalled our way through traffic, a beautiful thing happened. Maybe it was the last pothole, but the theme line, full-blown, popped into my head: GE . . . We bring good things to life." (2005: 4).

These advertising creatives concur that moments of inspiration arrive to them most often in nonwork transitional spaces and at unpredictable times. It seems that while on the way to somewhere, after coming from somewhere else, an idea arrives out of nowhere. These moments are similar to transitional spaces of liminality as described by Turner (1967). Different from Turner, however, the insights of creatives describe ordinary moments of between-ness not related to the social dramas or ritual processes in which Turner was interested. The muse arrives, rather, during ordinary but unplanned moments that occur between fixed boundaries—such as home and office, or between meetings. David Ogilvy, chief creative director and founder of Ogilvy and Mather, recounts his most creative moments occurring apart from work, such as on frequent vacations, when walking in the country, bird watching, listening to music, taking long hot baths, or gardening. He reasons that, "while employed in doing nothing, I receive a constant stream of telegrams from my unconscious, and these become the raw material for my creative work" (1965: 206–7). Ironically, it is during Ogilvy's self-professed transitional moments of "doing nothing" when he was quite active in being creative.

We can speculate that, for Ogilvy, while in the solitude of his walks in the woods or during the quietness of gardening, he may have arrived at slogans such as, "At 60 miles an hour the loudest noise in the new Rolls Royce comes from the electric clock" (Ogilvy 1985: 10). Or perhaps Dusenberry was influenced by the frustrating situation of sitting dead in a cab while crawling through New York City traffic when he arrived at the line, "GE . . . We bring good things to life." Their brief descriptions of *when* creative inspiration occurred for them reflect the very indeterminate qualities of between-ness that define transitional places. The situations that these advertising creatives describe also indicate qualities of transience: a sense of bodily motion of one form or another, a keen awareness of their circumstance, and the gathering or reordering of thoughts that bear on a work-related idea while away from work and in transition.

Malefyt spoke with a creative executive at BBDO about her work on a cable TV brand, and she detailed a similar situation of arriving at an insight during an odd time and off place. The copywriter mentioned that she was at a movie theater watching a film when an idea for an out-of-home campaign came to her. She said that the thought came to her not while at work or at home watching programs on TV, but when she least expected it. She had sought an escape, to take a break and let her mind rest. The temporality of the cinema provided a sudden flash of insight that marks the character of creative thinking. On another occasion, Malefyt spoke with a creative director who maintains that he regularly goes out shopping, perusing a store to clear his mind of work. Often, ideas would come to him in these unexpected times and places. In these moments, a sense of time and place reach a kind of epiphany of experience. Such culminations of mind and body are realized in the temporality of between-ness because they stand in relation to dwelled-in places and routine ways of thinking at work and home. The duality of place that generates insights for advertising creatives in temporal situations, such as in movie theaters or shopping excursions away from work, compares to the way anthropologists conducting consumer research gain insights away from corporate offices.

Ethnography and Place

In contrast to other forms of corporate research, anthropologists are charged with going out to the field to gather insights from consumers. As such, the issues they face in observing and interviewing consumers in locales are enmeshed with the dynamics of place. The ethnographer's task is to attempt to understand local forms of culture as it is experienced, shared, and communicated by local people in interpersonal settings of place (Basso 1996: 56). To an ethnographer, writes Geertz, context is everything since the shapes of knowledge are always local ([1983] 2000: 4). However, while anthropologists attempt to understand local knowledge in the places that consumers dwell, they themselves are temporary guests trying to absorb locality, but always one-off. They are transient objects themselves, experiencing the indefinite, uncertain sense of place. Nevertheless, they can learn to use this sense of between-ness to their advantage as a way to gather creative thoughts about self and consumers.

The first order of localized fieldwork is to recognize our bodies as the primary instrument for gathering data. Since the mind and knowledge are embodied (Kant), what happens in and to our bodies in fieldwork affect our perceptions. We interact in the world of the informant and with our own thoughts and feelings toward the subject. As the body is our primary means for assessing the culture of others, it also experientially recedes whenever we become fully engaged in daily activities and in conversations with others. The lived body in fieldwork, writes Feld, is characterized by this duality of switching back and forth in attention, engaging both a tuning in to ourselves and our concerns, and tuning out to the activity at hand (1996: 92). This dynamic transience of both presence and absence of the body and our perceptions of place is a key dimension for heightened awareness in gathering insights from ethnographic fieldwork.

Ethnography practiced as true participant observation reflects this paradox of two incongruent perceptions that arise out of a duality of time and place. Participant observation operates from two distinct domains of experience, itself an oxymoron of perceptions (Behar 1996). Participation involves subjective attachment of the interviewer to the informant, "being there" physically and emotionally as an embodied self. Yet observation of the subject requires objective detachment, a distance of the analytic self from the subject (Dewalt and Dewalt 2000: 262). This paradox of between-ness, of distance and engagement, instills a sense of incongruity. Indeterminacy here allows for the duality of being occupied with observing, listening, and discussing with others while being detached to take in ideas or see connections not otherwise apparent.

The sense of belonging and not belonging to a place and our transience of being there yet detached can aid in observing contradictions and paradoxes in others. People's lives are naturally full of inconsistencies and contradictions. By being aware of our own dualities, anthropologists can more carefully attend to the confusing and disjointed parts of consumer experience and look for the embracing conceptual logic that makes sense of the whole person. For instance, during a project conducted for a packaged goods client, Malefyt interviewed a staunch environmental supporter who discussed her passion for "green" products and proudly advocated for others to do the same. Yet Malefyt was surprised to observe that she also drove a large, gas-guzzling sport utility vehicle. In probing further, Malefyt listened for a unifying logic. The respondent said that she used her vehicle to car-pool her own and other children, and she admitted she felt most "protected" in a large vehicle. Her passion for the environment was expressed in generalized concerns of protection for the planet as well as for her family. Anthropologists notice such apparent contradictions and look for the internal logic that connects two separate domains into a unified whole.

Confusion, Ignorance, and Being Wrong

The practice of listening for contradictions, bridging disjointed concepts, and being attuned to paradoxes in consumers' stories takes getting used to, even for experienced anthropologists. Such encounters may lead us to feel surprised, unsure, even confused. Nevertheless, in states of confusion anthropologists can also experience creativity and notice connections not otherwise apparent. Confusion not only disarms former blocks of knowledge but also triggers an immediate search for meaning by sorting out structures of signification (Geertz 1973: 9) and domains of experience in self and others. Rosaldo writes that ambiguity and confusion are the very grounds for creativity: "Far from being devoid of positive content . . . indeterminacy enables a culturally valued quality of human relations where one can follow impulses, change directions, and coordinate with other people" (Rosaldo 1993: 256). Confusion results in increased attention to our immediate surroundings, listening more attentively, and, most importantly, a new readiness to look for causal connections where none appear to make sense. Uncertainty and confusion encourage us to make insightful connections in apparent disunity and see what we might not normally see.

Uncertainty and ignorance in the ethnographic process can be a great resource for learning and insight. Gray (2003) writes that knowledge stands in the way of perception, since solved problems tend to stay solved and people seek answers in what is already known and safe. Ignorance helps discard old preconceptions, hardened knowledge, and stereotypes as we initiate an exploration for fresh ideas in well-worn subjects of study. The resulting errors are themselves adventures in new thinking. Schultz (2010), in her book *Being Wrong*, celebrates error as a form of learning, adventure, and exploration. She claims that being right is basically static since it starts out with prepositions that are only validated. However, to err is "to wander, create movement and find adventure through discovery" (2010: 40).

To acknowledge error in fieldwork is to accept that points of confusion in conversations with consumers are opportunities rather than barriers to insights. When ethnographic discussions proceed opportunistically, we arrive at unknowns by following new thoughts that emerge in junctures of conversation. This often happens when interviews between interviewer and respondent are mutually constructed and proceed as an open and flexible communicative process that explores emergent contingencies. Alternatively, insights are less likely to happen when interviews are fixed and follow strict protocols of set discussion guides and questionnaires. Like a "drama that unfolds" (Holstein and Gubrium 1995: 17), improvisational styles of wandering and exploring in discussions with others invokes a between space for creativity to happen. This sense of awareness and openness is aided by our own displacement and sense of transience in place.

In a study conducted for an athletic shoe company, Malefyt was armed with knowledge from previous research, which claimed that runners run to keep healthy and physically fit as a brand benefit. Yet in conversations that wandered from the discussion guide, runners began to open up about how running integrates a different set of values in their lives. Malefyt followed this line of thought, questioning how the experience of running compared to other types of life experiences. An insight came when runners described the pleasure of running as not physical at all but rather mentally fulfilling. For them, running offered a private uninterrupted time for themselves, a way to be alone, reorder daily priorities, and relieve stress from work. One respondent expressed this clearly in an analogy that running helped "empty the garbage in his mind." Reporting these findings back to BBDO led the advertising creatives to develop a campaign idea around personal satisfaction of running as "my time," within the larger context of people's busy lives.

As this case demonstrates, the anthropologist can use his own awareness of indeterminacy to prompt people to think anew when unexpected responses emerge in conversations. Creativity becomes evident in the ways people formulate new thoughts and feelings about the brand in response to the anthropologist's queries. Questions that juxtapose different domains of consumer experience allow people to reflect on and create new associations, which generate unconsidered brand associations for advertising ideas and new product development. Responding to the unexpected thus promotes a human capacity for improvisation, which celebrates a cultural value of creativity (Rosaldo 1993: 256).

Participant observation is then about embracing the duality of the observer-self in transitional states of being that arise from a transient sense of place. Fernandez writes that daily interactions with people often bring together different domains of human experience in unexpected ways. He sees human creativity in argument and discussion, when ideas juxtapose the unknown with the known, producing "revelatory incidents." Such incidents in fieldwork are opportunities for gathering incongruities and connecting meaning through metaphor (Fernandez 1986). These dialectical moments between self and other and between ideas and experience are central to fieldwork and lie at the heart of reflexivity that informs anthropological knowledge (Behar 1996: 82; Feld 1996: 91).

Creativity in Advertising and Anthropology

We are now ready to explore more closely the connections between these two diverse professions: advertising creative work and anthropological inquiry. We may ponder what advertising creatives in their creative assignments and anthropologists in their fieldwork of others have in common in their use of transitional spaces. What traits are shared, and why might each require indeterminate moments and frequent excursions to places of the between for generating creative thought?

Both anthropologists and advertising creatives represent professions that require drawing on creativity regularly for the work they produce. Both become inspired by movement into transitional zones that are indeterminate relative to the fixed places they depart from. Being open to ambiguity relative to their own experience of movement, rearrangement of thoughts, and new perceptions, anthropologists and advertising creatives become alert to new ideas. In other words, an aspect of being inspired in thought and feeling by transitional place is identified in the fluid boundaries and permeable thinking that such sites engender. The quality of permeability as a feature of creative thinking and relative to indeterminacy is best understood by noting how it contrasts the fixed and determined and often named features of dwelled-in places.

Named Places, Fixed Boundaries, Ordered Thinking

In one sense, an essential attribute of dwelled-in places that defines them is that places, like persons, support individual names that provide a fixed identity (Frake 1996: 235). Named places such as New York's Fifth Avenue, Madison Avenue, and Las Vegas possess histories, memories, and characteristics that define particular identities, such as attitudes toward fashion, notable advertising company locales, and even boundaries to moral behavior or a lack thereof ("What happens in Vegas, stays in Vegas"). For the Western Apaches, Basso informs us that the mere mention of a named place can evoke a story (Basso 1988). Frake explains, "unlike persons, whose creation precedes naming, places come into being out of spaces by being named" (1996: 235). Yet, in another sense, when places are named, they also become objectified in ways that can be imagined, controlled, and limited, with endless adaption to apply rules over people, regions, religions, language, and so forth, as Benedict Anderson (1992) demonstrates in the rise of nationalism. Even if the dimensions of named places vary, from small points to almost limitless spaces, they enclose a boundary such that "The limits of a name serve, like a verbal fence, to enclose an individual place as a spatial self" (Frake 1996: 235). While named places possess an identity, a story, and social orientation, their fixed parameters can also be objectified, manipulated, and ordered, if not by their geographical features, then for their effects on shaping the imagination. This is antithetical to creativity.

In contrast, the nameless quality of transitional zones provides no fixed identity, bears a lack of control, and so is not objectified in the mind, which therefore offers greater potential for stirring the imagination. Transitional sites become meaningful through the fluidity of their boundaries and often nameless characteristics. Rather than being identified, controlled, and ordered from afar as in many dwelled-in places, the permeability, transience, and indeterminacy of between places require physical presence, an open awareness, and perceptions in the moment. They are defined not by an enduring or imagined identity but by a coming-into-being emergence that only makes sense being there, bodily. Thus, they are better described as *events* of person, thought, and activity that converge in the moment, such as in a ride on a bus, a dream in bed, a bath after a long day, to reference Boden's earlier example. Casey notes that an aspect of sensing place is *in the events* that characterize it, which is *not* limited by determinant boundaries. There has to be a permeable margin of transition for a place to become an event, since any event involves change and movement (Casey 1996: 42). While buses, beds, and baths are places that are typically not named, they are creatively significant for their influence on stirring the body and mind through temporality, transition, and movement. They are valued for what they do, for their effect on persons, and as transformational events that are occupied bodily.

In the field of advertising, as we have seen, the nameless sites, transient places, and porous thinking that transitional places of cab rides, movie theaters, and gardening afford, keep advertising creatives fluid and open to new thoughts and ideas relative to work assignments. Paradoxically, the transitional movement and fluid thought of creatives necessitate their counterpoint in the fixed and determined structures of business in order to function. The brands creatives work on are, in a sense, like dwelled-in and named places: they possess in their bounded features a certain identity, a story, and a social orientation; they are characterized by an indelible name, trademark, or symbol (Aaker 1996; Malefyt 2008a); and they develop long-term relationships with consumers. Brands are further bounded and determined by the countless advertising effectiveness measures, copy testing, and brand positioning work of advertising agency life. Still, the ordered world of brand marketing contrasts and complements the fluid imagination of the advertising creative. Relations thrive in a field of distinctions, where contrast and opposition enliven positions relative to other positions and to the field as a whole (Bourdieu 1993). Creatives in advertising, then, require the rigorous dwelled-in features of brands and the client's structured campaign requirements from which to work against. Frequently crossing boundaries from the domain of rigid deadlines, client meetings, and named brands, to the domain of fluid movement and porous thinking in and out of transitional spaces provides advertising creatives the necessary between-ness for new thoughts to flourish.

Anthropologists are also skilled at permeating boundaries. They operate between ideas from both sides; between a people under study and a home college, university, or corporate office environment; between flows and changes in thinking and perceptions. Porosity is a feature of their work. Paul Stoller addresses the anthropologist's relation to permeable ideas and boundaries: "Indeed, anthropologists are always 'between' things—between 'being there', as the late Clifford Geertz put it and 'being-here', between two or more languages, between two or more cultural traditions, between two or more apprehensions of reality. Anthropologists are the sojourners of 'the between'" (Stoller 2009: 4).

Stoller exhorts that being between can be negative, simultaneously pulling us in two directions, or, using Turner's description of liminality, in a state of betwixt and between, between indecision and confusion. He also affirms that if we draw strength from both sides of the between and embrace the creative air of indeterminacy, "we can find ourselves in a space of enormous growth, a space of power and creativity" (Stoller 2009: 4). Behar (1996) also speaks eloquently about her personal fieldwork experiences, which draw us in emotionally between the bounds of her past self and the places and women she encounters. Anthropologists use the between in their own personal experience of fieldwork to bridge other realities of the places they study with their own inner impressions, connecting others to selves, far off lives to close daily experiences.

Indeed, ethnography itself, as a methodological practice and form of analysis, operates between the humanities and social sciences and between descriptive facts that compare and contrast and impassioned stories that draw us in emotionally. Ethnography is a bridge that informs us here and now of a sense of locality elsewhere. Places we read about become elevated in our minds. We feel a consumer's excitement for a brand or sympathize with his or her frustration. Ethnography connects, in Geertz's expression, "there" and "here," deepening our sensitivity to the human condition in other places. Ethnography can be a path that entwines lives and places of others to our more familiar sense of place. The between that anthropologists create informs a place that is richly textured and deeply felt. Our clients, their brands, and our work are better off for embracing it.

When advertising creatives and anthropologists attune to the duality of boundaries and focus on ideas in transition, they open themselves to creative thought. It is as much the sense of place as it is a focused placing of the senses that transitional zones evoke, as Feld describes. Tuning in rather than tuning out, as Fernandez (1986) puts it, enables creative realization in key moments of place. Those of us in professions of mobility and temporality, of attending conferences, conducting consumer research, leading focus groups, and giving panel discussions, live in the between. In the ways that advertising creatives and anthropologists keep moving, become displaced and re-placed in and out of transient places, may we recognize and appreciate such moments of between-ness as creativity in the making.

Part III
Applying Anthropology
in Advertising Agencies

−7−

Advertising, Automobiles, and the Branding of Luxury

A curious thing happened in the U.S. luxury automobile market in 1990 and 2002. Two car manufacturers launched new vehicles with advertising campaigns that led to opposite results. General Motors (GM) developed a new Cadillac automobile line that was introduced to the public by the successful "Breakthrough" advertising campaign celebrating the idea of crossing boundaries and charting new territory. Sales increased within the target population. Nissan entered the luxury car market with the Infiniti automobile line and an advertising campaign that associated luxury with the serenity of nature. Sales did not reach the intended mark.

As anthropologists who conducted ethnographic work for both companies, Timothy Malefyt and Maryann McCabe (hereafter, the plural personal pronouns *we*, *us*, and *our* refer to Malefyt and McCabe) were internal observers of how the branding and advertising efforts unfolded. This chapter examines these two outcomes, one a feat, the other a folly, and focuses on branding as an economic and cultural process that engages producers and consumers in capitalist practice. Our purpose is to identify the dynamics between producers and consumers in developing brand meaning and hence to contextualize the location of agency in production and consumption.

In examining two automobile advertising campaigns, we contend that branding reveals a complex, dynamic, and ongoing process that involves negotiating layers of representation and interpretation by producers and consumers. Corporate marketers assign meaning to products and create brand identities based on their understanding of research on what products mean to consumers and on their own schemas and agendas for fitting their organization's lineup of products and brands into the competitive marketplace. Consumers, in turn, respond to both product and brand image through their own lived experiences with the brand. Because consumer response to product and/or brand image may be positive or negative (and, if negative, lead to further rounds of representation and interpretation), we argue that interactivity becomes a critical and necessary symbolic field of interaction and even contestation between marketers and consumers that leads to a negotiated meaning of the brand. Sometimes companies get it right, as Cadillac did with its "Breakthrough" advertising campaign, while other times companies need to redo their marketing strategy and advertising campaign, as did Nissan with its initially failed Infiniti ad campaign. The benefit of framing the brand as an interactive process of representation and interpretation is that it locates human agency on both the production and consumption side of capitalist society.

Our vantage point on interactive branding comes from our direct relationship with General Motors and Nissan North America and more generally from our professional work conducting ethnographic market research for corporate clients. At the time the ethnographic research was conducted for Cadillac, Malefyt was employed at D'Arcy Masius Benton and Bowles (D'Arcy), Cadillac's advertising agency of record in Detroit, Michigan; and McCabe, also a corporate anthropologist, joined the research team as consultant. This research was conducted in 2001, prior to the launch of the Cadillac "Breakthrough" advertising campaign on February 3, 2002. It was through McCabe's consulting practice that a relationship with Nissan developed that included consumer research for Infiniti in 1990 and again in 1991, completed in collaboration with Nissan's advertising agency of record, Hakuhodo in Tokyo. These long-term client relationships and employment positions in advertising agencies afforded us the opportunity to work closely with the companies and their advertising agencies on research projects and brand strategy and to compare the effectiveness of advertising campaigns. As a result, we helped to identify concepts for branding purposes while we observed how these concepts were negotiated and implemented in advertising campaigns at corporate and agency levels.

Case Examples

Cars are integral to the cultural environment in which we express our humanity, writes Miller (2001). Cars signify the totality of all people as an aggregate of vast systems of transport; and yet we are highly personal in our choice and individual relationships with them (Miller 2001: 2). As objects of material culture and subjects of the way we express ourselves, luxury cars have biographies (Kopytoff 1986). We will enter the cultural biographies of Cadillac and Infiniti at particular moments in time to understand what these brands meant to individuals at that time, to describe how the representation of the consumer target was constructed for each brand, and to compare consumer responses to the formulation of the two brands in advertising campaigns.

Our case examples are based on five ethnographic research projects: two for Cadillac and three for Infiniti. Although the methodologies varied somewhat by project, they were tailored to the learning objectives of each project and the theoretical orientation of the anthropologists. Specific methods included one-on-one interviews conducted in homes, with home tours and driving experiences in luxury cars, group interviews held in a local research facility, plus respondent homework assignments such as collages and photo journals. The number of respondents per project ranged from eighteen to ninety-six depending on how many consumer segments were involved. For instance, in the first Cadillac project, we had eighteen respondents from one segment, while in the largest Infiniti study, there were ninety-six respondents divided among three segments. Markets also varied, from singular markets of southern California for the first wave of Cadillac research, to three U.S. markets (San Francisco, Chicago, and Connecticut) for the second wave of Cadillac research, and to five U.S. markets (New York, Atlanta, Chicago, Dallas, and Los Angeles) for the largest Infiniti study. Anthropologists working in the business sector have adapted the traditional field method of long-term social immersion to suit their needs in gaining the respondent perspective and the time horizon of their clients, but the ethnographic endeavor remains the same: to understand the cultural assumptions, beliefs, values, and practices of a group of people and in a commercial setting in relation to a product category and brand.

Anthropologists who work in industry note the valuable contribution of cultural analysis in an ethnographic approach to market research (Sunderland and Denny 2007; Wasson 2000). Analysis for the case studies described here proceeded from linguistic and symbolic analysis within an interpretive framework. This allowed us to situate the Cadillac and Infiniti examples within the broader context of interactivity among consumers and producers in the branding process.

Cadillac

Cadillac and Lincoln were once the rulers of the luxury automobile market in the United States, but by the end of the twentieth century, Cadillac had lost the luster of its glory years. In 2000, it slipped to sixth among luxury car manufacturers. European and Japanese imports (Acura, Audi, BMW, Lexus, Mercedes-Benz) had eroded Cadillac's supremacy in the marketplace. According to advertising journalists (Halliday 2001), Cadillac was hurt not only by increased competition from abroad but also by lackluster products and an aging buyer base. The median age of the Cadillac buyer in 1995, for instance, was seventy-five years old (Walcoff 2006). With a dose of humor in its reporting style, the *New York Times* said that Cadillac had become the brand for "geriatric men looking for something with leather seats that can take them to their next tee time" (Hakim 2002).

In response, Cadillac developed a new line of automobiles that we know as the Escalade, CTS, SRX, XLR, and STS. The Escalade, Cadillac's first sport utility vehicle and the first of the new line to be rolled out, was intended to herald the "new" brand's singularization in the luxury vehicle marketplace. After its debut in 1998, other revised Cadillac models followed during the years 2002 to 2005. GM spent $4 billion (Walcoff 2006) in attempting to resurrect its flagship brand including consumer input during the product development phase, which had indicated that consumers described Cadillacs as "large floaty boats" and would prefer more agile vehicles with a less boxy design. Translating this consumer perspective into materiality, GM hoped the new Cadillac models with their edgy styling and hard, angular lines would reach a younger audience, increase its customer base, and compete more effectively against imports.

With these newly designed and developed vehicles imminently ready for market, the company decided to engage in market research to figure out how best to communicate with a younger audience than the brand had previously targeted. As ethnographers, each of us interviewed "leading-edge" consumers, thirty to forty-nine years old, in the test bed of car culture (southern California) who were selected on the basis of age, "innovator" qualities, and current or prospective luxury car ownership. We queried views of self, aspirations, the meaning of luxury, and perceptions of Cadillac. Cultural analysis of the ethnographic data and a subsequent ethnographic study in other U.S. markets led to Cadillac's successful advertising campaign called the "Breakthrough" campaign, which had a much-heralded four-year run, from early 2002 to early 2006. The national advertising campaign was first launched on February 3, 2002, for the Super Bowl, before an estimated viewership of eighty million people. It subsequently ran in numerous marketing outlets: a Times Square billboard, event sponsorship at the U.S. Tennis Open, and the Daytona and Indianapolis 500 race events. Cadillac dealerships brought the new vehicle models out to shopping malls, town squares, and sporting events to invite consumers for firsthand views and test drives. Cadillac also purchased prime product placement in popular feature movies, such as *The Matrix Reloaded*. The consumer response was largely positive. We examine here how this multimedia launch of "Breakthrough" was developed to represent the target audience.

Respondents in our interviews spoke of life as a process of becoming, where one defines and redefines oneself continually over time and through key life events. People told stories of themselves carving out new experiences, learning, growing, and becoming new selves as they succeeded in obtaining new jobs, promotions, new relationships, and so forth. There was nothing static about this forward-looking mindset. For these respondents, defining and redefining the self involved imagination, dreaming outside the box, crossing boundaries, not feeling constrained by either social rules or family wishes, and breaking through old restraints, both metaphorically and literally. Respondents added that anyone can dream, but one must pursue dreams avidly and persevere because success is achieved by hard work; slouchers fail. Finally, they said that achieving each step of a dream warrants celebration, with the purchase of luxury goods a possible venue for celebrating.[1] Moreover, rather than quiet or subdued celebrating, as this target was recruited for Cadillac, consumers felt celebration called for an obvious, almost ostentatious display. In the subsequent ethnography,[2] respondents likely to buy Cadillac or who had purchased Cadillac in the past were interviewed in their homes, where pictures of festivities, commemorative markings, and awards, posters, and emblems, were prominently displayed. For many aspiring Cadillac owners, celebration of their success was evidently well marked.

The main concept for the "Breakthrough" campaign was born from the ethnographic insight about dreaming outside the box and boisterously marking success. However, this idea ran contrary to respondent perceptions of the brand at the time. Cadillac was "my grandparent's car." While respondents considered the brand old and out of date, they also expressed a wish for the brand to reinvent itself and speak to their generation. They wanted Cadillac, an American icon in their view, to become "cool again" and "the leading luxury car in America." In other words, their discourse revealed correspondence between image of self and hopes for the brand: dream outside the box and reinvent oneself.

In the subsequent study, more ethnographic research revealed that "Breakthrough" resonated with consumers as a call to action for the company as well as for themselves to celebrate their achievements. In light of the new line of Cadillac automobiles and the compelling insights from our research, the advertising agency D'Arcy was challenged to create a dramatic campaign. Gary Topolewski, the chief creative director of D'Arcy at that time, sought advertising that would break through former stereotypes of Cadillac as a "soft luxury" brand. Mark LaNeve, the general marketing manager of Cadillac, chose Led Zeppelin as the "hip and cool" image of the brand for the largely baby boomer audience Cadillac wanted to attract. Ironically, the advertising agency initially selected "Break on Through," a song by The Doors with near perfect lyrics to match the "Breakthrough" advertising tagline. But the rock group's drummer, an avid environmentalist, didn't like Cadillac's gas-guzzling image, and so declined to sign a contract (LaReau 2005). It was then that Cadillac and D'Arcy executives trolled through other iconic symbols from baby boomers' coming-of-age period and agreed on Led Zeppelin's "Rock and Roll." They were able to get the signing rights as well (Halliday 2002).

Consumers largely resonated with the Led Zeppelin song "Rock and Roll." Indeed, they felt the song's lyrics, "it's been a long, lonely time since we've rocked and rolled," referred to the fact that Cadillac had been absent in their lives and that the company now recognized and owned up to its absence in the U.S. auto marketplace by offering more attractive cars. "Breakthrough" resonated with consumers not only for the sense of "doing" but also for the brand reinventing itself—a key belief of success in the United States. "Breakthrough" then operated for consumers both metaphorically and literally. Because the "Breakthrough" campaign concept was based on ethnographic insight, it was able to embody an accurate representation of the consumer. Cadillac, now a reinvented brand metamorphosed from the past with a refurbished heritage, could resonate with the target audience. The transfer of meaning from the context of consumer lives to the new identity of the brand represented in the advertising campaign forged a powerful connection between consumer and car. No wonder the campaign is given credit for helping to bring the Cadillac division of General Motors out of the red and into the black. During the four-year run of the "Breakthrough" campaign, Cadillac sales rose and profits increased. From 2000 to 2005, with the rollout of new models and the new advertising, Cadillac sales increased 24.5 percent, even as other GM divisions declined 10.1 percent (Walcoff 2006). The company was successful in appealing to younger consumers. The average age of the Cadillac owner was reduced from someone in their seventies to someone in their fifties.

Infiniti

When Japanese automotive companies first entered the U.S. luxury car market, the debut of Toyota's Lexus preceded Nissan's Infiniti. The Lexus was introduced in 1988, and the Infiniti followed in 1989. While the launch of the Lexus was successful, the launch of the Infiniti faltered. Sales were disappointing, and the brand's slow start in the marketplace was attributed to the company's initial advertising campaign (www.autotropolis.com). Our knowledge of this failed advertising campaign comes from working with the company in the aftermath of the failure and conducting three ethnographic research projects for the brand in 1990 and 1991.[3]

There had been a predilection at Nissan to sell the Infiniti on the basis of Japaneseness, arguably to give the car a Japanese heritage and thus differentiate it from other luxury car brands. The initial advertising campaign made an assumption that Japaneseness can be translated as serenity in the U.S. marketplace. Scenes from nature were employed to evoke a sense of serenity—leaves reflected in a rippling pond, waves rolling over an ocher beach, and geese gliding across the sky in curvilinear pattern. Underlying the Zen-like state depicted in the advertisements was an equation between nature, comfort, and luxury. However, these ads failed to bring about brand awareness and lead consumers to clamor for the vehicle.

The "Nature" advertising campaign did not reflect the symbolic formulation of luxury cars among members of the U.S. target, young professionals open to a Japanese luxury car because they previously owned Japanese cars. The most obvious reason for lack of consumer response to the campaign was that the ads did not show the car or the performance of the car navigating the road. Luxury, in all its minimal serenity, was presented as the peaceful absence of objects, whereas ethnographic insight determined that U.S. consumers felt luxury should embody and demonstrate the abundance of things (gadgets, amenities, and, most of all, performance). In addition, by trying to link luxury cars to a Zen-like conception of being one with nature, the ads misrepresented U.S. cultural attitudes toward nature as something to dominate and control. A sense of comfort may be an emotional benefit of driving a luxury automobile, but it arises from prevailing over nature, not being united with it, as U.S. consumers informed us. Consequently, the campaign did not represent targeted consumers and their perceptions of self and luxury. It did not offer meanings that could be used for the construction and performance of identity.

As a postscript to this moment in the biography of Infiniti, although Nissan shelved the now notorious "Nature" campaign, it did not give up the idea of positioning the brand on Japanese-ness. In subsequent market research conducted in 1991, the company wanted to retranslate Japanese-ness not as serenity but as simplicity. The research revealed that simplicity is a multivocal symbol with many meanings, negative as well as positive. Based on the research, Nissan chose to reposition the Infiniti on two meanings of simplicity related to luxury cars—performance and aesthetics— which more clearly represented the consumer target. This strategic approach has been followed through the years. A recent tagline from TV ads, for example, claims that Infiniti "uses the power of design to create dynamic, beautiful automobiles." Since the disastrous first year of the "Nature" campaign, Infiniti sales have grown consistently. This indicates that consumers had not rejected the physical car but the advertising message conveyed with its introduction to the market. In fact, in the first study for Nissan, the Infiniti had compared well to other luxury car imports on physical dimensions (style, aesthetics, performance, etc.).

Social Theory and Brand Meaning

Social scientists generally agree that brands mediate relations between production and consumption in capitalism, but the process by which brands assume meaning remains theoretically unclear. Some anthropologists and scholars (Holt 2004; McCracken 2005; Miller 1997; Twitchell 2004) consider brands as cultural texts designed by corporations and advertising agencies that infuse brands with cultural attributes. From this view, brands are produced as meaningful narratives based on corporate perceptions of what provides symbolic differentiation for consumers. This theoretical position has led to the notion that brands are devices offered to consumers who use them to fashion and perform identity.

Taking another approach to brands as media objects, some sociologists and cultural studies scholars (Arvidsson 2006; Lury 2004; Manovich 2001) define the relation between producers and consumers as "interactivity" in contrast to interaction to indicate a kind of communication that involves indirect rather than direct conversation. This theoretical position goes beyond a linear model of communication and conceives of brands as a somewhat vague medium for the exchange of information between producers and consumers. Based on this perspective, a brand performs symbolic work through its logo, such as the Nike swoosh and Cadillac crest, a kind of intellectual property that reveals meaning.

We seek to expand the current discussion of brands by developing a more precise location of human agency in the interactivity between producers and consumers. We argue that the interaction of agency more purposefully involves the directed actions of consumers and producers than vague notions of indirect conversations. In this, we seek to dimensionalize and address interactivity by means of the mediation of agency between producers and consumers. How is a brand brought into existence and maintained over time without face-to-face interaction? How is agency distributed and mediated within the network of economic actors who are party to interactivity? And, finally, how do new interactive marketing approaches alter the relation between producers and consumers in the branding process?

Marketing scholars Schroeder and Salzer-Morling call the space between production and consumption a "theoretical space between strategic concepts of brand identity and consumer interpretations of brand image" (Schroeder and Salzer-Morling

2006: 2). The term *brand identity* refers to the cultural idea constructed by producers to capture the meaning of a brand, and this idea is increasingly anchored in the lived experience of consumers, as companies and advertising agencies rely on an ethnographic approach to gaining market knowledge. *Brand image*, on the other hand, implies the consumer labor of evaluating text put forward by the producer to encode brand meaning. Brand image is what the brand symbolizes in the minds of consumers. It is the value added to a product (Lury 2004).

Rather than decoding the extensive marketing discourse filled with various brand terminology (brand essence, brand promise, brand equity, brand architecture, etc.),[4] we seek to identify the theoretical space where interactivity comes into play. By separating brand identity from brand image, Schroeder and Salzer-Morling carve out analytic room for considering what occurs between producer and consumer in the branding process, and they conclude, correctly we think, that "brand meaning is not wholly derived from the market. Culture, aesthetics, and history interact to inject brands into the global flow of images" (Schroeder and Salzer-Morling 2006: 5). We are talking about social actors and the cultural beliefs and values they bring to the work of constructing brand identities, expressing them in advertising campaigns, and evaluating the advertisements. The social actors include brand managers at companies, account managers, account planners and creative staff at advertising agencies, and the consumers to whom advertisements are directed. The theoretical space that exists between production and consumption involves representation and interpretation in a commercial setting.[5]

Representation and Interpretation in Qualifying Products

The concept of qualification put forward by Callon and his colleagues provides a useful starting point to describe the degree of interaction (or, in their terms, conflict and negotiation) between producers and consumers involved in branding practices. For Callon, a product is a changing entity that constantly goes through transformations and at any point in the sequence of transformations can be called "a good" with a certain set of defined stable characteristics. Callon pursues the idea that objects of material culture have a biography (Kopytoff 1986). Providing a car example, Callon writes:

> As an economic good a car is an object, a thing with a well-defined shape, which is used to meet specific needs and which has an established value in a market context. But it is more than that. It is also an object that has a life, a career. Seen from the angle of its conception and then production, it starts off by existing in the form of a set of specifications, then a model, then a prototype, then a series of assembled elements and, finally, a car in a catalogue that is ordered from a dealer and has characteristics which can be described relatively objectively and a with certain degree of consensus. Once it is in the hands of its driver the car continues moving, not only on roads but also, later, for maintenance

purposes to workshops, then to second-hand dealers. At times it becomes again an object on paper, which takes its place alongside other cars in the guide to second-hand car prices in specialized magazines. (Callon, Meadel, and Rabeharosoa 2002: 197–98)

Qualification includes the materiality of products as described above as well as more presentational aspects such as advertising. The good is made meaningful to consumers through relational dynamics that have particular intrinsic value (becoming singularized in Callon's terms; see also Kopytoff [1986]) beyond its generalized commodity function. Callon notes that brands are one type of characteristic that can qualify, describe, and distinguish similar products from one another as singular in meaning to the consumer, although he does not further elaborate on branding as part of the qualification process. Still, the concept of qualification is useful to apprehend how brands engage the interaction of producers and consumers in two ways.

First, a wide array of people are involved in qualifying products, from the design, production, marketing, distribution, and consumption facets of the capitalist enterprise. In other words, a dialectical relationship between producer and consumer is incorporated into the concept of qualification: "consumers are just as active as the other parties involved. They participate in qualifying available products. It is their ability to judge and evaluate that is mobilized to establish and classify relevant differences. There is no reason to believe that agents on the supply side are capable of imposing on consumers both their perception of qualities and the way they grade those qualities" (Callon, Meadel, and Rabeharosoa 2002: 201). Agency exists on the demand as well as the supply side. As Callon further claims, when goods become singularized, they create a close relationship between what the consumer wants and expects and what is offered by the company (Callon, Meadel, and Rabeharosoa 2002: 202). This effort in capitalist society of moving commodities into singular goods is what drives brand loyalty, the holy grail of marketers. Indeed, consumption is reconsidered, turning the old production-consumption formula on its head. It is no longer viewed as the passive end of production but rather offers an "active and creative means for people to interact, express their attitudes, beliefs, and values, to self and others" (Malefyt 2008b: 80).

Second, the concept of qualification makes provision for change in products and their competitive environment over time, resulting in the need for qualification and requalification or, in marketing discourse, positioning and repositioning. This happened for both Cadillac and Infiniti. Around 2000, following a period of stagnation in sales and loss of market share, the Cadillac line was redesigned and a new fleet of vehicles was put on the market. General Motors had come to realize that luxury car owners considered the Cadillac a big, klutzy box that would be driven by their grandparents, not by themselves. At the time Cadillac was redesigned as a material object, it was also requalified as a brand with a new meaning on which the "Breakthrough" advertising campaign was based. The Infiniti, after suffering a much slower-than-hoped-for start in its 1989 foray into the U.S. marketplace, was eventually requalified with new brand identity. Nissan had recognized that its brand identity and initial "Nature" campaign failed to connect with luxury car owners.

A key issue in articulating relations between production and consumption is the source of meaning for brand narration. How is the content of the narrative constructed? Who tells the story and who listens to it? We have argued that meaning is produced in the lived experience of consumers in an ongoing process of interactivity involving representation and interpretation. By representation we refer to the way one describes the ethnographic other.[6] In the commercial context of branding, representation plays an important role because interactivity implies some kind of filter through which producers and consumers apprehend each other. Debate about representation in the world of consumer research in the United States has focused largely on targeting minority groups such as African Americans (Sunderland and Denny 2007) and Latinos (Davila 2001; Sunderland, Taylor, and Denny 2004).

We claim representation in consumer marketing and advertising is not merely produced but carefully mediated through purposeful interactions between consumers and producers. In our case, one luxury car manufacturer accurately represented its target audience through advertising, while the other failed. Steel writes that the best and most effective advertising must involve consumers, both in the communication of messages and in its subsequent and continued development (Steel 1998: xiii). He further reiterates, "Advertising works better when it does not tell people what to think, but rather allows them to make up their own minds about its meaning. They participate by figuring it out for themselves" (Steel 1998: 6). In other words, corporations and their advertisers are not arbitrarily drawing on whatever cultural meaning they prefer but invest effort to express precise consumer meaning by accurately representing consumers in advertising communication. Without accurate consumer representation, the advertising will largely fall flat, as was the case with the initial Infiniti advertising.

Through ethnographic research, companies learn how people generate meaning with use of a product in their everyday lives. What product use reveals about identity and social relations becomes cultural knowledge, part of a company's store of knowledge about customers gained from multiple sources over time. A company tries to reflect that cultural knowledge in creating brand identity and developing advertising materials. On the supply side, then, the question of success or failure becomes how well the company represents the consumer in brand communications. Does the information about a brand contained in advertising text and image capture the meaning a product holds for the target audience? On the demand side, the question becomes how the consumer interprets brand imagery. Does it make sense to consumers in terms of their own beliefs, practices, and values? Does the consumer recognize his or her voice in the brand communications?

A primary question that arises when assessing an advertising campaign, then, is whether such utilized concepts express an accurate representation of the target segment. This ultimately measures whether a campaign, in all its extensive marketing and media expenditure, will succeed. Can consumers recognize an authentic voice and therefore take possession of brand meanings to incorporate into their identity and relationships with others? As we attempted to demonstrate in our case examples, the answer was yes for Cadillac and no for Infiniti.

The case examples show that the representation of consumers in an advertising campaign can have a positive or negative impact on consumer behavior depending on whether the representation is accurate. Relying on the concept and imagery of "Breakthrough," the Cadillac campaign captured the worldview of the target audience. Using the brand as metaphor for self and for a U.S. company that reinvents itself, the campaign expressed how these consumers conceived of their lives as a process of becoming as it foregrounded dreaming outside the box, crossing boundaries, and not being constrained. Consumers interpreted "Breakthrough" as an expression of living the American dream and achieving mobility. As a result, the campaign resonated with the target segment and had felicitous consequences for the brand. The brand communications offered consumers an opportunity to take possession of meanings for constructing and performing identity and social relationships in their everyday lives.

"Breakthrough" is a key symbol (Ortner 1973) that indexes beliefs and values in U.S. culture. "Breakthrough" evokes individualism, entrepreneurship, and even reinvention as ingredients for success or remaking success. It taps into the ethic of hard work, long considered a necessary part of success. It encompasses others by emphasizing democracy and inclusivity; in the mind of the consumer target, anyone can dream outside the box, work hard, and succeed.[7] In short, "Breakthrough" rests on the notion of consumer goods as extensions of the self in a "doing" versus a "being" mode of existence (Belk 1988). Doing is a strong component of the way personhood is defined in U.S. society and also how consumers want to perceive the auto companies from whom they purchase cars. Cadillac ads portrayed the brand (metaphorically, the self and the company) acting and accomplishing this in the world.

In comparison, the Infiniti "Nature" campaign presented objects of material culture as extensions of the self in a passive being mode of existence. The Infiniti ads suggested that driver, car, road, and environment are all encapsulated in Zen-like time and space. This execution of a being mode of existence, perhaps more redolent of Eastern versus Western culture, did not mesh with the meaning of nature nor of luxury as cultural categories in the United States and failed to fire the imagination of its intended audience. The meaning of words such as *nature* and *luxury* are not transparent and require cultural analysis (Sunderland and Denny 2007). In effect, the campaign misrepresented the consumer target and its relationship with a culturally constructed nature in which the driver surmounts obstacles on the road and subdues the external environment; the representation was contested and rejected by the target segment.

From these case examples, we see that branding encompasses ongoing two-way mediation, where consumer agency in the form of acceptance or rejection of circulated images mediates the various material artifacts of production. Launching car advertisements on television and as texts in magazines, product placements in popular movies, vehicle test drives in car showrooms, and so forth are precise moments of interaction when consumers accept or contest the process of production and consumption. Producers display agency when they integrate the insights and results of ethnographic research into the strategic work of a company. This process is social, where brand managers and advertisers negotiate how to construct brand identity, shape advertising campaigns, and develop creative materials. Representing the consumer, that is, the symbols that are employed and the way they are executed in ad campaigns and marketing plans remain under the discretion of the corporate and advertising hands that participate in bringing a campaign to fruition (Moeran 1996). Consumers display agency when they interpret brand communications, assess whether they make sense in the context of their lives, shop, test out brands, and make purchase decisions.

* * *

Brands are *transactable* entities between producers and consumers in capitalist societies. In the branding process there is a dialogic transfer of meaning to and from the brand (Malefyt 2008a). We have argued that the source of this meaning comes from the lived experience of consumers and from symbolic material circulated by producers. Consumption of branded goods does not mean that the brand as cultural imagery is something that consumers *add* to their lives; rather it comes *from* their lives. A brand can resonate with the consumer and succeed in the marketplace because it rests on the quality of ethnographic storytelling or an ongoing process of representation and interpretation through thoughtful advertising and other means. This way of thinking about interactivity between producers and consumers shifts the view of advertising away from its critique as a one-way media of persuasion, telling consumers what to buy (Schudson 1984), and reveals, instead, how advertising has attempted to become more interactive and representational of consumers. Perhaps this antiquated notion of advertising has become distasteful in the public eye because it leaves out the sense of involvement and doing that are important to the construction of personhood in U.S. culture (Strathern 1999).

Indeed, Lury (2004) writes that marketing has greatly changed, moving away from relations focused on one-time purchases to those developing ongoing dialogue with consumers. Companies are using new forms of media to produce advertising messages for consumers based on customized models of communication, the Internet, event marketing, direct-to-consumer mailings, product placements, and other engaging means beyond the thirty-second advertising message (Malefyt 2009: 204). Likewise, consumers are more interactive, gathering information and entertainment from various sources beyond TV, such as downloaded information, video games, online chat rooms, and cell phones. As media formats become more interactive to keep pace with changes in consumers' broadening media tastes, advertisers are moving into new and emerging media formats that are more engaging emotionally with consumers (see chapter 5, "Advertising Emotions"). By producing more integrative media that tap into a broader range of consumer experiences with brands, new media messaging translates into more authentic representations of the consumer. In advertising terms, this change in marketing messages and media outlets reflects a reprioritization of research approaches, such as calling for the use of ethnography to inform more approximate descriptions of the consumer's lived experience with goods.

If goods are materialities that stabilize and destabilize more frequently in the branded era of capitalism than in previous times, we would suggest one reason is that brands are not deterritorialized (Downey and Fisher 2006). Place and time do matter. In a marketplace where segmentation orients outreach to consumers, brands are localized to target segments at particular moments in time. Destabilization can occur when representation of the segment in advertising does not keep up with the flow of meaning in consumer lives. What would luxury car owners say now, for instance, in terms of carbon emissions and damage to the environment? From a marketing perspective, brand management requires continuous engagement with consumers as generators of new meaning or it risks entering a field of contestation.

The whole process of qualifying goods in advanced capitalism may appear more responsive to consumer needs and desires than previously thought. Ethnographic research is being utilized from product development and design perspectives (Wasson 2000) through marketing, distribution, advertising, and the sculpting of shopping venues (Sherry et al. 2009). Yet giving theoretical recognition to the role of consumer agency in the qualification of goods is not to claim that consumers actually possess greater agency in advanced capitalism than in earlier times but rather that there is now greater interactivity between producers and consumers (Malefyt 2009: 204). As Turow (2006) points out, manufacturers and retailers rely on digital information technologies for interacting with people in order to segment customers, customize product offerings, and tailor advertising. Producers and consumers live in co-constructed relationships. The rise of interactivity between producers and consumers invites collaboration and contestation, accommodation and resistance, which are only intensified by the new media technologies that increase communication between producers and consumers.

–8–

Business Anthropology Beyond Ethnography

A pharmaceutical corporation was planning to solicit proposals from marketing research companies for a study on diabetics. The research would enable them to better understand four psychologically and behaviorally defined patient segments they were evaluating as targets for a new prescription diabetes medication. The company sought a study that would probe deeply into diabetes sufferers' attitudes, emotions, and behavior and deliver insights that would help it determine which target segment offered the highest market potential and inform a strategy for direct-to-consumer advertising. Several months before the request for a proposal (RFP) was to be issued to research suppliers, the marketing research director responsible for the project invited Morais to visit the corporation's headquarters to give a presentation on ethnography, which was the methodology that she believed would be best to achieve her team's goals. About halfway through the presentation, the research director stopped Morais and said she wanted to brief him on what she called the "Portrait" study so that he could begin thinking about how his firm would design the research. As she described the goals of the project in detail, it became clear to Morais that in-depth one-on-one interviews (IDIs) in a focus group research facility, rather than ethnographic research, would be a more appropriate methodology to reach her objectives. Ethnography, he counseled the research director, was not needed for the client's learning needs and it would be an inefficient use of research funds. Morais suggested that *after* the patient segments representing the most sales potential were identified, ethnography would be an excellent way to learn about their everyday lives as diabetics. He made this recommendation with trepidation, hoping that his company would not lose an opportunity to work with the client, but he felt strongly that IDIs would be a superior research methodology for the client's needs. The research director and a colleague from the marketing department listened attentively, and a few months later Morais's firm received the RFP. Relieved that his company was being considered despite his methodological challenge, Morais proposed a series of ninety-minute IDIs in a focus room facility. He proffered research techniques drawn from his company's skills as PhD-level psychologists and anthropologists. To underscore the difference in his design from the primarily psychologically oriented approaches that he thought the competition would propose, Morais highlighted several techniques and topics that his firm borrowed from anthropology:

- Mining patients' fundamental definitions of diabetes, wellness, and sickness as if the marketing and marketing research team had no knowledge of these concepts
- Identifying patients' rituals regarding the management and treatment of diabetes
- Discovering patient transformational experiences, exemplified by different attitudinal and emotional states, throughout their diabetes life cycle
- Exploring patients' feelings, if any, about belonging to a diabetics "tribe" and what this means for their attitudes, emotions, and behavior
- Researching myths and beliefs about diabetes treatments
- Exploring beliefs in contrast to empirical thinking regarding diabetes medications
- Learning how interactions with health care professionals impact self-management of diabetes

Morais's company won the assignment. When he asked the client research manager why she and her colleagues chose his firm, she said, "We really liked the anthropology." A senior manager from the advertising agency who was also involved in the RFP review process also mentioned anthropology as the agency's reason for endorsing Morais's firm for the project. Ethnography, often conflated with anthropology in marketing research, was a not factor in the decision.

***

Marvin Harris, writing about Franz Boas's influence on anthropology, observed, "His mission had been to rid anthropology of amateurs and armchair specialists by making ethnographic research in the field the central experience and minimum attribute of professional status" (Harris 1968: 250). Boas's undertaking was indisputably successful; for over a hundred years, ethnography has been the requisite technique for sociocultural anthropological investigation. For most anthropologists engaged in marketing and advertising research, ethnography is their unique selling proposition. They promote ethnography as a means to access consumers' ideas, practices, and social relations and to investigate how brands and buying connect to culture in ways that no other marketing research methodology can match. However, despite the recognized value of ethnography as a technique, limited time and budgets mitigate against more frequent adoption of the methodology by marketers. For these reasons, and because some business executives still do not know precisely what ethnography is or comprehend what practical heuristic purpose it serves, their methodology of choice for qualitative research is typically a focus group. Consequently, when business anthropologists restrict their research capability to ethnography and eschew focus groups as an inferior research technique, they limit their opportunities for business employment. This chapter suggests that business anthropologists should incorporate focus room interviews into their repertoire. We will demonstrate how perspectives and techniques that anthropologists apply in business ethnography can and should be adapted in focus room settings, specifically in focus groups and in-depth one-on-one interviews. Our agenda can be stated simply: anthropologists can contribute to the identification and assessment of marketing and advertising opportunities in a myriad of ways. Traditional ethnographic techniques, especially when informed by anthropological theory, will continue to provide value to manufacturers, advertising agencies, design firms, and other commercial enterprises. However, anthropologists can make additional contributions and expand their business employment by adding research in focus room settings to their methodological skill set.

Ethnography in Business

U.S. business became enamored with ethnography beginning in the 1980s, when corporations began "tapping into a heretofore unheralded discipline: anthropology" (Louis 1985: 3).[1] The term *ethnography* soon replaced anthropology as the descriptor for naturalistic observation in commercial projects, and, over the next several decades, suppliers of the technique with and without formal training in anthropology proliferated in industry. As Malefyt asserts, the intensity of competition among research firms offering ethnography has now compelled suppliers to distinguish themselves through branding, abetted by innovative observation technologies (Malefyt 2009). In marketing and advertising trade articles, ethnography is occasionally confused or conflated with anthropology; for example, "executives refer to this sort of qualitative research as 'anthropology'" (Murphy 2005: 42). More typically, trade writers understand that ethnography was developed within the field of anthropology (e.g., Monari 2005: 28; Sanders 2002: 8; Wasserman 2003: 21; Wellner 2002: S2). The attraction of ethnography to business as a marketing research technique is clear: it is believed to be an advance over the formal, artificial setting of focus groups and the structured, often superficial questions of quantitative surveys. Advocates of business ethnography contend that the technique yields more bona fide consumer responses and allows for observation of actual consumer behavior rather than recollections or misrepresentations of actions—the difference between what people do and what people say they do. For academically trained business anthropologists, ethnography is their raison d'être, and they link the technique closely with anthropology. Thus, Jordan argues that the "goal of anthropology . . . requires the study of human behavior in natural settings" (Jordan 2003: 21). Moreover, every business anthropologist with whom we are aware stresses ethnography in their descriptions of how and why they are different from other kinds of market researchers.[2] The Ethnographic Praxis in Industry Conference trumpets its mission as "the premier international forum bringing together artists, computer scientists, designers, social scientists, marketers, academics and advertisers to discuss recent developments and future advances around ethnographic praxis" (from the American Anthropological Association Web site). Numerous organizations on LinkedIn, the online business networking Web site, revere ethnography—for example, Ethnography Forum, The Anthropology Network, and Ethnosnacker. As business ethnography has exploded, some anthropologists in business have voiced concerns that the anthropological theory is "invisible in business ethnography" (Denny and Sunderland 2008; cf. Morais 2009a; Sunderland and Denny 2003).[3] Based upon our industry experience, much of what is termed ethnography in business is more observational than anthropological in practice. This state of the method traces to two factors: Many practitioners of business ethnography are not trained anthropologists, and many clients desire naturalistic settings for consumer interviews but are uninterested in complex anthropological insights.

An Overview of Focus Groups

The focus group industry is robust with spending on this type of research in excess of $1 billion (Wasserman 2003).[4] Focus groups are used for a wide range of data gathering in addition to business, including, but not limited to, political opinions, consumer perceptions of the state of the economy, and social trends. Located in and around major cities, focus group facilities consist of three or more double rooms that are divided by a one-way mirror allowing observers in the back room to witness the sessions conducted in the adjacent room. Some rooms are decorated to resemble living rooms to create a natural-looking and presumably more relaxed conversational environment. Focus groups are normally ninety minutes to two hours in length. Group size ranges from two respondents to ten, depending upon the topic and client preference. In-depth, one-on-one interviews are often conducted in focus room settings and are typically one hour to ninety minutes in duration. Respondents for focus groups and IDIs are recruited through a screener that specifies desired characteristics, including demographics, psychographics, brand usage, and related attributes. Respondents who meet the criteria are accepted; respondents who do not match the requirements are not invited to participate in the session. There are two cost components to respondent recruitment: the fee that the facility charges to recruit the respondents and the incentive paid to the respondents for their participation in the sessions. Facilities also charge for room rental, video recording, and food.

The person responsible for conducting focus groups is known in the industry as the moderator and, for IDIs, the interviewer. Many of these professionals operate independently; others are employees of marketing research companies. Moderators work with focus room facilities that provide the respondents and the interview space.[5] Focus group moderators may or may not have formal interview training. Many begin their careers in advertising agencies as account managers or account planners and transition to moderating; some emigrate from client research manager positions. Moderators may hold degrees in the social or behavioral sciences, ranging from an undergraduate sociology degree to a doctorate in psychology. Still others earned a master's degree in business. A moderator's interviewing skills and style have an impact on the respondents' involvement, volubility, and veracity, and moderators' business success will be tied to these abilities and to their understanding of client needs and culture. Some moderators contribute strategically to the marketing challenge at hand, but most are interviewers rather than strategists. Their post-session impressions of the proceedings are solicited, but their conclusions tend to be extensions of the interview findings rather than leaps of insight, with the exception of moderators with strong strategic skills. Moderators who contribute to a strategic analysis are especially valued and more highly compensated than those who merely elicit responses to questions written in the moderator's guide and add little more to the learning process. The skill set of moderators has several parallels with that of cultural anthropologists who can bring additional dimension to the interviewing process and analysis. On this basis, anthropologists who have spent time in the field are capable of functioning as moderators after they have immersed themselves in the marketing research aims. Some may choose this function if they wish to move beyond the role of field ethnographer in business research projects. Other anthropologists may prefer to occupy a space in the back room and observe while a moderator conducts the interviews. The back room anthropologist can use the separation from the proceedings to view the interviews from a broader perspective, offering interpretation while the sessions are in progress and interacting directly with the back room marketing and advertising team as a tactical and strategic partner. The choice of role is subject to personal preference and career objectives. Either function will move the anthropologist beyond the ethnographer designation toward an expanded position on the marketing and/or advertising team.

When a focus group or in-depth one-on-one interview is in session, the observers in the back room include marketing and, as needed, advertising or design executives. Many on the team have helped plan the research, and all have a stake in the outcome of the sessions. Initially, all of the spectators attend studiously to the proceedings, often engaging in conversations about what is seen and heard along with implications for brand marketing and/or advertising. Over the course of six to eight hours of interviews, observers' attention often drifts, e-mails and phone calls interrupt their concentration, and casual side conversations siphon their focus. For most of the time during the sessions, however, the back room witnesses listen and watch closely as consumers speak their minds (for more on focus group practices, see Grandclément and Gaglio 2011; Morais 2010; Stewart, Prem Shamdasani, and Dennis 2007).

Focus Groups: Critiques and Commentaries

Despite the widespread use of focus groups, many marketing and advertising professionals express ambivalence about their merits. On the one hand, industry executives choose focus groups as a fast, cost-efficient technique to gain knowledge about consumer attitudes and desires, reactions to advertising, responses to new product concepts, and the appeal of packaging or design innovations. On the other hand, some business professionals are concerned about misdirection from small samples of consumers and are troubled when respondents in focus rooms express hostility to creative ideas that they might more readily accept online, in print, on the radio, or on television. Others maintain that focus groups, as a verbal forum, do not access consumers' unconscious thinking (Singer 2011). Advertising executive Jon Steel represents the industry's mixed sentiments about focus groups, first offering sharp criticism and then later lauding their value (1998: 79, 202–5). Business anthropologists sometimes itemize the weaknesses of focus groups in order to merchandise their ethnographic approach (for example, Serf 2007), and others offer additional critiques (Grandclément and Gaglio 2011). Some business anthropologists who use ethnography as their primary technique believe focus groups have value. Sunderland and Denny, for example, argue that the talk in focus groups is rich in meaning (2007: 175–79), and anthropologists have documented the use of focus groups as a component of a multimethod approach (Sengir et al. 2004; Trotter et al. 2008; Hautzinger 2012). As is evident from the case history that opened this chapter, Morais often integrates anthropological techniques in focus groups and one-on-one interviews.[6]

For most anthropologists, focus groups are antithetical to their naturalistic mode of inquiry. A focus room, even one warmed by homey art and comfortable seating, is not the ideal environment for accessing consumers' lives. Most focus groups and IDIs in focus room settings are highly structured and adhere to an outline (the moderator's guide) that disallows the more respondent-directed discovery process in ethnography. Promoters of ethnographic encounters over focus groups assert that the fixed agenda in focus groups is a formulaic process where informants are interrogated while ethnography is adaptive and fluid. If in focus groups the respondent is a provider of answers, in ethnographic interviews the respondent converses with the interviewer as a complete person. Moreover, unless respondents are engaged in an individual interview or are seated among friends or relatives who have been recruited with them, they are among a group of strangers. As a result, they may withhold their most personal reactions or be reluctant to express a point of view that differs from that of the other respondents. They are aware of the observers on the other side of a mirror and that the sessions are being recorded, which can make them self-conscious or compel them to engage in a performance for their audience, in contrast to the more interactive and personally warmer ethnographic process. That said, moderators help respondents feel comfortable so that they do not dwell on the potential distraction of behind-the-glass observers. Experienced moderators and patient clients allow interviews to stray from the predetermined format when the flow yields interesting findings.

Even with a highly capable moderator and understanding clients, some attributes of a focus room setting cannot be overcome. The environment causes respondents to pay greater attention to advertising being shown than they normally would to ads they see on their television, hear on the radio, or read in print or online elsewhere. The formal atmosphere and direct questioning can compel consumers to become hyperlogical. They may object to a nonlinear narrative or reject an advertising execution that is highly innovative. New product ideas that are outside consumers' comfort zones may be summarily dismissed in a focus room; the products might receive more consideration in a store. As ethnographers know, respondents are more relaxed and expressive in natural settings than in a focus room. In addition, homes, offices, and other locations provide stimuli that reveal behavior, attitudes, and sentiments and their cultural correlates. This is one of the reasons ethnography took root and blossomed in marketing and advertising research and why ethnography is often selected as an alternative methodology to focus groups.

The focus room location imposes limitations on what can be learned from consumers, but there is malleability in the design and process of interviews in these settings. Focus groups and IDIs can be free flowing and the interview co-created by the moderator and the respondents conducted with what Holstein and Gubrium (1995) characterize as an active interview process. When anthropologists contend that ethnography, and not focus group interviews, enables them to probe deeply into consumer's lives, they miss the possibility that focus group interviews and IDIs can be constructed to accommodate many types of inquiry, including modes that are anthropological. Even the empathy that ethnographers argue moves them beyond a prescribed set of questions and drives insights can be approximated in a focus group room. A moderator can connect with respondents and gain admittance to their lives with careful planning, rapport, close questioning, and thoughtful interpretation of respondent answers as they are given. In ethnographic research, anthropologists look for apparent contradictions in what respondents say and listen for a unifying logic to generate an insight, as discussed earlier. This discovery process can occur in a focus room as well as during ethnography.[7] Moreover, focus groups offer opportunities for learning about consumers that ethnographies cannot. Ethnographies rarely bring strangers together under a common theme for discussion. In a focus group setting, like-minded consumers of a particular brand of luxury sports car or beverage can be recruited to discuss their shared enthusiasm, or divergent brand advocacy subgroups can engage in a debate. The session can become highly charged, and respondent passion can be amplified by the group setting. As Steel writes, respondent views "can be taken to a higher level, much more rapidly, in focus groups, by using the very group dynamic that many researchers fear" (1998: 204) bringing to mind the way Turner (1969, 1974) characterized the charged "effervescence" in the communitas of social gatherings and the power of social dramas in rituals to move people emotionally. Precisely because focus groups and IDIs are framed by clear boundaries, within certain time limits, and among unfamiliar others, respondents can potentially become more creative and expressive than they would under more comfortable ethnographic conditions. An anthropologist can use the focus room environment to compare and contrast ideas in ways that more natural settings would be unlikely to spark. In this sense, a focus room allows consumers to act in ways they might not act otherwise and express thoughts they might not normally express. The outcome can inspire strategic and creative thinking among marketing and advertising agency executives.

Debates about the relative merits of ethnography and focus groups aside, the marketplace reality is that focus groups and IDIs vastly outpace ethnography as a research choice in business. They are selected over quantitative surveys when executives seek expansive responses to their questions and when they desire an observational experience that brings them close to their customers. The cost efficiency of focus groups relative to ethnography is striking. A single day of focus group research with four ninety-minute groups, each group composed of five respondents for a total of twenty individuals, costs about $20,000. This expenditure includes the moderator's professional time for writing a screener, crafting the interview guide, conducting the sessions, writing a report, and multiple client conversations and meetings regarding these actions. It also includes facility rental, respondent recruitment and incentive costs, food, and video recording. The expense of $1,000 per respondent compares with a cost of about $4,000 per ethnography respondent in addition to the many days the ethnographic team, including marketing and advertising executives, spend in the field, away from their offices. This is one of the main reasons that, while ethnography has a place in marketing research, its cost and time are not justified for all types of learning needs. In addition, focus groups are used at several stages in the advertising development cycle: first, for initial exploration of a category to define strategic direction; second, for a read on specific advertising ideas; and, third, for assessment of advertising before or instead of quantitative testing.

Anthropology in Focus Rooms

Elevation of ethnography as a methodology above focus groups has practical consequences for business anthropology. In essence, it has frozen many practicing anthropologists in the ethnographer role and prevented them from engaging in additional marketing research functions. Many business anthropologists welcome the ethnographer moniker because ethnography is how they differentiate themselves from other qualitative marketing researchers, especially focus group moderators. Ethnography, in contrast to anthropology, is, for many anthropologists, their only access point to marketing research, because business executives view ethnography as an appealing alternative to focus groups and an anthropologically informed perspective is a more difficult sell to executives. Anthropology sounds exotic to most business professionals, and what it means in practice is not clear to them, except for those executives who actually value the exoticness of anthropologists (cf. Suchman 2007). Ethnography is more tangible and accessible. Anthropologists in business should continue to leverage their ethnographic expertise and, when clients are receptive, the theoretical acumen that sets them apart from researchers who claim to be ethnographers but lack knowledge of anthropological theory (Morais 2009a). However, business anthropologists will be well served if they accept that ethnography is not the sole means for the application of anthropological practices and ideas. Just as anthropological theory should inform marketing ethnography, anthropological theory can and should be adapted in nonethnographic settings. The approach can be promoted to business executives in the context of a familiar, cost effective option and couched in terms that are accessible to business professionals, as the illustrations below reveal. The specific applications that we will discuss include focus groups and one-on-one focus room interviews because anthropologists are well equipped to conduct these kinds of sessions or serve as behind-the-mirror back room analysts. Anthropologists are experts at close listening and observation; they have strong interviewing skills; they possess analytical abilities informed by culture theory that can inspire marketing innovation and bring perspectives that are of immeasurable value to business executives. Some of the examples contained here incorporate concepts and techniques from psychology and are not purely anthropological. As discussed in the next chapter, we believe that business anthropologists should incorporate social and behavioral science theory and methodologies that extend beyond anthropology.

Marketers from Mars

Ethnographic fieldwork is approached with a purposeful naiveté that enables the ethnographer to clearly perceive and fully deconstruct everyday behaviors. This perspective, which both academic and business anthropologists sometimes describe as "being from Mars," can be revelatory when used to advance an understanding of consumers. It can be applied in focus rooms as well as in the field and has considerable value in marketing research. Marketing and advertising executives often enter a focus room setting with assumptions regarding consumer thinking and with desired results in mind—for example, a favorite advertisement or a new product that management is pressuring the team to launch. The anthropologist, as an objective observer, can remind colleagues that knowledge and insights regarding consumers are best gained by setting aside predispositions. In this way, the anthropologist will protect executives from their own biases and better serve the research project. A case that is detailed in the next chapter, focus room–based research on a breakfast cereal, was revealing when the team stepped back from what they thought was known about breakfast and asked respondents to define breakfast as an occasion, a meal, a memory, and so on. If this exploration had not been conducted, the interviews would likely have missed the transformational, ritual-like components of the meal. In the pharmaceutical research example that opened this chapter, the research team began with questions about respondents' fundamental definition of diabetes and then asked them to provide their experientially based thoughts about the nature of wellness and illness, particularly as they progressed through their lives with their illness. Inquiries regarding stories and beliefs about diabetes, rites of passage, and interaction with health care professionals were framed as if each interview was the first and the culture of the respondent was alien. This enabled the team to paint rich portraits of the lives of the respondents. These kinds of questions add value to interviews in focus room facilities, just as they do in ethnographic interviews, and they would not typically be asked by interviewers without an anthropological perspective.

Observation

Marketing executives laud consumer ethnography as a method to discern the difference between what people say they do when buying or using products and what they actually do. For many marketers, ethnography is their only access to consumer behavior. Focus rooms, despite their inherent limitations, can be a setting for close observation of consumers. If the manufacturers of a chocolate chip cookie mix need to determine fresh ways to speak to consumers about the baking experience of their brand, in-home, kitchen-based ethnography is an excellent research choice. If client time, funding, or inclination rule out this methodology, a focus room facility can provide a kitchen with an oven to meet these objectives. Over the course of a session, observers can watch consumers as recipe instructions are processed, witness how manageable and enjoyable (or difficult and frustrating) the baking experience is, and listen to the ways that consumers characterize the tastes and textures of the cookies they have made. Consumer actions and words during the baking experience will probably be different than their recall from memory of the process. The anthropologist, as the designer and observer, and perhaps moderator, of this study would provide the client with insights they would be unlikely to obtain from a typical focus group. For clients who are interested in understanding consumers' shopping experience, a focus room can be arranged to resemble a supermarket, and shoppers can be observed as they scan shelves and select brands. Shopping scenarios can be presented to groups of friends recruited to a focus group for a discussion on shopping for clothing. With clothing racks and tables within reach and a private changing room available, back room spectators can observe consumer conversations and debates. A focus room is not identical to an actual supermarket, clothing store, or other shopping setting, and the ambient noise, lighting, crowds, and other stimuli are absent. For a more complete understanding of how consumers are influenced by environment, in-store ethnography or observation in test market stores is essential. However, when ethnography is not possible or desired, behavior can be observed in a focus room setting, and much can be gleaned from the analysis.

Interaction

Ethnography often entails observation of individuals interacting with those who influence their behavior. Observation of interactions can also be obtained in focus rooms, as noted above. Interactions that are not possible in naturalistic settings can also be arranged. For example, in the United States, observation of health care practitioners and their patients in professional settings can be problematic given health care privacy law. To answer client needs regarding these kinds of interactions and abide by the law, Morais's firm devised a simulated interactional technique (Morais and Barnhart 2007). The method enables pharmaceutical marketers to see and hear practitioners and patients discuss conditions and treatments in real time rather than having to retrieve the interaction from memory. To conduct research of this type, patients who suffer from the target medical condition and professionals who treat the condition are recruited. Prior to the interaction, both parties are informed of the goals of the research, and then they are introduced in a focus room, told to behave as if they are engaged in an office or hospital-based visit, and left alone. Patients describe their health problem, physicians probe to make a diagnosis and recommend treatment, and patients respond. After the interaction, each party is debriefed separately by an interviewer as the marketing and advertising team (and sometimes the other party) observes. In a study on a prescription topical skin care remedy by Morais's firm, interactional research revealed that the doctors and patients did not communicate clearly, and the teams' observations helped elucidate why relationships between professionals and patients sometimes broke down in the real world. One example: patients felt that the doctors failed them when a treatment was not effective and never returned to that doctor; doctors assumed that when they did not see the patient again, the condition was addressed effectively. The research encouraged the pharmaceutical manufacturer to create communication materials that improved doctor-patient dialogue regarding treatment outcomes.

Language and Meaning

Anthropologists' skills in linguistic analysis and their ability to elicit classification systems can expand marketing executives' understanding of how their customers think. During focus group sessions on advertising for toilet bowl cleaners, Morais asked respondents to list the benefits of their regular brand, and they omitted a benefit that was a· centerpiece of category advertising: "leaves the bathroom fresh." At Morais's suggestion, the marketing team agreed to explore the possibility that "clean" not only meant free of dirt but also connoted fresh smelling. As the interviews progressed, the research indicated that the benefit of "leaves the bathroom fresh" was embedded in the word *clean*. The layered meaning of clean for consumers had implications for advertising because a fifteen-second television commercial contains about forty words. Clean could convey both the visual and olfactory benefits of a brand. Classification systems used by respondents can also be explored in focus room settings. Consumers can be questioned, for example, on types of headaches they encounter. Classification and experience-rich descriptions of cold-related headaches, sleep-deprivation headaches, and tension headaches can generate ideas for new products and extensions of brands into new categories. Jordan's elicitation and analysis of corporate domains in an office environment could have been conducted in a focus room as effectively as it was in a work setting (Jordan 2003: 26–27).

Life Histories during In-Depth Interviews

Anthropologists have long used life histories in ethnographic settings to gain entry to individual psychology and cultural systems (Dyk [1938] 1967). A modified life history approach is also valuable in focus room contexts. In a study conducted by Morais's firm on a mouthwash for smokers, respondents were asked to transpose their sentiments regarding their self-characterized pariah status to other times and contexts in their lives. Several respondents talked about their experiences in middle school, when emotional pain from social stigmas caused them to wish to be invisible. This revelation inspired an advertising strategy that stressed smokers' desire for invisibility and differentiated the smoker's mouthwash from mouthwashes that emphasized breath freshening. The advertising for this product depicted a couple meeting at a restaurant, kissing. The woman, not sensing the usual hint of tobacco asks, "Did you quit smoking?" The man replies, "Did I?" The implicit promise of the brand was that it rendered the smoker's habit invisible. The research also revealed that smokers were unwilling to abandon their habit, and they resented advertising that encouraged them to quit smoking. The man's "Did I?" response allowed him to wink conspiratorially to the viewer that he successfully masked his continued smoking. The dubious value expressed in this advertising—that the brand allowed him to deceive his romantic partner and perpetuate an unsavory and unhealthy habit undetected—was not a barrier to the success of the commercial in prebroadcast testing and in the marketplace.

Culture

Grant McCracken believes that when corporations ignore culture, which he defines as "the body of ideas, emotions, and activities that make up the life of the consumer," they place their organizations at risk in the marketplace (McCracken 2009: 1). Culture is an elusive but intriguing concept to marketing and advertising executives. Yet many marketers who embrace ethnography do not comprehend how a cultural perspective on ethnographic observations can advance new product development and advertising thinking (Sunderland and Denny 2003). They must be educated on the value of cultural understanding as a marketing asset—a task that can be challenging but ultimately rewarding to both the client and the anthropologist practitioner (see Denny and Sunderland 2008). The application of culture as an analytical construct is as feasible in focus room settings as it is in ethnographic studies; connections between consumer buying attitudes and behavior and culture can be identified in much the same way they can be discovered in the field. Focus room interviews can be settings for questions derived from anthropological ideas, exploring culture-bound rules and behaviors. Consumers in a focus room can be questioned about their shopping habits and practices and their related attitudes and sentiments. Consumption can be tied to a larger cultural movement, as when Morais, listening to focus group respondents, suggested that the client's brand of orange juice, Simply Orange, be linked in marketing to a cultural trend toward living simply. Culturally defined status and roles of parents and children can be explored in a focus room by observing them interact as they discuss buying food or apparel.

Focus groups often spark strategic thinking about how culture impacts consumers along with tactics for marketing initiatives. Morais was involved in a branding project for Major League Soccer that was initiated to increase the fan base of this U.S.-based league. Focus group interviews revealed that professional soccer is seen by Americans as a foreign sport. Soccer, in essence, is not in Americans' DNA like baseball, football, and basketball. Morais suggested that Major League Soccer should be branded as a distinctively American sport for American fans to more readily accept it. Questions during the focus groups about fan "tribal" associations led to a fresh way to frame marketing opportunities. Using an extremely successful Major League Soccer franchise, the Portland Timbers (Belson 2011), as an example of a team with "tribal tendencies," Morais and the consulting team analyzed their behavior in terms of four dimensions: ritual, hero narrative, community connection, and cultural identity. Morais bolstered the consulting group's analysis with explication of the meaning of tribe. Several new marketing initiatives were developed, and the client meeting that presented this line of thinking was highly successful.

In a separate discussion, a senior executive from Major League Soccer sent the following e-mail:

> was reading book on fans this weekend and author observed that fan avidity was increasing over time as historical "tribes" (religion, families, loyal employers, etc.) were breaking down, i.e., new and longer lasting sense of identity. I'd like your cultural anthro to express an opinion on this notion.

The idea that sports provides a powerful spiritual experience that substitutes for religion has been discussed by many scholars (for a recent example, see Dreyfus and Kelly 2011). Morais forwarded a few popular articles on the topic and a reference to the Dreyfus and Kelly book but noted that accurate measurement of sports fan avidity over time is elusive. He also referenced Robert Putnam's *Bowling Alone* (2000), which analyzes the patterns and implications of societal disintegration. To offer an actionable recommendation, Morais pointed out that online social networks provide a venue for connection and group identify formulation when face-to-face interaction is not desired or possible (something Putnam foresaw in 2000). Morais suggested that Major League Soccer use virtual social networks to enhance fan involvement.

Focus groups are often conducted to assess advertising, and anthropologists can direct marketers' attention to how well respondents identify with an advertisement on a cultural level. Is a beer commercial that celebrates male bonding relatable for men in the second decade of the twenty-first century? Does advertising that disparages competitive brands conflict with cultural trends about fairness? How can Internet ads appeal to consumers without intruding on what they perceive as their personal space online? As these examples illustrate, a wide swath of consumer habits, attitudes, beliefs, and ideas can be examined in focus rooms, and culturally informed insights can be generated even though the context is not ethnographic.[8]

The Evolution of the Business Anthropologist

The anthropologist as consumer ethnographer is an observer and analyst but is rarely a full participant in the marketing and advertising strategic planning process. This is especially true for suppliers of research to corporations. Ethnographers plan a study, conduct ethnographic encounters, write a report, present it to executives, and usually have no further contact with their clients until a new project is assigned. In contrast, when an anthropologist is in the back room during interviews or immediately after having led a focus room session, that anthropologist has a greater opportunity to engage in discussions and play a more active part in advancing marketing ideas to the commercial world. To the extent that business anthropologists desire to function strategically (Anderson 2009), expansion of their role will lead to more frequent and higher-level involvement. As they become more intimately engaged with their client's business, anthropologists will become partners in the generation of both consumer understanding and brand growth. In the process, they will enhance their status and their value to the executives who hire them.

* * *

Boas's call for firsthand immersion in the lives of the subjects studied was a correction to speculation and misrepresentation during the nineteenth century. In twenty-first century marketing research, ethnography is one of several means to access consumer ideas, rules, symbols, and behaviors. Ethnography will continue to have appeal as a research tool for manufacturers, advertising agencies, design firms, and other enterprises. If anthropologists choose to expand their methodological repertoire as suggested here, they will generate additional employment options and differentiate their expertise from that of untrained practitioners who offer basic observational research and call it ethnography. Marketing and advertising executives will welcome those anthropologists who wish to make broader contributions to the challenges they face as they compete for market share.

–9–

Ethics in Advertising

In his 1961 book *Culture Against Man*, Jules Henry devoted an entire chapter to a relentless critique of advertising. He argued that "advertising is unable to see its ethical position relative to traditional orientations" (1961: 94) and observed that "youngsters with a traditional ethical sense avoid it" as a means of employment (1961: 97). A quarter of a century later, Michael Schudson's book title itself telegraphed his sentiments: *Advertising: The Uneasy Persuasion*. If that title was not clear enough, he stated emphatically in his final chapter that "the pseudopopulist rhetoric of 'discovering needs' and giving the public what it says it wants is misleading" (1984: 235). These kinds of analyses, countless other commentaries on advertising in mass media, and the low ethical ranking by consumers of the advertising profession (Steel 1998: ix–x) have undoubtedly contributed to what Marietta Baba calls an "uneasiness that some anthropologists sense in the use that may be made of their work in ethically questionable sales" of products and services (Baba 2006: 47). In our experience, we have found that many academic anthropologists feel that the application of anthropology to advance the effectiveness of marketing and advertising is not only ethically dubious, it is nefarious.[1]

A central question confronts anthropologists who work in marketing and advertising research. Do anthropologists who use ethnography or other anthropologically informed ways to understand consumer experiences and their motivations for buying brands behave unethically when they help corporations engage in the art of persuasion? Related to this question are considerations regarding specific guidelines in the ethical code of the American Anthropological Association. Our objective in this chapter is not to debate the ethical merits of capitalism as an economic model. We agree with Daniel Miller, who suggests that commerce expresses and enriches culture and facilitates personal transformations. Miller asserts, and we concur, that we need to acknowledge the developmental changes of materialism and consumption in Western society as we have transitioned from industrial to consumer capitalism (Miller 1995a, 1995b). According to Miller, Karl Marx laid blame for the alienation of the worker on the dehumanizing order and exploitation of the world market by owners of private property in capitalist society (Marx 1954, 1987). Marx's analysis remained focused on production, the factory, wage labor, and the stock market. Nevertheless, he neglected consideration of an equally vital development in the presentation of commodities in the rise of department stores (Bowlby 1985; Wilson 2003) and in the social, personal, and exchange value that purchased objects afforded consumers. This development fostered outlets and exchanges for consumer desires in goods across all social strata, including the worker. The nature of capitalism evolved from the industrial capitalism, as Marx knew it, to the consumer capitalism of today. For us, then, capitalism itself is not an issue. However, the role of the anthropologist in advancing brands in the context of capitalist systems is of concern, at least in part because of anthropologists' historical questions about ethical behavior in dealing with native populations.

The Historical Context of Anthropological Ethics

Anthropology developed initially as a discipline to record and comprehend non-Western cultures, often through direct contact. This legacy has been discussed and criticized within the field of anthropology, particularly in terms of the ethics of unacknowledged colonialist agendas that often accompanied ethnographies (Pratt 1992). In a historical review of anthropological ethics, Murray Wax discusses Project Camelot, a defining case study in the ethics of disclosure and political agendas in anthropological fieldwork (Wax 1987; see also Lowe 1966). In the *Handbook on Ethical Issues in Anthropology* (Cassell and Jacobs 1987), of twenty-five case studies, only one touches on commerce. This example, "Power to the People," addresses conflicts regarding relationships with the community to be studied, which is not relevant to marketing researchers who do not maintain relationships with their subjects beyond the limited time of the study. The lack of close attention to ethics in business anthropology is unfortunate given anthropology's increasing presence in industry. Rare discussions of business ethics for anthropologists can be found in the work of Ann Jordan (2003) and J.F. Sherry (2008). Jordan contextualizes ethical issues in business within covert military projects such as Camelot and suggests that, between 1960 and 1980, American Anthropological Association criticism of unpublished research led to a moratorium on business anthropology because industry needed to protect corporate secrets from competition and did not permit public dissemination of research findings (Jordan 2003: 14–15). She notes that, by the 1980s, the American Anthropological Association did not discourage proprietary research, and business anthropology flourished. Jordan raises the issue of the impact on consumers of anthropological marketing research: "Will this research assist the corporation in convincing people to buy a product that they don't need and is harmful, thereby increasing corporate profit at the expense of the consumer?" (2003: 54). Her conclusion:

> The primary responsibility is clear enough: anthropologists should not cause harm to those who are the subjects of their studies. In real life, applying this ethical rule is difficult. Each anthropologist must think through the issues in each case and reject those projects she feels are harmful. (2003: 56)

We will return to Jordan's and Sherry's comments later because the question of harm to consumers is complex and it requires fuller discussion.

During the past few decades, another level of discourse on ethics among anthropologists emerged out of a self-directed critique in gathering cultural data through ethnography (Clifford 1988; Clifford and Marcus 1986; Marcus and Fischer 1986). The concerns focused not on doing direct harm to informants but rather on the subtle and potentially subversive ways that writing about native others furthered positions of authority, authorship, and additional forms of dominance without equal representation by the informants. The tasks of ethnography, the types of relationships anthropologists engaged in with informants, post-fieldwork authoritative writings about native culture, and the potential for co-opting of information through cultural contact were reflected upon and often found wanting. Ethical considerations centered not only on the implications of anthropological inquiry but also on the ways in which ethnographers conduct themselves with others and what this means in terms of their descriptions and analysis of their subjects. As a consequence of these critiques, Marcus and Fischer (1986) remark that anthropologists have entered an age when more ethnographer-subject dialogue is sought.

> Dialogue has become the dominant imagery for expressing the way anthropologists (and by extension their readers) must engage in an active communicative process with another culture. It is a two-way and two-dimensional exchange, interpretive processes being necessary both for communication internally within a cultural system and externally between systems of meaning. (Marcus and Fischer 1986: 30)

Culture is now viewed less as a "text" to be read through ethnography, as Clifford Geertz (1973, [1983] 2000) suggested, than as a process that entails dialogic interactions with informants (for example, Behar 1996; Tedlock and Mannheim 1995; Marcus and Fischer 1986). This dialogue reflects knowledge that is co-produced through interactions and entails active exchange even more than the empathy that many anthropologists associate with ethnography (cf. McCracken 2009). Anthropologists no longer just read culture or imagine they enter the minds of informants; they *communicate* with others in a manner that involves negotiation and adjustment over time. Meaning in ethnography is thus collaboratively produced, not merely observed and recorded.

Coincidently, as academe experienced its crisis of representation, business models of consumers and how to engage them through brands became more reflexive. The dialogic approach paralleled the rise of reflexivity in marketing and advertising research over the past decade, which produced novel modes of responsive interaction between corporations and consumers (Callon, Meadel, and Rabeharosoa 2002; Fisher and Downey 2006; Thrift 2000; also see chapter 4, "Fieldwork in Advertising Research"). Consumers were not to be merely studied as subjects, given surveys to respond to, or tracked for their consumption patterns but rather to be engaged as co-creators of product innovations, marketing strategies, and advertising. As Malefyt notes, this level of "brand interaction allows marketers to extend their relationships with consumers on multiple levels, mediating between individuals and corporations in reflexive exchanges of consumption and production" (Malefyt 2009: 204). Many leading marketers now attempt to develop deeper relations with consumers by shifting consumption away from one-way purchases to ongoing "dialogues" (Lury 2004: 44). Direct interactions with consumers are ever more possible through the Internet, including Twitter feeds, Facebook updates, branded events and sponsorships, and other forms of individualized marketing approaches that go well beyond the anonymous mass marketing of the past. This exchange allows brands to act as an interface in "how consumers relate to producers and how producers relate to consumers" (Lury 2004: 7). Consumer research, including ethnography, is one way that marketers put into practice the dialogic exchanges between corporations and consumers. As anthropologists call for more dialogue with their informants and are more sensitive to informant representation, consumer marketing research is responding, knowingly or not. As we discuss, this shift is one reason why the ethically based perception of consumers as passive receptors of marketing and advertising advances is outmoded and misguided.

Defining Ethics in Marketing and Advertising

To bring perspective to our discussion on ethics in marketing and advertising research, we begin with marketing experts Philip Kotler and Gary Armstrong (1991, 2004). Two issues regarding ethics bear on our discussion here: the social responsibility of companies as entities and increased advertising and marketing ethics in the consumer marketplace.

Kotler and Armstrong claim that social responsibility in business has grown dramatically over the past twenty-five years. Companies such as Ben & Jerry's and The Body Shop, for example, have pioneered the notion of what the authors describe as "values-led business" (2004: 627). These and other companies have spearheaded the role of business in ameliorating impoverished social conditions by donating a significant share of profits to charities and environmental causes over the years.[2] These businesses are also raising awareness of social concerns through informational Web sites and advertisements. The notion of profit-earning corporations as caring is not without its critics. Kotler and Armstrong state that having a "double bottom line" of values and profits is difficult to maintain. However, among the newer generation of entrepreneurs, the authors suggest, the notion of running a business is linked to a greater sense of mission and purpose that goes beyond pure bottom-line profits. For some businesses, being competitive today means taking a wider perspective on how they can and should operate. It remains to be seen how newer socially responsible companies fare down the road. The fact that such topics have entered public discourse demonstrates that the ethics of business is evolving.

Kotler and Armstrong also address social criticism of marketing and advertising. According to them, marketing, and particularly advertising, are wrongly blamed by some for many of society's ills: inducing people to buy things they do not want or need; driving up the cost of products; deceptive practices; or simply wasting consumers' money. In their 1991 edition, Kotler and Armstrong indicate how, in response to widespread criticism, the American Association of Advertising Agencies (AAAA) launched a campaign to defend the use of advertising and highlighted its economic benefits and social importance. The campaign states that advertising is incapable of generating false needs to persuade people to purchase things they do not want or need.[3] Kotler and Armstrong concur that the power of advertising to generate and perpetuate false needs is greatly exaggerated: "Marketers are most effective when they appeal to existing wants rather than when they attempt to create new ones" (1991: 633). They also claim, "if Americans are highly materialistic, these values arose out of basic socialization processes that go much deeper than business or mass media could produce alone" (1991: 632). Needs and wants, they continue, are shaped at a foundational level of society by deeper sets of values from family, peer groups, religion, ethnicity, and levels of income and education. Moreover, legislation and consumer protection actions have been created to protect consumers from deceptive practices. Kotler and Armstrong argue that most companies avoid deceptive practices and false advertising because it harms their business in the long run. If consumers are displeased with products, they switch to competitive brands or inform others about a product's oversell, which has deleterious effects on a company. Most consumers are aware of a marketer's intent to sell a product and are therefore cautious about their purchase, occasionally to the point of not believing the true product claims (2004: 631).

The AAAA campaign detailed by Kotler and Armstrong also rebukes other criticisms of advertising, such as advertising unnecessarily driving up the cost of items and constituting a waste of money. Instead of raising product prices, the AAAA campaign contends that advertising has the opposite effect: lowering prices. Their explanation is that advertising helps products sell, which creates a competitive environment for goods and lowers prices for the benefit of the consumer. Finally, the campaign disclaims accusations that advertising makes people purchase inferior products. Choice and selection is so pervasive in the United States that if a product performs inadequately, it will not be purchased again, and, as a result, that product will likely fail (1991: 632). The AAAA campaign, along with Kotler and Armstrong, concludes by suggesting that advertising is *beneficial* to society because, ultimately, it offers consumers the freedom of choice. We agree with much in these arguments. However, our experience has taught us that some of these glossy statements about the virtues of advertising are not, to put it kindly, completely true. More objectively, the marketing industry has sometimes been rightly accused of misleading consumers (see, for example, Singer 2011; for additional recent perspectives on advertising ethics, see Beltramini [2011] and Drumwright and Murphy [2009]).

Other discussions on advertising ethics are being generated from within the advertising community. Noted advertising executive Alex Bogusky has brought advertising industry attention to the responsibility of ad agencies for ethical behavior (Bogusky 2010). He contends that advertising agencies should refuse the targeting of children, even against the wishes of a client, because children are highly susceptible to persuasive messages. He also affirms that, while children are vulnerable, adults possess a healthy level of judgment and discernment to filter and choose. Therefore, while Bogusky condemns advertising to children whom he wants to protect, he condones advertising to adults for whom he believes advertising can expand options and generate excitement. Bogusky's contribution suggests that the ethics of advertising should be evaluated, mediated, and even policed by its own community of practitioners.[4]

Sunderland and Denny (2007) address ethics in their own marketing research enterprise, the Practica Group, when they discuss the use of photographs and representation in Cuba, and wonder if they are complicit in the exploitation of their respondents. They generously and candidly admit to culpability (2007: 309–10). Speaking more broadly about ethics in marketing research, they comment, "In our own consumer research work, we take ethical and moral issues seriously and we strive to maintain moral and ethical standards from multiple vantage points: that of the project, the clients, and the respondents" (2007: 310). This is a laudable and actionable aim for all business anthropologists. However, Sunderland and Denny qualify their remark by adding that they have little or no control over the uses of their findings, but are comforted in knowing that their clients have strict legal, moral, and ethical codes (2007: 311). We suspect they know, as we do, that, while most corporations have high moral standards, some clients occasionally compromise absolute truth in the interest of profit objectives. We believe that when an anthropologist is complicit in the procurement of data, he or she holds some responsibility in the application of the research. We will return to this point later, but we note here that client legal constraints and ethical codes cannot always be trusted to protect practicing anthropologists from misuse of their research findings.

What of the ethics of anthropologists' relationship with respondents, which we discussed earlier in the context of ethnography? We hold that in marketing research the relationship with respondents can often stand on higher ethical ground than is typically the case in academic fieldwork. For instance, in marketing and advertising research, respondents are recruited openly and voluntarily, informed of the nature of the project, briefed on the scope of expectations and conditions under which they are interviewed, and are remunerated quite generously for their time. The relationship, and the reciprocity entailed, is undoubtedly of an economic nature. In traditional ethnographic fieldwork, the relationship is more ambiguous. The question of representation as raised by Marcus and Fischer (1986) and Clifford (1988) addresses the issue of anthropologists' responsibility to informants and audiences and of crossing moral and ethical boundaries in writing about them. We understand from colleagues in academia that this issue persists today. What does it mean to build rapport with informants and the community in which one studies, be invited to events, share lives, foster trust, and so forth, and then leave the field to write about personal conversations and experiences in a detached way without compensating them? Is this ethical? Are the bonds we form with informants acts of performance? Are the friendships genuine or spurious? Do we leave the field implying lifelong relationships that terminate, in fact, after a few years or even months apart? In marketing and advertising research, there is no pretense of friendship. By design, marketing research is arguably more straightforward than much academically oriented ethnography, which is more open to vaguely defined relationships with informants. Perhaps this latent misrepresentation explains the extreme sensitivity to ethics in the academy-based anthropological discipline. We suggest that academic anthropologists could learn from business practices and, when appropriate, adhere to the definition of relationships with respondents that we practice.[5]

The Role of the Consumer

Changing views toward advertising and marketing trace to an evolution in ways of conceptualizing consumer autonomy and agency. The notion that advertising surreptitiously manipulates unwary shoppers into consuming unnecessary wants and needs is a carryover from a time when perceptions of shopping dynamics held consumers to be impressionable and submissive characters without agency of their own (cf. Henry 1963; Schudson 1984). As we have suggested, this perspective is inconsistent with current practices and with our experience in the advertising and marketing research industries. We agree with Baba, another anthropologist who has worked in business:

> Consumers and the marketplace were viewed as territory exterior to the business, a place that products and services were sent outward *to*. Often, firms made products first and then looked for the consumers afterwards, dictating what consumers would have to accept. Now, because of ever-intensifying competitive pressures, companies have been forced not only to listen to what consumers want, but also have come to view consumers as potential sources of innovation that they must draw knowledge inward *from*. This new perspective on the value of consumers, and the need for creative exchanges with them, has transformed the way consumer behavior is conceptualized and acted upon as firms create new products and services and take them to market. (Baba 2006: 42)

And later Baba writes: "Consumers are not passive adopters of products, but active innovators who also resist, mutilate, and reconfigure what they find in the market to suit their emerging interests. As active co-producers, consumers have powerful impacts upon products, services, and corporations" (2006: 44). As Sherry puts it: "Consumers are neither cultural dopes nor cultural dupes" (2008: 90).

Eric Von Hippel also discusses consumer agency from the perspective of product innovation. He has shown that when consumers become passionate about an activity, such as windsurfing, mountain climbing, or creating homemade radios, purchased equipment is often modified and knowledge shared with others. Innovation, he suggests, is cultural, not individual. The best inventions arise not from product and design teams within corporations but from among users, who, he estimates, generate 77 percent of product innovation (Von Hippel 2005). Corporations must pay close attention to the ways consumers use their products, because it is consumers who interact with a product, modify it to suit their liking, and share it with other enthusiasts without a motive for monetary profit.

As perceptions of consumer agency have shifted from passive to active, so have accompanying views of the role of advertising and marketing. In recent years, sea changes have occurred in marketing practices and corresponding views of consumers and how they shop for and purchase brands. Rachel Bowlby (2001), in her analysis of the rise in modern shopping, notes that after World War II marketing was guided by a different set of values and beliefs in consumers, which advocated that consumer behavior was a measurable science that could be manipulated. Behavioral psychology in the 1950s assumed that all shoppers reacted similarly to the same stimuli and could be persuaded for "wants" once their resistance or "inhibitions" were removed (2001: 172). This ideological assumption was followed by the development of in-store research techniques that measured and tracked consumer shopping patterns. Because consumers were viewed as passive agents, the compelling idea for marketers and advertisers was to introduce "impulsive" influences, such as in-store ads, promotions, and purchases in unexpected locations, thus encouraging consumers to deviate from their normal shopping routine (2001: 237). Notably, the passive/receptive view of shopping and shoppers described by Bowlby corresponded to social views of women as being fulfilled by their subservient role in housekeeping. Advertising was regarded as the primary brainwashing influence on the "mindless" housewife of the 1950s, making her open to suggestions she might not otherwise take (Bowlby 2001: 200). This view was supported in the late 1950s by Vance Packard's famous book, *The Hidden Persuaders* (1957), which capitalized on rising public fears of coercive marketing practices and the use of subliminal messaging in advertising.[6]

The development of self-service retail in the rise of department stores and supermarkets changed the way consumers had access to goods. As Bowlby writes, consumers now could choose or refuse, see or disbelieve, desire or ignore. It was the difference between doing shopping—a chore of the past—and going shopping—a modern open-ended pleasure. The self-service format shifted human agency away from store owners and their services to consumers as discerning agents of choice. With the advent of self-service, choice was elevated to a status of exemplary good sense that extends far beyond shopping itself. The shopper is no longer a "jellyishly susceptible mass" but an individual endowed with rights and free will, "the embodiment of modern individuality" (2001: 7).

The Responsibility of the Business Anthropologist

U.S. consumers have free choice; they can accept or reject marketing messages based upon their evaluation of the promises made (cf. Beeman 1986). In this context, caveat emptor applies. Consumer decision making is more informed than ever; with Internet search engines, Web communities, and online social networks, people have more information available to them than at any other time in history. The fact that consumers often reject marketers' claims explains why advertising is not 100 percent effective. As Kotler and Armstrong (1991, 2004) point out, and as our own advertising research experience confirms, few consumers accept advertising promises wholeheartedly, and the majority of them place their purchase interest below the "definitely would buy" quintile.[7] Given consumers' active part in message evaluation, we see anthropologists' role in advertising research as reporters and interpreters who seek consumer input that will inform marketing initiatives and help optimize brands to suit consumer needs. We make observations and ask questions; we bring our clients news of what consumers like and dislike about products and communication; we build insights about consumer beliefs, values, needs, and desires that inform advertising strategies. Our contribution as anthropologists lies in accessing unprecedented and often deeper consumer input than is obtained by other marketing research techniques. In this sense, we enable consumer co-creation of brand innovation.

We also know and accept that we are occasionally complicit with advertisers in the manipulation of consumers. Kotler and Armstrong (1991, 2004) and the AAAA's campaign notwithstanding, we have been in conference rooms when clients press us for ways to distinguish their brands through imaginative selling propositions that appeal to consumers' needs, desires, values, or fears in a manner that their brand can own. We cannot deny that some advertisements are highly seductive, promising better health, improved appearance, greater competence, higher self-esteem, a more robust romantic life, and so on. As we listen to our clients' demands for more compelling advertising, we nod our heads, smile, and, unless we believe the client's claims are patently false and harmful to consumers, we accept the call to action. In our combined forty-plus years in advertising and marketing research, we have yet to walk out of a room during one of these kinds of client meetings.

To what extent is exaggeration or hyperbole in advertising an ethical issue? Marketers and advertising agencies have the means to convey to consumers that their brand is better than the competition, even when, by strict standards, it is not. A brand may be superior based on objective evidence: "Nine out of ten doctors recommend Brand X." Brand superiority can also be implied. Verizon telecommunication service's long-term advertising theme, "Can you hear me now?" suggests to consumers, but does not state explicitly, that their competition does not deliver equivalent service. There is no legal burden on this claim unless it is accompanied by a map that shows that Verizon service covers more regions than its major competitors. That said, even if Verizon does provide service in areas that its competition does not, the advertising pushes truth to the limit, and it can be difficult for consumers to know when they are being misled.[8] Manufacturers also attempt to impress target consumers with image advertising or imply directness in their advertising to convince consumers of their sincerity and authenticity.

To illustrate our involvement in what some might label consumer manipulation, we offer two case histories from our professional lives. These stories illustrate ethically ambiguous situations, and we each offer our own thoughts about our personal roles.

Morais

I worked for more than ten years on Sensodyne toothpaste, an over-the-counter brand targeted to sufferers of dental sensitivity, which entails tooth discomfort upon exposure to hot and cold foods and beverages or pressure from a toothbrush. For many years, sales of Sensodyne and its marketplace competitors were sluggish relative to the number of people who experienced tooth sensitivity. In the late 1980s, I was a member of an advertising agency team that developed a highly inventive advertising strategy intended to ignite Sensodyne's sales. The strategy was created through a leap of insight that led to repositioning Sensodyne to dental professionals and consumers. Focus groups and surveys of dental professionals (dentists and hygienists) and consumers who suffered from dental sensitivity demonstrated that one of the barriers to broader and more frequent use of sensitive toothpastes was that many consumers toughed out the pain of sensitivity without feeling compelled to buy a more expensive, specialized toothpaste to address the pain. The explanation, we learned, was that consumers did not believe that tooth sensitivity was a serious problem; they were willing to tolerate the momentary discomfort that sensitivity caused rather than buy Sensodyne or another sensitivity brand. My advertising agency reasoned that perhaps the solution to generating increased usage of Sensodyne would be found not by emphasizing the ability of the brand to solely relieve the pain of sensitive teeth but rather *by enlarging the issue* of dental sensitivity and *increasing the urgency* for consumers to buy the brand and for dental professionals to recommend it. The agency created advertising based on what we termed a "serial consequences strategy"; sensitivity sufferers were informed that the pain from brushing a sensitive tooth could cause them to stop brushing that tooth and lead to a sequence of plaque buildup, gingivitis, periodontal disease, and ultimately tooth loss. Advertising research with target consumers and dental professionals documented that the serial-consequences commercials, which used the metaphor of falling dominoes to graphically dramatize the outcome of not addressing tooth sensitivity, could drive Sensodyne purchases more aggressively than a simple pain-relief approach. I helped write the new advertising strategy for Sensodyne and was a leading member of the team that sold the advertising to the client, produced it, and devised the media plan. I devoted most of my efforts to the consumer target and contributed to dental professional-targeted marketing initiatives. Sensodyne's marketplace performance was impressive as sales grew dramatically following the airing of "The Domino Effect" television advertising.[9]

I knew then and know now that the Sensodyne advertising was effective because it compelled many tooth sensitivity sufferers to make a purchase that was not absolutely necessary because the probability of suffering the consequences depicted was not high for most people. The advertising advised consumers to consult with their dentist about Sensodyne, so it could be argued that the dentist, who received a professional version of the domino campaign in print and through a sales force that visited dental offices, acted as a gatekeeper. However, consumers could buy Sensodyne without consulting their dentist. Was I guilty of manipulation? The consumer did have a choice and a professional advisor, their dentist. The advertising concept was technically true. I can rationalize the ethics of the campaign, but I am also aware that the serial-consequences strategy represented a truth that served the marketing corporation more than typical dental sensitivity sufferers.

Malefyt

On one ethnographic project, I assisted in developing a strategy that capitalized on associating the benefits of a brand of soft drink with overcoming human longings for connection and security. In 2003, a global beverage manufacturer, a long time client of BBDO advertising, entered the fast-growing lemon-lime soft drink category with a new carbonated soft drink called Citrus Splash (a pseudonym).[10] Lemon-lime soft drinks appeal to a diverse youthful audience, roughly aged eighteen to twenty-nine. Rivals Sprite and 7UP had increased their sales by advertising heavily to this audience. The global beverage manufacturer enlisted BBDO to conduct ethnographic research on heavy users of lemon-lime sodas. The assignment was given to my in-agency ethnographic group to better understand the emotional connection of this youth target to the lemon-lime category and Citrus Splash in particular. We focused on life-stage changes of this audience, especially on the transitory period between youth and adulthood. Our hypotheses going into research suggested that humor and laughter played an important role in their lives, easing some of the anxieties this target felt about transitioning to adulthood. We would then advise our creative team and subsequently the client on ideas for an advertising campaign.

We interviewed and observed Citrus Splash enthusiasts and delved into how soda made them feel. The respondents we spoke with were entering new careers, relationships, and living situations. They reported feeling excited but also anxious about their future. We discovered that humor and laughter were indeed important social by-products of the many activities, friendships, and outings in which respondents were involved. This confirmed other studies that note the importance of laughter in fostering feelings of belonging and social connectedness (Provine 2000). In our interviews, soda enthusiasts associated Citrus Splash with lightness, clarity, refreshment, and movement. Gathering these insights, we formulated a marketing strategy for

Citrus Splash that aligned its lighthearted lemon-lime product features—bubbly, clear, and sweet—with imagery and associations of overcoming difficult situations, using humor to lighten up, feel destressed, and move forward in life. Citrus Splash, a "life-stage salve," would help anxious young people overcome odds and adjust to new life responsibilities through clever humor, good spirits, and levity. The creative campaign "Surprisingly Invigorating" aired successfully in its run from 2004 to 2007, depicting savvy young consumers outsmarting "hot and compromising" social situations with clever, cool humor and, of course, Citrus Splash. The campaign won an Effie award for demonstrating advertising effectiveness. The brand gained large increases in TV and brand awareness, product perceptions, and volume sales and sourced business from key competitors of Sprite and 7UP. As a result, the new brand attained national distribution, gained market share against competitors, and established it as a long-term contender.

The ethical issue I confronted dealt not with my involvement in helping to position a product category, a soft drink, with dubious health benefits. Rather, it involved sequestering consumer research findings that centered on people's insecurities and helping to associate those insights with a product's positive features. I questioned the ethics of suggesting to consumers that a product like soda can be lighthearted and somehow substitute for, or enhance, real human relations. Our research on the lives of youth in transition provided an opportunity to leverage an apparent weakness, with brand associations of humor acting as a salve for emotional insecurities and a proxy for real human relations. Is it ethical when marketers and researchers seek an upper hand in product persuasion by drawing on people's emotional sensitivities? Advertising increasingly culls emotional territory over rational linkages to human dispositions (see chapter 5, "Advertising Emotions"), and this research was an example of how this is manifested.

Ethical Dilemmas and Decisions

The way we frame ethically questionable situations in marketing depends on where we locate the idea of individual free will, choice, and human agency. We believe that business anthropologists who consider the ethics of their work should assess the impact of their contributions on the target audience, even when the ultimate decision about buying is up to the consumer. This process is not always simple. A good example of this conundrum is direct-to-consumer (DTC) prescription drug advertising. The benefits and liabilities of this multibillion-dollar mode of consumer communication are hotly debated (Spatz 2011). Advocates contend that DTC advertising builds awareness among sufferers of underdiagnosed conditions, leads to needed treatment for these conditions, and reminds consumers to take their medication, thereby improving public health. Critics argue that DTC advertising profits mainly pharmaceutical companies, contributes to overmedication, and places physicians in the uncomfortable position of talking their advertising-influenced patients out of medications that they do not need. Given that both sides of the argument have merit and are discussed openly, we believe that the decision to accept or refuse a DTC assignment must be a personal one for the researcher.

Other advertising categories are more or less problematic. Cigarettes are unequivocally harmful to human health, but freedom of speech allows some degree of marketing and advertising of these products. We would not choose to participate in cigarette marketing research because we see no redeeming value in the products, but other anthropologists might argue that these products deserve representation and that consumers can decide for themselves whether to purchase them. Children's sugar-laden cereals provide scant nutritional value, but mothers feed them to their children because they feel these cereals are the only food their children will consume in time-compressed mornings. Hard-surface disinfectants protect individuals from contagion, but they may reduce the broader population's resistance to bacteria. Credit cards bring convenience but can result in unmanageable debt. Candy and other junk foods are satisfying when consumed but represent empty calories and contribute to obesity. Some fast-food companies claim their offerings are more nutritious than their competition—for example, grilled versus fried hamburgers. Is the highly salted, fatty beef offered as a healthier option *really* healthy? Political advertisements can be combative and stress only the truth that is advantageous to one side.

A cigarette campaign that aims to increase smoking or surreptitious surveillance on government projects for war efforts, as in the Camelot affair, are two examples where most anthropologists would refuse cooperation. However, deciding on the degree of ethical responsibility for many consumable categories is difficult. Moreover, we recognize that we are complicit in muddying consumer evaluation of brands when we highlight their positive attributes, such as soda for its taste enjoyment, and downplay its negative dietary impact, or when we stress the most dire consequences of not attending to the pain of tooth sensitivity. At the same time, we have observed that corporate profit and consumer fulfillment are not mutually exclusive, as in a zero-sum game. Many consumers derive pleasure and obtain no deleterious consequences when they drink soda in moderation, some of which is sugar-free, and they protect their teeth when they brush with a toothpaste for sensitivity. Both the buyer and the marketer win. In the end, we feel that consumers usually have access to information that enables them to make an informed choice about the brands they consider. Assuming that a marketing researcher believes that the client's essential claims are valid and that the consumer has enough information available, each of us must weigh the merits in developing advertising that might influence consumers toward potentially detrimental ends.

The Code of Ethics of the American Anthropological Association

The Code of Ethics of the American Anthropological Association (AAA) (www. aaanet.org/issues/policy-advocacy/upload/AAA-Ethics-Code-2009.pdf) is silent concerning business, but in any discussion on business ethics for anthropologists, the code must be considered.[11] Foremost among the AAA guidelines is the statement that no researcher should intentionally engage in a project that will cause serious, unquestionable "harm or wrong" (2009: 2) to the people studied. As is evident from our earlier discussion, we believe that all business anthropologists should consider any assignment in this regard. The code also states that anthropologists "should not agree to conditions which inappropriately change the purpose, focus or intended outcomes of their research" (2009: 4). This is not a realistic condition in business research. We produce research findings, but our clients own the research, and they can use it as they wish. Were we to state conditions for the use of the studies we conduct, our clients would select another research resource. Moreover, conditions agreed upon at the onset of a project may change over time. In our experience, the scope, objectives, and occasionally the target audience of a project are sometimes adjusted as new learning is gained. We must use our judgment in working with clients whom we trust will not abuse our findings. AAA guidelines concerning advanced consent of those studied (2009: 3) may also constrain business anthropologists. In our studies, respondents are fully aware of our objectives. However, a marketing research practice known as covert ethnography is not consistent with the AAA code. An article in a widely read marketing research magazine states, "A popular definition of ethnography is found in Hammersley and Atkinson (1995: 1): 'In its most characteristic form it involves the ethnographer participating *overtly or covertly*, in people's lives for an extended period of time, watching what happens, listening to what is said, asking questions'" (Ritacco 2010: 18; emphasis added). Paco Underhill, who identifies himself as a "retail anthropologist," takes this point further: "It is crucial to our work that shoppers don't realize they're being observed. There is no other way to be sure that we're seeing natural behavior" (1999: 14). Underhill's work is decidedly observational, surveillance at a distance, over ethnographic interaction. We suggest that if such observation poses no harm to those observed and they remain anonymous, it should be allowable, but we recognize that some anthropologists will disagree. Finally, the AAA code suggests that researchers: "disseminate the results through appropriate and timely activity" (2009: 2). Competition in business requires confidentiality, and the dissemination of research findings would violate this mandate. The AAA code allows that, in cases of intellectual property protection, confidentiality is permitted. Marketing and advertising research falls within this area. In fact, most of our clients require us to sign nondisclosure agreements.

* * *

Human interaction demands that we make judgments every day that have moral and ethical implications. Should we walk by the homeless woman or stop to give her spare change? Is it acceptable to use a hand sanitizer to prevent illness while contributing to the spawning of superbug bacteria in the broader community? Should university professors, well aware that the job market for PhD anthropologists is dismal (Baba 2006; Editorial 2010; Pannapacker 2011) decrease the size of graduate programs and suggest alternative careers to prospective students? Are we all above reproach in our responses to questions such as these? Taking this argument further, must anthropologists be advocates for the public good? This is a noble calling, but is it central to the practice of anthropology in the twenty-first century? During anthropology's historical period in the early twentieth century, when the field's objectives were often intertwined with colonial aims and "powerless natives" needed protection, anthropologists could rightly be called upon to play activist roles. We have suggested that business is not an all-powerful force; consumers have the freedom to reject marketing and advertising messages. Other than in cases of malfeasance, consumers do not require advocates. Consequently, we do not believe that advertising and marketing researchers need to take on a protective role for consumers. (See Malefyt and Moeran 2003b: 18–20 for a related discussion on power as it impacts relationships between the informant and ethnographer.)

Ethics are ultimately defined and negotiated in public discourse as well as by individual decision making. We and other practicing anthropologists with whom we are acquainted constitute a community that views ethics as certain appropriate and responsible behavior in the context of our businesses. We value our communal discussions, professional meetings, and informal lunches where we vent frustrations, discuss our concerns, and inform one another of the issues we face. It is, in part, through communities like these that we arbitrate what is ethical and what is not. Our personal values inform our judgments and actions in our business conduct as well. Through both communities and personal experiences, we evolve guidelines for our business conduct. As our stories revealed, we have, at times, felt conflicted. A decision to turn away work is not easy, and we find ourselves more likely to rationalize accepting a client in a gray area than refusing to work on a project on moral grounds. We have boundaries, but we do not pretend that we hold ourselves to a lofty standard of pure truth in advertising. We also accept that some academic anthropologists might find the profit motives of business abhorrent and consumer manipulation repugnant. We hope that they will recognize the ethical considerations most marketing and advertising anthropologists try to abide by in our working lives. We also urge academic anthropologists to embrace cultural relativity and accept that advertising anthropology can be not only a viable career path but also an ethical one.

–10–

Hybrid Research Methodologies and Business Success

The "Get a Mac" series of advertisements (also known as "Mac vs. PC") that ran nearly forty different iterations from 2006 to 2010, is regarded as a highly successful advertising campaign. Throughout a series of different situations, a casually dressed youthful man introduces himself as a Mac, "Hello, I'm a Mac," while an older, corpulent man dressed more formally in a suit and tie introduces himself as a PC, "And I'm a PC." In each advertisement, the two men act out humorous vignettes in which the capabilities and attributes of Mac and PC are compared. The PC, characterized as formal, stuffy, and overly concerned with work, is frustrated by the laid-back demeanor and superior capabilities of the Mac. The campaign received the Grand Effie Award in 2007 for effectiveness, is said to have increased Apple computer market share from a 2–3 percent share to a 6–8 percent share, and helped Apple become the solid number three seller of computers in the United States (Bulik 2010).

One reason the "Get a Mac" advertising campaign was so successful is because it uses the psychological technique of personification to encourage viewers to consider similar inanimate objects (Mac and PC computers) as living individuals with distinct attributes. Personification techniques, such as asking people to describe a brand as if it were a car, an animal, or a person, are a common practice in qualitative marketing research. This type of inquiry is valued because it enables marketers to access consumers' higher-order (i.e., deep emotional rather than functional) thoughts about brands. Higher-order consumer insights allow marketers to differentiate brands, especially when brands' functional properties are essentially indistinguishable. Marketers know that brands become meaningful to people beyond their generalized commodity function through psychological dynamics that have powerful emotional value. This is what enables a brand to be unique or "singularized" (Callon, Meadel, and Rabeharosoa 2002) and obtain a personal "biography" (Kopytoff 1986). As Csikszentmihalyi and Rochberg-Halton observed, "Things embody goals, make skills manifest, and shape the identities of their users" (Csikszentmihalyi and Rochberg-Halton 1981: 1).

Psychology as a way to gain consumer understanding has long been a natural fit for the advertising and marketing industry. The singular unit of the brand in marketing aligns with the singular unit of the individual in psychology. The coherence of psychology with branding in marketing has become so ingrained over the years that they form tacit knowledge (Polanyi 1958) in the business world. Indeed, psychology in business serves not only as a model of and for analyzing human behavior in marketing; the language of psychology is also a component of colloquial conversations. Psychological terms have entered everyday parlance, from hearing about one's "co-dependent" behavior to "scapegoats" to discussions on the subject of "everyday psychology" used to better understand issues in parenting, education, career, and workplace to explaining crime and violence. It is no wonder that psychology has the reign in our culture that it does.

Most business anthropologists fail to embrace this phenomenon and express their ideas only in terms of culture. Make culture more "visible" is one battle cry (Sunderland and Denny 2007). As anthropologists, we agree with this call to action. At the same time, the concept of making culture visible can be problematic for business executives because they have little, if any, idea what culture, as anthropologists define it, means. The language of culture, as anthropologists have developed it in scholarly studies of kinship systems, structural analysis, or, more broadly, interpretations of culture, is useful for categorizing relationships, practices, cognitive structures, and symbols. However, rarely is the language of culture as anthropologists construe it heard in everyday conversations, let alone in business settings. Moreover, the language of culture as applied in ethnographic and other anthropological business research is sometimes vague and often referenced in business, ironically, through psychological concepts as a "separable singularity" (Sunderland and Denny 2007: 321). For these and other reasons that we will discuss, we propose that business anthropologists broaden their perspective to incorporate additional theory, language, and methods from psychology.[1] This hybrid approach does not negate the value of cultural analysis. Rather, it provides more ways to comprehend consumer behavior, ideas, attitudes, and sentiments surrounding consumption. Our proposal also constitutes an adaptive strategy for business anthropologists in that it will improve their relationships with corporate executives who tacitly or explicitly embrace psychological models of human thought and behavior. A hybrid methodology also enables business anthropologists to be seen as experts in understanding the breadth of human behavior rather than solely as research ethnographers. Throughout our own careers, we have experienced the use of psychology as the core method and analytical framework for understanding consumer behavior. In our work, we regularly apply both psychological and anthropological approaches. We do not value one framework over another; we believe that integrating approaches leads to better results. We have found that is what our clients want, need, and expect.

We see hybrid approaches in the business setting as a kind of advanced applied anthropology, working, as it were, between two or more distinct cultures with different perspectives and adopting them for the benefit of our clients' understanding as well as our own. These contrasting views are represented by anthropologists who think and do anthropology per se (often ethnography in business practice) and their clients, manufacturers, and advertising and design agencies, who think mainly in terms of psychology (Sunderland and Denny 2003: 190–91). The psychological models of human thought and behavior that marketing and advertising executives use view consumers as operating on individualistic levels. This perspective corresponds to marketing models of purchase decision making and the ways that marketers appeal to consumers through advertising, package design, price incentives in coupons, retail store shelf placement, and so on. To access consumer attitudes and behavior, marketing and advertising professionals typically rely on psychological tools. This process ranges from the explicit application of psychological theories such as Maslow's "Hierarchy of Needs" (Malefyt 2003; Maslow 1968) to questions that are asked of respondents regarding individual perception, intention, and behavior, which rely on methods such as personal histories, surveys, psychologically oriented focus groups, and projective techniques. As anthropologists, we are aware that consumers are subject to cultural systems, beliefs, and values that impact their cognition and behavior. Although marketing and advertising executives are generally aware of the interaction of culture, behavior, and attitudes, they are often indifferent to this process. Their research and strategic planning methodologies are constructed as if consumers select goods for themselves and others from an individualistic mode. Even when marketing and advertising companies hire anthropologists to conduct ethnographic studies, as Sunderland and Denny point out, "ethnographic inquiry is too often embraced as a means to obtain a deeper psychological understanding of a target audience" (2003: 188). This way of thinking can stoke contentious debates between anthropologists and their clients. When Sunderland and Denny speak of marketers and anthropologists as "talking past" one another (2003: 188), we are not surprised. We have experienced the same discursive incongruence in our work, and we have developed ways to ameliorate the problem. This is the heart of the matter at hand; business anthropologists must learn the language and culture of their corporate clients as they would learn the language and culture of their informants in the field. In marketing and advertising research, we believe that anthropologists should integrate psychology with anthropology to create hybrid methods and analysis that will serve the business problem *and* the anthropologist-client business relationship. We will illustrate our argument by showing how we apply this convergent methodology and how it informs our research and enables us to mediate between client psychological and our own inherent anthropological perspectives. Our integrated approach relies on anthropological skills of listening, interpreting, and conversing across and between modalities. In the process of learning about our respondents' ways of thinking and being, we better connect with our clients' ways of thinking and being. We contend that anthropologists in advertising and marketing research who retain their pure anthropological perspectives without regard for their clients' perspective risk their jobs and, in fact, are not practicing as anthropologists should—as keen observers and navigators of different cultures.

Despite the penchant in marketing and advertising for psychological analysis, some anthropologists are reluctant to expand their perspective. These anthropologists, like Sunderland and Denny (2003), frame their work in marketing research as a disciplinary prizefight: psychology versus anthropology. From our perspective, rather than stress disciplinary competition, we propose that difference be seen in terms of complementarity and have attempted to educate the industry in this regard (Morais 2009c). We suggested in the previous chapter, and will illustrate further here, that a means to expand anthropology's contribution to business is to convince industry that anthropology is more than conducting ethnography; it entails a way of thinking about culture, observing behavior, and asking questions and incorporating trends and fads as well as deep-seated beliefs, even in focus group or other research and analytical settings. As we incorporate both psychological and anthropological modes of inquiry in a variety of research contexts, we find that many business executives, indifferent to academic theory, welcome any perspective that will gain them access to the ways their customers think and behave. Through our hybrid methodology and analysis, we secure both consumer insights and client acceptance.

Anthropology and Psychology: A Brief History

During anthropology's formative years, a convergence of anthropology and psychology was manifested in culture and personality, which was a dominant subfield, stimulated by the early work of Mead (1928) and Benedict (1934) and later by Kardiner and his associates (1945), Whiting and Child (1953), Hallowell ([1955] 1967), and Sapir (1970), among others. By midcentury, culture and personality suffered critical blows (Bock 1980: 131). Unbowed, but influenced by critics, anthropologists produced a spate of books during the 1960s and 1970s on culture and personality; its successor in name, psychological anthropology; and the related subdiscipline of cognitive anthropology (see, e.g., Barnouw 1973; Cole and Scribner 1974; Hsu 1972; Hunt 1967; Levine 1973, 1974; Spradley 1972; Tyler 1969; Wallace 1961). These schools of thought were not immune to additional reevaluation (Harris 1968; Shweder 1979a, 1979b, 1980). In this context, Clifford Geertz noted, "Anthropology is a conflicted discipline, perpetually in search of ways to escape its condition, perpetually failing to find them . . . fissures within cultural anthropology as such, the heart of the discipline, have proved increasingly prominent and less easy to contain" (Geertz 1995: 4). His thoughtful review of two books on Captain Cook's life and death in the Pacific focused on competitive cultural and psychological interpretations of the events. Although Geertz sided with the cultural analysis, evidence that psychological and cognitive anthropology remained vibrant through the 1980s and 1990s is found in publications by Shweder and LeVine (1984); Schwartz, White, and Lutz

(1992); and D'Andrade (1995), among others, and in more recent work by Shweder (2003) and D'Andrade (2008), along with the enduring vitality of *Ethos*, the journal of the Society for Psychological Anthropology.

The theories and research techniques of psychological and cognitive anthropology have much to offer business, especially marketing and advertising, as do methods and concepts from psychology that anthropologists have not typically used—for example, deprivation scenarios, personification as a projective technique, locus of control, mindfulness, and cognitive dissonance. In our work, we have found that marketing and advertising executives value a close examination of the relationship between culture-driven beliefs, rituals, and classification systems and consumer perceptions, attitudes, and purchase motivations. The convergence of disciplines informing this examination is an evolutionary step for psychological anthropology. It will help advance the subdiscipline and increase opportunities for anthropologists who choose to engage in business practices.

Anthropologists and Clients: A Way Toward Mediation

For anthropologists to bridge the cross-cultural gap with regard to their psychologically oriented clients, they must accept a duality in their role. They must retain their identity as cultural anthropologists able to make distinctive contributions in a business setting, and they must also incorporate the perspective of their clients who pay the bill for their research. The following case study, based upon a meeting Morais attended, illustrates the need for duality in an advertising agency–client relationship, one similar to the anthropologist-client relationship.

The president of an advertising agency was under extreme pressure. He was informed by his agency's largest client the previous day that the account was being placed in review, meaning that the client intended to ask competing agencies to pitch for the assignment. His agency had much to lose, and the president called a meeting with senior account management and creative staff to determine a plan of action to protect their assignment. He explained the conditions of the competitive pitch. All of the participating agencies would present creative work written to the same strategy, the work would be tested among consumers, and the assignment would be awarded to the agency whose creative work achieved the best test scores. He noted plaintively that he saw this coming because the client had expressed dissatisfaction with recent agency creative work and the interpersonal chemistry between senior agency and client executives was increasingly poor. He said he considered resigning the account but felt that the future of the agency would be in jeopardy. He contended that the agency had an opportunity to demonstrate their superior understanding of the client's brand and surprise the client with winning work. As he ended his summary of the position the agency was now in, the president said that one of the reasons the agency was in this predicament was because they had been not been sensitive enough to the client's way of doing business. He underscored that agency executives' relationships with the client were tense and creative presentations had not gone well in recent months; even when creative ideas were sold to the client, the client did not seem happy. Then the agency president said, "We have to be like them and not be like them." He meant that, to win back the client's loyalty, the agency needed to do a better job of understanding and adapting to the client's corporate culture, their interactional style, their operational processes, and the kind of creative work that they were most likely to accept. At the same time, he said, the agency must demonstrate a distinctive creative voice; otherwise why would the client retain them? After this meeting, the agency went to work. They tried to deliver on the president's objectives. However, after several months, the agency lost the account to a competitor.

The agency president's phrase—"We have to be like them and not be like them"—expresses the duality that anthropologists engaged in marketing research must practice. Business anthropologists must be like them in that they must learn and function effectively within their client's culture or risk alienating them. At the same time, business anthropologists must not be like them and retain their distinctive professional identities, which provides value to their clients. We know from our experience that an effective way to attain this duality in marketing and advertising research projects is to accept the notion of a convergence between clients' psychological mode and our own cultural perspective. This duality is not duplicitous; it is a way to mediate the cultural divide that otherwise leads to anthropologist-client contentiousness and, ultimately, incompatibility.

Hybrid Approaches: Two Examples

To illustrate our argument, we have selected two case studies from successful projects that each of the authors has managed. These examples demonstrate how ideas and methods from psychology and anthropology offer complementary means of probing how consumers think and feel. We will show that blending methods and theories from these two disciplines leads to productive results for marketers and for the researcher-client relationship. We have focused on marketing research for advertised brands, which is our domain, but we have no doubt that, together, psychology and anthropology can benefit other areas of industry.

Malefyt: Understanding the "Dinner Dilemma"

An international client who specializes in a packaged food sought to better understand how middle-class American women typically create a family meal for each day of the week. The advertising agency assigned to this project decided to use in-home ethnography conducted by anthropologists and observed shopping patterns of consumers to understand the ways in which women thought about, prepared, and created meals for their families. The research methods for the project included a blend of psychological and anthropological methods such as observations and interviews around meal planning, preparation, and mealtime consumption. In addition, before the scheduled ethnographic visit, the anthropologists who conducted the research asked each woman to keep an in-depth journal of her daily thoughts and feelings around meal planning over the course of a week. These combined approaches led to new thinking about the role of women in meal preparation.

The anthropologists discovered that both experienced and novice home cooks receive and share recipes and meal ideas through a social network of other women, including women in their family, friends, neighbors, associates at work, and in the local community. The anthropologists reported that when women searched for meal ideas, they usually were informed about a recipe or meal idea from a woman coworker, friend, or relative and then carried out the recipe or checked for close alternatives on Web sites or in cookbooks or magazines. This learning reflected the powerful influence of personal connections in the daily task of generating meal ideas for the family. The idea of a successful family meal intertwined both food features (i.e., combination of vegetables, meat, and starch) and the relational outcome of such meals (family enjoyment and socializing). Success was determined by what family members liked to eat and the resulting shared feelings of happiness and togetherness such meals produced. For example, a sister might strongly recommend a meal idea or recipe that she had used successfully to make a "happy meal occasion," and pass this recipe to her sibling or other women. Indeed, the anthropologists discovered that the world of food and recipes is highly contextual of lived situations, where food is intertwined with personal stories and social connections. As Harris points out, "Food, so to speak, must nourish the collective mind before it can enter an empty stomach" (1985: 15). Food is ultimately social and personalized, since face-to-face connections significantly influence meal ideas, choices, and outcomes.

The success of this project lay in coalescing an understanding of the range of psychological states that women bring to meal preparation along with an anthropological perspective on the importance of social exchange in meal ideas and recipes. Especially insightful was the analysis of women's daily journal logs, since women wrote about their varying emotional states, such as when they felt creative, inspired, bored, and even frustrated coming up with meal ideas on a regular basis. In addition, the anthropologists discovered that women resolve such frustrations through sharing information with other women who might be experiencing similar emotional states. As Maslow writes, healthy individuals are motivated by higher-order needs in which sharing their "potentials, capacities and talents" helps fulfill a sense of mission (Maslow 1968: 25). In this way, a friend or sister with whom recipes are exchanged occupies the same psychological space as another familiar or close woman, and the sharing of meal ideas helps to identify and align women with similar thoughts and feelings about cooking for their families. By blending a psychological perspective on cooking as it relates to the emotional state of the self with an anthropological perspective on social networking and recipes producing relations of reciprocity, the anthropologists discovered that strong emotions were attached to the idea of recipes as "re-creating the family" as a social unit through the family meal.

These insights from the anthropologists helped the advertising agency create a range of strategic and tactical marketing solutions to assist women in planning their weekly meals beyond just using recipes from the client's Web site and magazine. For example, the advertising agency recommended that the client's Web site could retain a psychologist to offer tips and advice on a Web site for new and experienced cooks on how to deal with feelings of stress in preparing the family meal—for example, offering content that addressed the whole person, responding to her at a moment of need in her particular life stage, and providing her the space to connect with the client's brand. The advertising agency also suggested ways for women to expand their meal options and offer recipe ideas for friends and advice on how to set up meals for different occasions and events as well as starting local cooking classes for beginner cooks. Finally, the agency employed a multidisciplinary approach to cover the range of women's emotional and activity states in thinking, planning, and creating meals for their families. The agency applied creative ideas that reflected modes of self-identity that Belk elaborates as "doing" states and "being" states (Belk 1988). The client praised the agency's findings and recommendations and has since implemented many of the suggested marketing plans.

Morais: Breakfast Cereal as a High-Stakes Experience

The U.S. cereal market is cluttered with brands that compete for a place on the consumer's palate. The client, a manufacturer of several well-known breakfast cereal brands, needed to learn how one of its brands could increase consumer selection in the store during the "moment of choice" when consumers scan the supermarket shelf. Instead of conducting in-store observations, the usual research choice for this kind of inquiry, the client asked the research company to explore consumer responses in a focus group setting to understand the consumer thinking that led to the in-store purchase decision. The client's reasoning for this setting was that it would allow for more expansive exploration into consumer beliefs, and a greater number of marketing and advertising team members could observe the proceedings in the back room of a focus group facility than could accompany the researchers in a store. The research supplier proposed, and the client agreed, that a combination of psychological and anthropological methods would generate new insights on the breakfast experience (when most cereal is consumed), the client's brand and competitive brands, and drivers of brand choice. The research firm also suggested that extended one-on-one interviews with consumers would allow for greater depth of inquiry and response than traditional focus groups. The client concurred. Ninety-minute in-depth one-on-one interviews were arranged with thirteen consumers. Prior to their arrival for the interviews, respondents were given homework assignments in which they created collages with images that illustrated how they feel when eating the client's brand and how they feel when eating other kinds of breakfast foods (noncereal). The use of images as metaphors to elicit respondent commentary is a technique used by many marketing research companies, championed by Zaltman (2003), and was a tool for early psychologically driven anthropological studies in the form of the Thematic Apperception Test (Bock 1980: 96–105). Respondents also kept two-week diaries concerning their breakfast experience and took photographs of home eating and breakfast food storage places, techniques that some marketers consider a kind of virtual ethnography (Malefyt 2009). During the interview sessions, the respondents were exposed to a model of a supermarket shelf set with a wide range of brands to replicate (in a general way) the supermarket setting, tasted the client's brand and competitive brands, and were asked about their feelings, beliefs, and rituals surrounding breakfast. A variation on life history elicitation was incorporated, mirroring efforts in anthropology dating back to Dyk's early Navaho work ([1938] 1967) and following a central practice in psychotherapy (Gabbard 2005; McWilliams 1999: 42). Respondents were asked to describe childhood breakfast eating experiences and to imagine their current life without their preferred brand, a psychologically oriented deprivation exercise with questions centering on their degree of loss and food substitutions.

This project called for an anthropological perspective on the meaning of food during a specific eating occasion, for a psychological interpretation of an eating experience, informed by observed consumption and additional insights into consumers' attitudes and feelings about their brand. Observation and analysis revealed that breakfast is a liminal space—an in-between, highly ritualized occasion during which personal transformations occur (Turner 1964, 1969). Early morning is a transitional period, when consumers move over a threshold from sleep to waking, from their private to public selves. The breakfast cereal brand they consume during the liminal phase defines the emotional content of their transformational experience. The client's brand's sensate attributes of sweetness and crunch made respondents feel happy, optimistic, and even joyful. This finding, first discovered during the formal interviews, was underscored during observation of consumer consumption of the client's brand. The positive feelings were expressed when respondents experienced a cascade of enjoyable flavors and textures. Drawing on a psychological definition of mindfulness, the research team concluded that eating this brand was especially mindful because it stimulated a charged awareness of a sensate experience (cf. Bishop, Shapiro, and Carlson 2004 for psychological definitions of mindfulness). The researchers and their clients agreed this quality of experience could help the client's brand gain ownership of breakfast. Other findings informed an understanding of breakfast and the brand. From a cognitive classification perspective, there was a sharp distinction between weekdays, which entail purpose and preparation, and weekends, which are more relaxed and loosely structured. Through the discussion of the collages and detailed description of the consumption of the client's brand and other breakfast options, breakfast was revealed to be psychologically linked to a kind of personal ownership and to be territorial, with respondents using phrases such as: "My breakfast"; "My time"; "My zone." These findings helped the research and client team realize that breakfast is high stakes; the wrong breakfast (e.g., doughnuts) can negatively affect eating choices for the remainder of the day, compromising mood, productivity, and self-image.

This research provided the client with a deep understanding of its brand and the means to position it in the marketplace more competitively. The study contributed an anthropologically informed analysis of the transformational nature of breakfast and the psychological attendants of that eating occasion. As expressed in the creative brief that served as a guide for advertising development, the client's brand releases the consumer's best, most optimistic self at the start of their day (paraphrased here for confidentiality). After the study was completed, the client lauded the research team's layering of anthropological and psychological methodologies and analysis and rewarded the research company with numerous additional projects. When new projects were assigned to the research company, the client insight director specifically asked the firm to blend psychological and anthropological approaches. She commented repeatedly that the appeal of the research company was largely in its ability to engage in this kind of hybrid research.

From Mutual Exclusivity to Mutual Benefit

Epistemologically, the academic disciplines of psychology and anthropology have clear distinctions, but in consumer marketing and research practices, the units of analysis are often intertwined. Furthermore, in business projects, the convergence of these disciplines is accomplished in abbreviated and condensed form. As Sunderland and Denny (2007: 325) acknowledge, a benefit of being anthropologists in business as opposed to academia is that working knowledge over perfect knowledge is welcomed and prioritized. In business there is no need, nor is there time, for the full application of pure theory. Rituals, gift or commodity exchange, or any other useful analytic model is sufficient and, in fact, appreciated, in truncated form. When we speak about these ideas and use theory in our work, we use the language of business rather than the language of scholarship. Our analyses, though informed by academic studies, are purposely devoid of academic jargon. We see working knowledge as a component of a hybrid approach and as eminently useful for both understanding consumer behavior and helping to bridge conceptual divides between business executives and the anthropologist researchers they hire.

In essence, we have argued here for what Wilson (1998) calls consilience. In this context, a convergence of psychology and anthropology yields both heuristic and occupational ends (cf. Belk 1988 for a multidisciplinary analysis of possessions).

We understand that the successful application of hybrid methodologies will require changes in the way business anthropologists think about their work and interact with their research respondents and their clients, but we believe that this interdisciplinary synthesis will positively shape the future of anthropologists in corporate work. We should underscore that we believe the cultural perspective of anthropology has value in and of itself, and the distinction between anthropological and psychological questions should be recognized. However, rather than engage in battles with business executives in an effort to educate them about differences between anthropology and psychology, we believe that it is wiser to consider how psychological and anthropological ideas interact in the interest of consumer understanding. In addition, corporate clients who distain theoretical distinctions embrace *any* knowledge that generates brand growth. In this way, we educate our clients gradually on anthropological concepts without engaging in contentious debates about an anthropological approach.

Being anthropologists in advertising and marketing research affords us a position in which we are able to play with accepted practices of psychology, expanding them to be more anthropological and to integrate psychological methods and modes of thinking with anthropological ones. We are not alone (cf. Rapaille 2006 for a popularized approach). In a sense, the business community may provide more freedom than academic settings in which to integrate disciplines, because business applications are less concerned with purity of theory, method, and application and are more focused on answering questions with marketplace value. Many anthropologists succeed in business while retaining theoretical purity. Other anthropologist practitioners face clients who find an exclusively anthropological perspective limiting or too arcane to be of value. For the latter segment, convergence between anthropology and psychology will open opportunities in applied anthropology as it makes the work and the working relationships of anthropologists in business more robust.

Part IV
Conclusion

The Future of Advertising Anthropology

When we reflect on our employment as anthropologists in advertising and marketing research, we are impressed by anthropology's advancement as a valued discipline in the corporate world. Our experience and observations have encouraged us to inspire more anthropologists to seek employment in our industry. However, even with our bullish outlook, we realize that there are hurdles to overcome. Misconceptions and false assumptions circulate in our industry and business in general concerning what anthropology is as a discipline and what it can offer business practices. Anthropology is still sometimes conflated with archaeology, as evidenced by the occasional queries we receive regarding how many digs we have been on lately. There still linger associations of anthropology with Margaret Mead and her work in Samoa—now many generations past and without any heir apparent to fill her public void.[1] Many marketers continue to misconstrue ethnography as interchangeable with anthropology, where both are assumed to be methodological rather than analytical means of uncovering truth about human behavior. Indeed, ethnography is perceived by business as more valuable than methods adapted from other social science disciplines for zeroing in on consumers' unarticulated desires, the holy grail of marketing. However, much of the analytical thinking that accompanies anthropologists' use of ethnography is still underutilized or misunderstood in marketing and advertising. In several chapters in this volume, we have expressed the different kinds of questions, processes, and lenses through which anthropologists can uncover meaning and generate value for business. We have suggested that, while ethnography is a method that anthropologists should continue to use in business, it is not the only way we operate. Anthropological analysis, whether by focus groups, ethnography, or thoughtful cultural perspectives, can enhance advertising and marketing initiatives by offering a broader view of culture, from its fads and fashions to its deep enduring structures.

Embedded in the persistent misunderstandings of what anthropology is lies a perception in business that anthropologists are inherently exotic. Lucy Suchman (2007) notes that, even after many years of reporting anthropology's use in corporations, it remains an exotic subject for media coverage. Citing a 2006 *BusinessWeek* article, "The Science of Desire" (Ante 2006), for which Suchman herself was approached as an anthropologist who worked for Xerox, she describes the corporate perception of ethnographers in contrast to other types of consumer marketing researchers. The role that anthropologists fill better than other social scientists, she postulates, is presumably "making the familiar strange"—that is, transforming what is otherwise mundane—such as middle-class homes, supermarket trips, cooking habits, breakfast routines—into material that is exotic and therefore of elevated interest to corporations, if only by the presence of anthropologists studying them. Anthropologists' chief role as investigators *of* the other is then juxtaposed with the anthropologist's own position in business settings *as* the other (2007: 6).[2] There is work to be done for anthropology in business settings to be seen as more practical and less exotic. We surmise that this state of affairs is partly the unfortunate result of anthropology still considered and practiced as ancillary to the core functions of business.[3] We suggest several possible trajectories below that may help ameliorate this condition.

As we have argued, anthropology in the corporate setting needs to move beyond the singular and limited use of ethnography as a methodology. This will lead to richer contributions for anthropologists in corporations who are skilled at understanding and integrating the larger impact of culture on a range of business practices. Expanding upon McCracken (2009), more positions for anthropologists need to be layered within corporations—for example, cultural brand managers in addition to, or perhaps rather than, a single elevated chief culture officer (CCO). We laud McCracken's passion for corporate embrace of senior-level chief cultural officers and envision such executives as valued strategic partners with the rising tide of global chief marketing officers (Neff 2011). However, we believe that more industry jobs will be available to professionally trained anthropologists and others with an anthropological sensibility in middle management. Indeed, some of these anthropologists may advance to the privileged position of CCO; we feel it will be highly beneficial and more likely to create an impact on business if the ranks of manufacturers, advertising agencies, marketing research firms, and design companies are populated with anthropologists occupying a wide range of management levels. Responsibilities of such executives could entail gaining a deeper understanding of their company's target consumers, emerging cultural trends and their impact on brands and targets, and linking these trends to societal beliefs and values that affect consumption. Internal corporate anthropologists would also contribute to understanding that enhances internal corporate operations, much as Elizabeth Briody did for nearly twenty-five years at General Motors. A path that anthropologists in advertising specifically and in business more broadly might take is one that situates them not so much as exotic outsiders who work *for* corporations, but rather as insiders who understand the business goals of an organization *from within* and who contribute actively to the crafting and managing of business strategies. In this role, anthropologists would become tightly woven into the corporate fabric and would ultimately have more direct management responsibility as opposed to the supportive research and advisory roles that anthropologists now usually play.

We anticipate a two-way bridge across what now exists largely as insular worlds separating those who practice anthropology in advertising and marketing research (and other businesses, too) and academics who study consumers and consumption.

We have advocated in our essays for more engaged conversation between academic and business understandings of consumption and consumers. Now is a moment to merge and coalesce mutual interests and understandings of the same subject matter. This conversation will be abetted by a greater attention to theory in business anthropology studies, as advocated by Maryann McCabe (2011). Even as academic literature in recent years has shifted to include discussions on the nature of capitalism, consumption, and globalizing forces—topical to both anthropological practitioners and academics—more often than not, academic anthropology stands apart, failing to acknowledge the work and ideas of practicing anthropologists and vice versa. We advocate for more anthropologists in business, including advertising and marketing, to fill the ranks in conference meetings, thus increasing cross-channel discussions. We are encouraged by the 2011 American Anthropological Association (AAA) conference proceedings that included seminars on marketing or advertising. At the same time, we have learned from several practicing anthropologists who are loath to attend AAA and similar academic meetings because they have had painful experiences of unfairly critical attitudes toward their business work. With the rise of the Ethnographic Praxis in Industry Conference (EPIC), the continuing efforts of the Society for Applied Anthropology, and other conference proceedings as well as two new business anthropology journals, we see greater receptivity occurring before our eyes. We urge all parties to reach a higher level of mutual intelligibility and for greater communication and acceptance between academic and practice discussions on anthropology, consumption, and consumer research. This will increase knowledge exchange between academic and practice vocations and lead to career advancement for new MAs and PhDs. Careers that cross-pollinate academia and business are desirable; they should not be mutually exclusive professions.

We have recommended that business studies become more interdisciplinary with greater interaction among anthropology, psychology, and other fields. In 2011, Malefyt attended an academic conference at the Copenhagen Business School that focused on the analysis of creativity in advertising, fiction writing, publishing, fashion design, and orchestral music production. These sessions were inspirational in that they included anthropologists, psychologists, and sociologists as well as fashion designers, musicologists, and musicians to share, discuss, and debate creativity from a multitude of perspectives. This conference would have been far less edifying from a solely anthropological viewpoint. Other conference proceedings, such as EPIC, contribute to cross-pollination with the inclusion of corporate anthropologists from marketing, advertising, and media along with journalists, creative designers, and researchers from design firms. Success in marketing and advertising *requires* that anthropologists move among disciplines, incorporating psychological and philosophical perspectives with anthropological ones. Cultural analysis in business is already infused with concepts of the person, discussions on emotions of individuals, what motivates the self, and other psychological constructs. We do not eschew these perspectives but rather incorporate them with hybrid cultural models of human behavior and meaning making to bring our clients a more complete understanding of their consumers.

We envision a major opportunity for business anthropology at the pedagogical level. We are sometimes inspired and at other times discouraged by the number of e-mails and phone calls that we receive from recently degreed anthropologists inquiring how they can begin a career in advertising or consumer marketing. We try to help them with advice and networking. However, we believe that universities can and should do more to train anthropologists for work in the corporate world. We are clearly champions of more master's- and PhD-level anthropologists engaging in business, especially in creative industries. To prepare these anthropologists for business, academic institutions should develop programs that educate them. More anthropology departments should partner with business schools and offer joint MA/MBA and PhD/MBA degrees. Pioneers in these cross-pollinating efforts include Marietta Baba at Michigan State University, William O. Beeman at the University of Minnesota, Brian Moeran at the University of Copenhagen Business School, Allen Batteau at Wayne State University, John Sherry at the University of Notre Dame, and Barbara Olsen at the State University of New York College at Old Westbury, among others. A few institutions, such as the University of Pennsylvania's Wharton School of Business, have implemented interactive programs with industry. Wharton's Consumer Analytics Initiative, in particular, integrates industry's desire for understanding consumer behavior with various academic approaches. The University of Southern Denmark has launched an undergraduate major in Management Anthropology.

We imagine future programs will set a new standard of academic excellence for business preparation of students in the emerging fields of culture, commerce, and consumerism. These curricula would not only prepare anthropologists for business careers but also provide business students perspectives to better deal with cultural complexities, today and tomorrow. Programs would incorporate theoretical approaches and applied perspectives. Coursework would include offerings from a wide range of disciplines, such as, but not limited to, American studies, anthropology, culture theory, literature, marketing, statistics, media, communications and journalism, philosophy, psychology, semiotics/linguistics, and sociology. Cooperative arrangements with advertising agencies and marketing research firms would educate students on the ways that anthropology contributes to these enterprises. In these settings, the uses of ethnography and cultural theory would be demonstrated and expanded upon. Internships would allow for real-world immersion in the businesses that are receptive to anthropological ideas. These programs would be especially valuable for anthropologists who need to learn about contributing disciplines.

We also feel that anthropologists who enter the advertising and marketing industries should assume responsibility for educating themselves in the concrete functions and goals of the businesses they serve. To contribute holistically, anthropologists employed by advertising agencies and marketing firms should not restrict themselves to anthropological analysis; they should actively seek to understand the roles and responsibilities of their subordinates, peers, and superiors in other domains. They should grasp corporate marketplace agendas and financial goals, know the competition, and become proficient in the language of business. They should be cognizant of corporate philosophies and comprehend how their particular assignments impact and are impacted by the larger business enterprise. Anthropologists who work in advertising, for example, should not only know the components of a creative brief, they should also be skilled in crafting one and be aware of where the brand they champion stands in the marketplace relative to other brands and how their client plans to build market share. Through these efforts, anthropologists will connect research and insights more effectively with the aims of their advertising and marketing partners. Equally important, they will maximize their value.

As anthropologists become enmeshed in the advertising business, we also encourage them to study the meaning of creativity and the process of innovation. Increasingly, advertising, marketing, organizational management, and education recognize creativity as instrumental in producing thought leadership in a knowledge-based economy. As we and others have noted, the core product of advertising agencies is creativity that helps sell products and services (Callahan and Stack 2007: 270). The commercial ends of these enterprises and the people involved in carrying out research, marketing, account management, and the creative work itself shape the type of discourses, ideologies, and practices that circulate in popular culture. Now is a moment for greater understanding of the social processes involved in producing creativity, not only from creative types—advertising copywriters and art directors—but also from within the structures and networks of people that make it happen in organizations. Scholars are beginning to unpack popular, but often incorrect, beliefs about the process of creativity, such as the image of the singular creative spark, the linear path to innovation, and the lone genius at work without social contact (Sawyer 2007). These misconceptions inhibit the potential for democratic creative growth in the advertising industry and beyond. Further study is needed to understand how creativity in organizations is distributed and embedded in social groups, emergent in collaborative networks, and channeled in organizations by generative practices, distributions across people, and by utilizing specific tools and proper environments (Csikszentmihalyi 1988, 1990a; Ingold and Hallam 2007; Sawyer and DeZutter 2009). Continued investigation on the ways that people and their ideas work together to produce creativity can augment many types of industries that require innovation to compete as well as benefit creative enterprises. More anthropologists working in advertising and marketing will help contribute toward these ends.

It is heartening to read that a growing body of practicing anthropologists, especially those concerned with engaging scholarship, is moving in the direction of collaboration, advocacy, and activism. In the June 2011 issue of the *American Anthropologist* we read that anthropological advocates continue to confront the complexities of cultural diversity, social justice, and racial (in)equality in interdisciplinary discourses on the environment, culture, climate change, and in archaeology and museum studies enlightening the public on how visions of heritage and the past shape contemporary life (Mullins 2011: 235). We hope that such collaboration and activism continues apace with those anthropologists interested in the advertising and marketing industries. Indeed, we have stressed throughout this volume that anthropology has already adapted to the business world, at least in terms of the ways it embraces a business-friendly methodological approach in ethnography. Anthropology as an interdisciplinary discipline, writes Feinberg (2009), adapts by its very nature. Feinberg anticipates that the future of anthropology will continue its "cross-disciplinary hybridization," a tendency, he notes, that marks the history of some of anthropology's greatest contributors. Boas trained in physics and geography; Malinowski studied math and physics; Firth earned an MA in economics; Mead majored as an undergraduate in English and psychology; Geertz studied philosophy (Feinberg 2009: 4). Anthropology adapts as a social science, a discipline of humanism, and as a form of social critique. We assert, by the same token, that anthropology adapts to advertising and marketing in ways that potentially demonstrate its greater usefulness as a global business model and as a way of mediating culture between producers and consumers. At the same time, though, we agree with DiFruscia's (2011) admonition that "Anthropology bears the marks of rough handling at being so summarily morphed into a participant in corporate expansion" (2011: 43). That said, anthropology has already been appropriated by business, whether anthropologists like it or not.

This volume has placed our years of practice within a critical framework of broader political, ethical, and socioeconomic reflection, relating the ways in which we have drawn from anthropological theory and applied it to our work in advertising and marketing. Our aim has been to discuss and stimulate debate on the practical and theoretical issues of practicing anthropology that we face every day. In the coming years, anthropologists may distinguish themselves by elevating the discipline to new levels of business engagement and commitment to industry practices. We hope we will have contributed along these lines. Our purpose has been to inform and inspire our current and future colleagues in the multiple ways that anthropology currently and will continue to contribute to knowledge making, creative production, and the success of commercial enterprises.

Notes

Preface

1. The governor of Florida, Rick Scott, said publicly in the fall of 2011 that liberal arts programs in his state's public colleges should receive far less funding than programs in science, math, and technology that lead directly to corporate jobs. He commented on anthropology in particular, saying in a talk radio interview, "We don't need a lot more anthropologists in the state."

Chapter 1: Anthropologists In and Out of Advertising

1. PhD production is based on 2006 National Science Foundation data; the academic job opportunities percentage was derived by Baba from the Anthropology Newsletter.

Chapter 2: Advertising Meetings and Client Relationships

1. Sherry (2005: 72–74) discusses liminality from a different, and extremely interesting, perspective.

Chapter 3: Rituals of Creativity in Advertising Agencies

1. David Parkin (1978) also argues that culture is a system of communication in which lexical categories persist as custom, even as the content of particular words change. Words may be given new meaning when redefined by group and individual use. However, to accommodate change, terms must be ambivalent, as is the case, we argue, with brands. See Moeran (1984) for an insightful discussion of this process in Japanese culture.
2. In the past fifty years, the outward appearances of account managers and creative executives have become more similar due to the pervasive influence of casual dress codes throughout all businesses. Still, the philosophical and operational differences remain.

Chapter 4: Fieldwork in Advertising Research

1. For a further discussion on how brands create interaction and engagement between consumers and companies, see Arvidsson (2006), Lury (2004), and Malefyt (2009).

Chapter 5: Advertising Emotions

1. See Malefyt's "Models, Metaphors and Client Relations" (2003) for a discussion on how consumer and brand models align to create affinity between the client and agency.
2. A touch point (itself a tactile term) is considered any tangible contact a consumer makes with a brand as well as intangible thoughts, feelings, and brand associations. QSRweb.com uses six similar touch points to describe optimal drive-through service for quick-service restaurants.
3. Undisclosed client branding document, 2002.

Chapter 6: Creativity, Person, and Place

1. The notion of "release" is similar to the psychological idea of "incubation," in which, after failed conscious efforts to arrive at creative solutions, ideas gestate unconsciously on their own (O'Looney et al. 1989: 314).
2. Similarly, Kasper Tang Vangkilde (2011) discusses the practice among fashion designers of going on inspiration trips to counteract and frame those instances in their work when they seem to have become "lost in the existing perspective of a brand."

Chapter 7: Advertising, Automobiles, and the Branding of Luxury

1. The meaning of luxury for respondents fits with their idea of life as a process of becoming with new experiences, exploration, and inner growth. Like the process of becoming, luxury was considered something internal, intuitive, and engaging. Shown mock-ups of the new Cadillac automobiles, respondents could begin to imagine interacting with the expression of luxury in car features. This reflected a generational shift in the meaning of luxury from elitism and outward badging to a sense of being drawn inward and connecting with the self. If their grandparent's Cadillac was an external status symbol, the new Cadillac would create an internal experience.
2. We acknowledge The Curious Company, and especially its founder, Pam Scott, for their efforts and ethnographic help in later studies.

3. We also acknowledge Practica Group, LLC, and especially Rita Denny for collaborative work on the initial Infiniti research and for helpful comments on earlier drafts of this essay.

4. See, for example, Aaker's (1996) popular work on brands, Aaker and Joachimsthaler's (2000) book on brand leadership, and Malefyt's (2009) discussion on branding in consumer ethnography.

5. For discussions on the inside workings of advertising agencies, see Malefyt and Moeran (2003a), Moeran (1996), as well as other chapters in this volume

6. We are indebted to theoretical work in anthropology on the concept of representation. Among anthropologists, concern with representation initially developed in the academy with feminist scholars and their interest in reflecting the female as well as the male voice in ethnographic encounters (Behar and Gordon 1995; Weiner 1976). In the postcolonial environment, concern with representation broadened to include larger issues of power and the historical context (Clifford and Marcus 1986). Recent emphasis in academic writing has been placed on representing immigrant populations, minority groups, and poor and oppressed peoples (Farmer 2003).

7. The belief among respondents that anyone can dream outside the box, work hard, and succeed follows the notion of the American dream in popular culture. Their belief, ignoring the reality of structural constraints on individuals in U.S. society, may constitute a rationale for their higher class position or perhaps a wish that the possibility of achieving the dream were a reality for all.

Chapter 8: Business Anthropology Beyond Ethnography

1. Significant ethnographic projects in business began during the 1980s. Bill Abrams, an advertising creative director, started Housecalls in 1983, which uses video recording as an observational technique (Abrams 2000). Housecalls does not incorporate anthropological theory, and Abrams did not realize when he started the company that he was engaging in ethnography (quoted in Wasserman 2003: 22). Anthropologist Steve Barnett was an early champion of business ethnography (Louis 1985). Baba comments that

> Barnett invented what were initially unorthodox ways of observing consumers and translating their behavior patterns for applications in marketing and advertising campaigns for major clients such as Campbell Soup, Procter & Gamble, Royal Dutch Shell, and Union Carbide. For example, in the early days Barnett invented the "unfocus" group, in which a cross-section of a firm's market is placed in a video observation room with a collection of objects and then given a (usually bogus) task of some sort; e.g., write a booklet for middle school students describing how electricity is generated, or build a "safe" nuclear reactor using kitchen gadgets. Analysis of the videotape rendered ideas to be turned into advertising images; e.g., a campaign to

raise electricity rates drew on consumers' lack of knowledge on the subject, or a campaign to gain approval for a new nuclear energy plant was based on consumers' desire to "lock" any radiation inside. (Baba 2006: 42–43)

We would argue that these sessions were, in fact, focus groups, but they were informed by an anthropologist's expertise. By terming these sessions "unfocus groups," Barnett was doing savvy marketing.

2. Marketing research companies with anthropologists include, for example, The Practica Group, Context, Research International, and Cheskin, along with Morais's company, Weinman Schnee Morais, among many others. Several corporations, advertising agencies, and design firms have anthropologists on staff, again, for example, Intel, BBDO, and Ogilvy and Mather. For many years, General Motors had a significant commitment to anthropology, as exemplified by Elizabeth Briody (Fiske 2007).

3. Coincidentally, in the decades during which business adopted ethnography, academic ethnography experienced substantial changes in its way of representing culture such as diary (Taussig 2003), novel (Hecht 2006), authentic native voice (Stewart 1996), and empathetic autobiographical engagement (Behar 1996). In recent years, ethnography has been applied to commerce (e.g., Ho 2009; Horst and Miller 2006; Kelty 2008) in addition to studies of advertising agencies, design companies, and manufacturing corporations that have been discussed elsewhere in this volume.

4. Focus group facilities host both focus groups and one-on-one interviews. The argument for the application of anthropological ideas and techniques applies to any kind of session that is held in a focus group facility. We use the phrase "focus room" to encompass interview sessions that may be held as groups or one-on-one interviews.

5. The term *moderator* will be used interchangeably with *interviewer* from this point forward.

6. Focus groups are valuable as a means to prescreen respondents for ethnographic encounters. Morais's firm has used focus groups to select a smaller segment of respondents for ethnographic studies on cereals, industrial lubricants, and household cleaning products, for example.

7. It is fair to mention at this juncture that business ethnography is, after all, a distant cousin to ethnography as practiced by academic anthropologists. In business projects, ethnographic encounters typically last a few hours; the business ethnographer cannot be as fully immersed in the lives of the subjects as the ethnographer who spends a year or more in the field. Naturalistic settings in business ethnography add dimension, but deep contextual cultural observation and understanding is limited by the time spent with respondents.

8. McCracken rightly suggests that attention to culture should be a systematic, sustained, corporate-sponsored enterprise that can be based on secondary re-

sources such as magazines, online publications, blogs, music, television, and other cultural products as well as primary studies (McCracken 2009: 193–204; cf. his blog, www.cultureby.com). He avers that cultural analysis is a rebirth of "armchair anthropology" (2009: 195). Morais suggests the term "culturalgraphics" for marketing-driven cultural analysis. Culturalgraphics is another level of analysis in addition to demographics and psychographics (Morais 2010). It does not carry the negative connotation of armchair anthropology.

Chapter 9: Ethics in Advertising

1. Sunderland and Denny observe, "The ingoing assumption about applied work was also that it was less 'pure' and always a little compromised. Moreover, if 'applied' in general was 'dirty,' consumer research or 'marketing' was filthy—wickedly so, in fact" (Sunderland and Denny 2007: 31). They recount a story about soliciting help from graduate students for research on fast food and discovering a student-to-student e-mail during the process with the subject heading, "Selling yourself to the devil for a few days." Sunderland and Denny focus here not on the ethics of conducting marketing research on fast food but rather the clients' personal characteristics as nice, intelligent people, and they defend marketing anthropology for its ability to engage "the analytic imagination" (2007: 31–32). Sunderland and Denny do address ethics later in their book, as we will discuss shortly. A colleague of Malefyt's submitted a paper for peer review at a medical anthropology journal and was chastised for engaging in the subject of her study on behalf of a multinational drug company and for paying her informants, which is a standard practice in marketing research.

2. Ben & Jerry's donates a percentage of pretax profits to support creative problem solving and hopefulness relating to children and families, disadvantaged groups, and the environment. The Body Shop donates a percentage of profits each year to animal-rights groups, homeless shelters, Amnesty International, Save the Rainforest, and other groups (Kotler and Anderson 2004: 627).

3. They spoof this claim by depicting an advertisement with a woman shaving, which is obviously meant to be taken as a joke, proof that advertising cannot get consumers to buy goods that are not relevant to them.

4. Cook (2011) offers a similar argument on the question of children's abilities to make decisions regarding marketing.

5. See Malefyt and Moeran (2003b: 19–20) for a related discussion on compensating informants in advertising research and Tian, Lillis, and Van Marrewijk (2010: 246–48) for a summary of ethical concerns in ethnography.

6. Ironically, writes Bowlby, the book itself became a model of and for subversive behavior of marketing.

7. Most quantitative advertising testing contains a purchase intent question, and consumers choose from the following after viewing the advertising: definitely would buy; probably would buy; might or might not buy; probably would not buy; definitely would not buy.

8. We contend academic writing take this approach as well. It claims a position and builds a persuasive case around it, often challenging other articles and authors or building upon them with a unique perspective.

9. This campaign aired for several years but was subsequently replaced.

10. The particular soft drink account has since shifted to another Omnicom agency due to political issues unrelated to the brand's success. BBDO still retains many other brands of the global beverage company.

11. The Society for Applied Anthropology and the National Association for the Practice of Anthropology also offer guidelines. These statements are variations on the AAA code. As of this writing, the AAA Code of Ethics was under revision.

Chapter 10: Hybrid Research Methodologies and Business Success

1. This chapter focuses on integrating psychological concepts and methods with anthropological approaches. Our work often adapts ideas and methods from sociology, literary analysis, and other disciplines in addition to psychology.

Chapter 11: The Future of Advertising Anthropology

1. Jeremy Sabloff (2011) examines the absence of anthropologists in the role of public intellectuals and suggests ways for anthropologists to address this opportunity.

2. The same 2006 *BusinessWeek* article that Suchman critiques also features a section on Malefyt. Ironically, exemplifying Suchman's remark that business typically regards anthropology as exotic, the photographer for the photo shoot instructed Malefyt to don a fedora and leather jacket like "Indiana Jones" and pose on the steps of Columbia University's Low Library for visual effect.

3. This issue stems from both anthropologists' unique cultural approach and being outside vendors. Working inside an advertising agency or a corporation would integrate and make these positions familiar.

References

Aaker, D. (1996), *Building Strong Brands*, New York: Free Press.

Aaker, D., and Joachimsthaler, E. (2000), *Brand Leadership*, New York: Free Press.

Abrams, B. (2000), *The Observational Research Handbook*, Chicago: NTC Books/ American Marketing Association.

American Anthropological Association (2009), "Code of Ethics of the American Anthropological Association," www.aaanet.org/issues/policy-advocacy/upload/ AAA-Ethics-Code-2009.pdf.

Amin, A., and Thrift, N. (eds.) (2004), *The Blackwell Cultural Economy Reader*, Malden, MA: Blackwell.

Anderson, B. (1992), *Imagined Communities: Reflections on the Origin and Spread of Nationalism*, New York: Verso.

Anderson, K. (2009), "Ethnographic Research: A Key to Strategy," *Harvard Business Review*, 87/3: 24.

Anderson, K., and de Paula, R. (2006), "We We We All the Way Home: The 'We' Affect in Transitional Spaces," in *EPIC Conference Proceedings*, September 24–26, Portland, Oregon: 62–75.

Anderson, K., and McClard, A. (2008), "Focus on Facebook: Who Are We Anyway?" *Anthropology News*, 49/3: 10, 12.

Ante, S. E. (2006), "The Science of Desire," *BusinessWeek*, June 6: 99–106.

Anthes, E. (2009), "How Room Designs Affect Your Work and Mood," *Scientific American Mind*, April 22.

Appadurai, A. (ed.) (1986), *The Social Life of Things: Commodities in Cultural Perspective*, Cambridge, UK: Cambridge University Press.

Appadurai, A. (ed.) (1996), *Modernity at Large: Cultural Dimensions of Globalization*, Minneapolis: University of Minnesota Press.

Arvidsson, A. (2006), *Brands: Meaning and Value in Media Culture*, London: Routledge.

Augé, M. (1995), *Non-Places: Introduction to an Anthropology of Supermodernity*, London: Verso.

Baba, M. (2006), "Anthropology and Business," in H. J. Birx (ed.), *Encyclopedia of Anthropology*, Thousand Oaks, CA: Sage.

Baba, M. (2009), "Disciplinary-Professional Relations in an Era of Anthropological Engagement," *Human Organization*, 68/4: 380–91.

Bachelard, G. ([1958] 1994), *The Poetics of Space*, Boston: Beacon Press.

Barnouw, V. (1973), *Culture and Personality*, rev. ed., Homewood, IL: Dorsey Press.

Basso, K. H. (1988), "Speaking with Names: Language and Landscape among Western Apache," *Cultural Anthropology*, 3/2: 99–130.

Basso, K. H. (1996), "Wisdom Sits in Places: Notes on a Western Apache Landscape," in S. Feld and K. Basso (eds.), *Senses of Place*, Santa Fe, NM: School of American Research Press.

Baudrillard, J. (1994), *Simulacra and Simulation*, Ann Arbor: University of Michigan Press.

Beck, U. (1994), "The Reinvention of Politics: Towards a Theory of Reflexive Modernization," in U. Beck, A. Giddens, and S. Lash (eds.), *Reflective Modernization: Politics, Tradition and Aesthetics in the Modern Social Order*, Stanford, CA: Stanford University Press.

Beck, U., Giddens, A., and Lash, S. (eds.) (1994), *Reflective Modernization: Politics, Tradition and Aesthetics in the Modern Social Order*, Stanford, CA: Stanford University Press.

Beebe, B. (2004), "The Semiotic Analysis of Trademark Law," *UCLA Law Review*, 51/3: 621–704.

Beeman, W. O. (1986), "Freedom to Choose: Symbols and Values in American Advertising," in H. Varenne (ed.), *Symbolizing America*, Lincoln: University of Nebraska Press.

Beeman, W. O. (2007), "The Performance Hypothesis: Practicing Emotions in Protected Frames," in H. Wulff (ed.), *The Emotions: A Cultural Reader*, Oxford, UK: Berg.

Behar, R. (1996), *The Vulnerable Observer: Anthropology That Breaks Your Heart*, Boston: Beacon Press.

Behar, R., and Gordon, D. A. (eds.) (1995), *Women Writing Culture*, Berkeley: University of California Press.

Belk, R. W. (1988), "Possessions and the Extended Self," *Journal of Consumer Research*, 15: 139–68.

Belson, K. (2011), "Soccer Sets Portland Abuzz (a Chain Saw Helps)," *New York Times*, June 24: A1, B12.

Beltramini, R. F. (ed.) (2011), "Special Section: Advertising Ethics," *Journal of Advertising Research*, 51/3.

Benedict, R. (1934), *Patterns of Culture*, New York: Houghton Mifflin.

Berger, J. (1972), *Ways of Seeing*, London: British Broadcasting Corporation.

Bishop, S. R., Shapiro, L. M., and Carlson, S. (2004), "Mindfulness: A Proposed Operational Definition," *Clinical Psychology: Science and Practice*, 11/3: 230–41.

Bock, P. K. (1980), *Continuities in Psychological Anthropology*, San Francisco: W. H. Freeman.

Boden, M. (1990), *The Creative Mind: Myths and Mechanisms*, London: Weidenfeld and Nicholson.

Boden, M. (2004), *The Creative Mind: Myths and Mechanisms*, 2nd ed., London: Routledge.

Bogusky, A. (2010), "The First Cannes Lion for Not Advertising at All by Alex Bogusky," www.litmanlive.co.uk/blog/2010/06/the-first-cannes-lion-for-not-advertising-at-all-by-alex-bogusky/.

Boorstin, D. J. (1965), *The Americans: The National Experience*, New York: Random House.

Bourdieu, P. (1993), *The Field of Cultural Production*, Cambridge, UK: Polity.

Bowlby, R. (1985), *Just Looking: Consumer Culture in Dreiser, Gissing and Zola*, New York: Methuen.

Bowlby, R. (2001), *Carried Away: The Invention of Modern Shopping*, New York: Columbia University Press.

Brooks, D. (2011), "The New Humanism," *New York Times*, March 7, www.nytimes.com/2011/03/08/opinion/08brooks.html?_r=1.

Bulik, B. S. (2010), "Marketer of the Decade: Apple," *Advertising Age*, October 18, http://adage.com/article/special-report-marketer-of-the-year-2010/marketer-decade-apple/146492/.

Burnett, L. (1971), *A Tribute to Leo Burnett: Through a Selection of the Inspiring Words That He Wrote or Spoke*, Chicago: Leo Burnett.

Callahan, R., and Stack, T. (2007), "Creativity in Advertising, Fiction and Ethnography," in E. Hallam and T. Ingold (eds.), *Creativity and Cultural Improvisation*, Oxford, UK: Berg.

Callon, M., Meadel, C., and Rabeharosoa, V. (2002), "The Economy of Qualities," *Economy and Society*, 31/2: 194–217.

Casey, E. (1996), "How to Get from Space to Place in a Fairly Short Stretch of Time: Phenomenological Prologomena," in S. Feld and K. Basso (eds.), *Senses of Place*, Santa Fe, NM: School of American Research Press.

Cassell, J., and Jacobs, S. E. (eds.) (1987), *Handbook on Ethical Issues in Anthropology*, Washington, DC: American Anthropological Association.

Cefkin, M. (ed.) (2009), *Ethnography and the Corporate Encounter: Reflections on Research in and of Corporations*, New York: Berghahn Books.

Certeau, M. de (1988), *The Practice of Everyday Life*, Berkeley: University of California Press.

Clifford, J. (1988), *The Predicament of Culture*, Cambridge, MA: Harvard University Press.

Clifford, J. (1997), *Routes: Travel and Translation in the Late Twentieth Century*, Cambridge, MA: Harvard University Press.

Clifford, J., and Marcus, G. (1986), *Writing Culture*, Berkeley: University of California Press.

Cole, M., and Scribner, S. (1974), *Culture and Thought*, New York: John Wiley.

Cook, D. T. (2011), "Commercial Epistemologies of Childhood: 'Fun' and the Leveraging of Children's Subjectivities and Desires," in D. Zwick and J. Cayla (eds.),

Inside Marketing: Practices, Ideologies, Devices, Oxford, UK: Oxford University Press.

Couvson, K. (2009), "China and the 'Creative' Idiom: A Study of an Advertising Agency in Beijing," unpublished dissertation, Cornell University, Ithaca, New York.

Csikszentmihalyi, M. (1988), "Society, Culture and Person: A Systems View of Creativity," in R. J. Sternberg (ed.), *The Nature of Creativity*, New York: Cambridge University Press.

Csikszentmihalyi, M. (1990a), "The Domain of Creativity," in M. A. Runco and R. S. Albert (eds.), *Theories of Creativity*, Newbery Park, CA: Sage.

Csikszentmihalyi, M. (1990b), *Flow: The Psychology of Optimal Experience*, New York: Hill and Wang.

Csikszentmihalyi, M., and Rochberg-Halton, E. (1981), *The Meaning of Things: Domestic Symbols and the Self*, New York: Cambridge University Press.

D'Andrade, R. G. (1995), *The Development of Cognitive Anthropology*, Cambridge, UK: Cambridge University Press.

D'Andrade, R. G. (2008), *A Study of Cultural Values*, New York: Palgrave Macmillan.

Davidson, M. (1992), *The Consumerist Manifesto*, London: Routledge.

Davila, A. (2001), *Latinos, Inc.: The Marketing and Making of a People*, Berkeley: University of California Press.

Denny, R. (1999), "Consuming Values: The Culture of Clients, Researchers and Consumers," in *The Race for Innovation*, Amsterdam: ESOMAR.

Denny, R., and Sunderland, P. (2008), "Engaging Ethnography's Ethnographic Muscle," *QRCA Views*, 7/1: 12–17.

Desjarlais, R. (1992), *Body and Emotion: The Aesthetics of Illness and Healing in the Nepal Himalayas*, Philadelphia: University of Pennsylvania Press.

Dewalt, K., and Dewalt, B. (2000), "Participant Observation," in H. R. Bernard (ed.), *Handbook of Methods in Cultural Anthropology*, Walnut Creek, CA: Altamira.

DiFruscia, K. T. (2011), "Review of *Ethnography and the Corporate Encounter: Reflections on Research in and of Corporations*," *Anthropology of Work Review*, 32/1: 41–43.

Douglas, M. (1966), *Purity and Danger: An Analysis of the Concepts of Pollution and Taboo*, London: Routledge.

Douglas, M., and Isherwood, B. (1979), *The World of Goods: Towards an Anthropology of Consumption*, London: Routledge.

Downey, G., and Fisher, M. (2006), "Introduction: The Anthropology of Capital and the Frontiers of Ethnography," in M. Fisher and G. Downey (eds.), *Frontiers of Capital: Ethnographic Reflections on the New Economy*, Durham, NC: Duke University Press.

Dreyfus, H., and Kelly, S. D. (2011), *All Things Shining: Reading the Western Classics to Find Meaning in a Secular Age*, New York: Free Press.

Drumwright, M. E., and Murphy, P. E. (2009), "The Current State of Advertising Ethics," *Journal of Advertising*, 38/1: 83–107.

Durkheim, E. ([1915] 1965), *The Elementary Forms of Religious Life*, New York: Free Press.

Dusenberry, P. (2005), *Then We Set His Hair on Fire: Insights and Accidents from a Hall-of-Fame Career in Advertising*, New York: Portfolio.

Dyk, W. ([1938] 1967), *Son of Old Man Hat: A Navajo Autobiography*, Lincoln: University of Nebraska.

Editorial (2010), "The Disposable Academic: Why Doing a Ph.D. Is Often a Waste of Time," *The Economist*, December 18: 156–58.

Elliott, S. (2005), "In an Industry That Has Historically Snubbed Research on Marketing, the Field Is Suddenly in Vogue," *New York Times*, April 18: C10.

Elliott, S. (2011), "TV Networks Expect a Jump in Spending on Commercials," *New York Times*, May 15, www.nytimes.com/2011/05/16/business/media/16adco.html.

Farmer, P. (2003), *Pathologies of Power: Health, Human Rights and the New War on the Poor*, Berkeley: University of California Press.

Farrell, M. P. (2001), *Collaborative Circles: Friendship Dynamics and Creative Work*, Chicago: University of Chicago Press.

Feinberg, R. (2009), "Bridging Science and Humanism: Thoughts on the Future of Anthropology," *Anthropology News*, 50/9: 4, 8.

Feit, J. (2007), "Neuromarketing and Diversity Go Hand-in-Hand," *Advertising Age*, November 2, http://adage.com/article/the-big-tent/neuromarketing-diversity-hand-hand/121687/.

Feld, S. (1982), *Sound and Sentiment: Birds, Weeping, Poetics, and Song in Kaluli Expression*, Philadelphia: University of Pennsylvania Press.

Feld, S. (1996), "Waterfalls of Song: An Acoustemology of Place in Bosavi, Papua New Guinea," in S. Feld and K. Basso (eds.), *Senses of Place*, Santa Fe, NM: School of American Research Press.

Fernandez, J. (1986), *Persuasions and Performances: The Play of Tropes in Culture*, Bloomington: Indiana University Press.

Fiasco, L. (2011), "Project: First Drafts," recorded by Alex Hoyt, *The Atlantic Magazine*, May 4: 60.

Finke, R. A., Ward, T. B., and Smith, S. M. (1992), *Creative Cognition: Theory, Research and Application*, Boston: MIT Press.

Fisher, M., and Downey, G. (eds.) (2006), *Frontiers of Capital: Ethnographic Reflections on the New Economy*, Durham, NC: Duke University Press.

Fiske, S. (2007), "Improving the Effectiveness of Corporate Culture," *Anthropology News*, May: 44–45.

Frake, J. (1996), "Pleasant Places, Past Times, and Sheltered Identity in Rural East Anglia," in S. Feld and K. Basso (eds.), *Senses of Place*, Santa Fe, NM: School of American Research Press.

Gabbard, G. O. (2005), *Psychodynamic Psychotherapy in Clinical Practice*, Arlington, VA: American Psychiatric Publishing.

Geertz, C. (1973), *The Interpretation of Cultures*, New York: Basic Books.

Geertz, C. ([1983] 2000), *Local Knowledge: Further Essays in Interpretive Anthropology*, New York: Basic Books.

Geertz, C. (1995), "Culture War," *New York Review of Books*, 42/19: 4–6.

Geertz, C. (1996), "Afterword," in S. Feld and K. Basso (eds.), *Senses of Place*, Santa Fe, NM: School of American Research Press.

Geurts, K. L. (2002), *Culture and the Senses: Bodily Ways of Knowing in an African Community*, Berkeley: University of California Press.

Giddens, A. (1990), *The Consequences of Modernity*, Sanford, CA: Stanford University Press.

Giddens, A. (1991), *Modernity and Self-Identity: Self and Society in the Late Modern Age*, Stanford, CA: Stanford University Press.

Gillette, F. (2010), "Don Draper's Revenge," *BusinessWeek*, November 24, www.businessweek.com/print/magazine/content/10_49/b42060742.

Gobe, M. (2001), *Emotional Branding*, New York: Allworth Press.

Goffman, E. (1959), *The Presentation of Self in Everyday Life*, New York: Doubleday.

Goffman, E. (1974), *Frame Analysis*, Cambridge, MA: Harvard University Press.

Goffman, E. (1979), *Gender Advertisements*, Cambridge, MA: Harvard University Press.

Goldman, R., and Papson, S. (1996), *Sign Wars: The Cluttered Landscape of Advertising*, New York: Guilford Press.

Grandclément, C., and Gaglio, G. (2011), "Convoking the Consumer in Person: The Focus Group Effect," in D. Zwick and J. Cayla (eds.), *Inside Marketing: Practices, Ideologies, Devices*, Oxford, UK: Oxford University Press.

Grant, J. (2002), *Understanding and Protecting Agency/Client Relationships*, The Management Series, New York: American Association of Advertising Agencies.

Gray, D. (2003), "Wanted: Chief Ignorance Officer," *Harvard Business Review*, 81/11: 22, 24.

Hackley, C., and Kover, A. J. (2007), "The Trouble with Creatives: Negotiating Creative Identity in Advertising Agencies," *International Journal of Advertising*, 26/1: 63–78.

Hakim, D. (2002), "Cadillac Recasts Itself as a Full-Line Manufacturer," *New York Times*, May 7: C2.

Hallam, E., and Ingold, T. (eds.) (2007), *Creativity and Cultural Improvisation*, Oxford, UK: Berg.

Halliday, J. (2001), "Has Lincoln, Caddy Lux Run Out?" *Advertising Age*, December 31: 4.

Halliday, J. (2002), "Caddy Goes 'Rock and Roll'; Spots Use Led Zeppelin's Classic Tune," *Advertising Age*, February 4: 4.

Hallowell, A. I. ([1955] 1967), *Culture and Experience*, New York: Schocken Books.

Hamilton, J. (2009), "Shifting Towards the Slow Food Way of Life," September 18, www.examiner.com/x-23716-SF-Wellness-Examiner%7Ey2009m9d18-Shifting-toward-the-Slow-Food-way-of-life.

Hammersley, M., and Atkinson, P. (1995), *Ethnography: Principles in Practice*, 2nd ed., London: Routledge.

Harris, M. (1968), *The Rise of Anthropological Theory*, New York: Thomas Y. Crowell.

Harris, M. (1985), *Good to Eat: Riddles of Food and Culture*, Prospect Heights, IL: Waveland Press.

Hausman, C. R. (1979), "Criteria of Creativity," *Philosophy and Phenomenological Research*, 40/2: 237–49.

Hautzinger, S. (2012), "Depending on Context: Counterintuitive Uses of Focus Groups in Mixed-Method Ethnographic Research," *Human Organization*, 71/1: 22–31.

Hecht, T. (2006), *After Life: An Ethnographic Novel*, Durham, NC: Duke University Press.

Heidegger, M. (1977), "Building Dwelling Thinking," in D. Krell (ed.), *Martin Heidegger: Basic Writings*, New York: Harper & Row.

Henry, J. (1963), *Culture against Man*, New York: Random House.

Hill, D. (2003), *Body of Truth*, New York: John Wiley.

Hill, D. (2007), "CMOs, Win Big by Letting Emotions Drive Advertising," *Advertising Age*, August 27, http://adage.com/article/cmo-strategy/cmos-win-big-letting-emotions-drive-advertising/120017/.

Hirschman, E. C. (1989), "Role-Based Models of Advertising Creative and Production," *Journal of Advertising*, 18/4: 42–53.

Ho, K. (2009), *Liquidated: An Ethnography of Wall Street*, Durham, NC: Duke University Press.

Holstein, J., and Gubrium, J. (1995), *The Active Interview*, Thousand Oaks, CA: Sage.

Hopkins, C. C. (1966), *My Life in Advertising and Scientific Advertising*, New York: McGraw-Hill.

Horst, H., and Miller, D. (2006), *The Cell Phone: An Anthropology of Communication*, Oxford, UK: Berg.

Hower, R. (1939), *The History of an Advertising Agency: N.W. Ayer & Son at Work 1869–1939*, Cambridge, MA: Harvard University Press.

Howes, D. (ed.) (2005a), *Empire of the Senses*, Oxford, UK: Berg.

Howes, D. (2005b), "Hyperesthesia, or, the Sensual Logic of Late Capitalism," in D. Howes (ed.), *Empire of the Senses*, Oxford, UK: Berg.

Hsu, F.L.K. (ed.) (1972), *Psychological Anthropology*, Cambridge, UK: Schenkman.

Hughes-Freeland, F. (1998), *Ritual, Performance, Media*, London: Routledge.

Hunt, R. (ed.) (1967), *Personalities and Cultures*, Garden City, NY: Natural History Press.

Inglessis, M. G. (2006), "For Marketers or Scholars?" *Quirk's Marketing Research Review*, December: 58–62.

Ingold, T. (2008), "Bindings against Boundaries: Entanglements of Life in an Open World," *Environment and Planning A*, 40/8: 1796–1810.

Ingold, T., and Hallam, E. (2007), "Creativity and Cultural Improvisation: An Introduction," in E. Hallam and T. Ingold (eds.), *Creativity and Cultural Improvisation*, Oxford, UK: Berg.

Jhally, S. (1987), *The Codes of Advertising*, London: Frances Pinter.

John-Steiner, V. (2000), *Creative Collaboration*, New York: Oxford University Press.

Johnson, S. (2006), "The Rational and Emotional 'Tells' to Get the Most from Agency Presentations," *Product Management Today*, January: 26–27.

Jordan, A. T. (2003), *Business Anthropology*, Prospect Heights, IL: Waveland Press.

Kantar Media Report (2011), "Kantar Media Reports U.S. Advertising Expenditures Increased 6.5 Percent in 2010," March 17, http://kantarmediana.com/print/1063.

Kapferer, J. N. (2004), *The New Strategic Brand Management: Creating and Sustaining Brand Equity Long Term*, London: Kogan Page.

Kardiner, A. (1945), *The Psychological Frontiers of Society*, with the collaboration of Ralph Linton, Cora Du Bois, and James West, New York: Columbia University Press.

Kelty, C. M. (2008), *Two Bites: The Cultural Significance of Free Software*, Durham, NC: Duke University Press.

Kemper, S. (2001), *Buying and Believing: Sri Lankan Advertising and Consumers in a Transnational World*, Chicago: University of Chicago Press.

Kertzer, D. (1988), *Ritual, Politics and Power*, New Haven, CT: Yale University Press.

Kirby, P., and Chesler, M. (2011), *Advertising Agencies: The Cost of Recovery*, January 7, London: Deutsche Bank.

Klein, N. (2000), *No Logo: Taking Aim at the Brand Bullies*, New York: Picador.

Kopytoff, I. (1986), "The Cultural Biography of Things: Commoditization as Process," in A. Appadurai (ed.), *The Social Life of Things: Commodities in Cultural Perspective*, Cambridge, UK: Cambridge University Press.

Kotler, P. (2003), "Brands," in P. Kotler (ed.), *Marketing Insights from A to Z*, New York: John Wiley.

Kotler, P., and Armstrong, G. (1991), *Principles of Marketing*, 5th ed., Englewood Cliffs, NJ: Prentice Hall.

Kotler, P., and Armstrong, G. (2004), *Principles of Marketing*, 10th ed., Englewood Cliffs, NJ: Prentice Hall.

Kover, A. J. (1995), "Copywriters' Implicit Theories of Communication: An Exploration," *Journal of Consumer Research*, 21/4: 596–611.

Kover, A. J., and Goldberg, S. M. (1995), "The Games Copywriters Play: Conflict, Quasi-Control, a New Proposal," *Journal of Advertising Research*, July/August: 52–62.

LaReau, J. (2005), "Who Really Picked Led Zeppelin?" *Automotive News*, July 11: 4.

Lash, S., and Urry, J. (1994), *Economies of Signs and Space*, London: Sage.

Latour, B. (1987), *Science in Action: How to Follow Scientists and Engineers through Society*, Cambridge, MA: Harvard University Press.

Latour, B. (1991), "Technology Is Society Made Durable," in J. Law (ed.), *A Society of Monsters: Essays on Power, Technology, and Domination*, London: Routledge.

Levey, R. (2004), "Emotion Can Make a Difference," *Direct*, March 1: 22.

Levine, R.A. (1973), *Culture, Behavior and Personality*, Chicago: Aldine.

Levine, R.A. (ed.) (1974), *Culture and Personality*, Chicago: Aldine.

Leymore, V.L. (1975), *Hidden Myth: Structure and Symbolism in Advertising*, New York: Basic Books.

Liep, J. (2001), *Locating Cultural Creativity*, London: Pluto Press.

Louis J.C. (1985), "It's Anthropological: Research Takes a 'Cultural' Bent," *Advertising Age*, January 14: 3–31.

Lowe, G.E. (1966), "The Camelot Affair," *Bulletin of the Atomic Scientists*, May: 44–48.

Lury, C. (2004), *Brands: The Logos of the Global Economy*, London: Routledge.

Lutz, C. (1988), *Unnatural Emotions*, Chicago: University of Chicago Press.

Malefyt, T. de Waal (2003), "Models, Metaphors and Client Relations," in T. de Waal Malefyt and B. Moeran (eds.), *Advertising Cultures*, Oxford, UK: Berg.

Malefyt, T. de Waal (2006), "The Privatization of Consumption: Marketing Media through Sensory Modalities," in J. Sinclair and C. Spurgeon (eds.), *Media International Australia, Culture and Policy* (theme issue on "Advertising and the Media: 30th Anniversary"), 119: 85–98.

Malefyt, T. de Waal (2008a), "Brand," in M. Erlhoff and T. Marshall (eds.), *Design Dictionary*, Basel, Switzerland: Birkhauser.

Malefyt, T. de Waal (2008b), "Consumption," in M. Erlhoff and T. Marshall (eds.), *Design Dictionary*, Basel, Switzerland: Birkhauser.

Malefyt, T. de Waal (2009), "Understanding the Rise of Consumer Ethnography: Branding Techno-methodologies in the New Economy," *American Anthropologist*, 111/2: 201–10.

Malefyt, T. de Waal, and Moeran, B. (eds.) (2003a), *Advertising Cultures*, Oxford, UK: Berg.

Malefyt, T. de Waal, and Moeran, B. (2003b), "Introduction: Advertising, Ethnography and Anthropology," in T. de Waal Malefyt and B. Moeran (eds.), *Advertising Cultures*, Oxford, UK: Berg.

Malinowski, B. (1989), *A Diary in the Strict Sense of the Term*, Stanford, CA: Stanford University Press.

Manning, P. (2010), "The Semiotics of Brand," *Annual Review of Anthropology*, 39: 33–49.

Manovich, L. (2001), *The Language of New Media*, Cambridge, MA: MIT Press.

Marchand, R. (1985), *Advertising the American Dream*, Berkeley: University of California Press.

Marcus, G. (ed.) (1998), *Corporate Futures: The Diffusion of the Culturally Sensitive Corporate Form*, Chicago: University of Chicago Press.

Marcus, G., and Fischer, M. (1986), *Anthropology as Cultural Critique*, Chicago: University of Chicago Press.

Marx, K. (1954), *Capital: A Critique of Political Economy*, vol. 1, trans. S. Moore and E. A. Aveling, London: Lawrence & Wishart.

Marx, K. (1987), *Economics and Philosophic Manuscripts of 1844*, trans. M. Milligan, Buffalo, NY: Prometheus Books.

Maslow, A. (1968), *Toward a Psychology of Being*, 2nd ed., New York: Van Nostrand Reinhold.

Massey, D. (2005), *For Space*, London: Sage.

Mayer, M. (1957), *Madison Avenue U.S.A.*, New York: Pocket Books.

Mayle, P. (1990), *Up the Agency: The Funny Business of Advertising*, New York: St. Martin's Press.

Mazzarella, W. (2003a), "Critical Publicity/Public Criticism: Reflections on Fieldwork in the Bombay Ad World," in T. de Waal Malefyt and B. Moeran (eds.), *Advertising Cultures*, Oxford, UK: Berg.

Mazzarella, W. (2003b), *Shoveling Smoke: Advertising and Globalization in Contemporary India*, Durham, NC: Duke University Press.

McCabe, M. (2011), "Business Anthropology, the Future and Pursuit of Theoretical Directions," in R. G. Tian, D. Zhou, and A. van Marrewijk (eds.), *Advanced Readings in Business Anthropology*, Toronto: North American Press.

McCracken, G. (2005), "Homeyness: A Cultural Account of One Constellation of Consumer Goods and Meanings," in *Culture and Consumption II*, Bloomington: Indiana University Press.

McCracken, G. (2009), *Chief Culture Officer*, New York: Basic Books.

McCreery, J. (2000), *Japanese Consumer Behavior: From Worker Bees to Wary Consumers*, Honolulu: University of Hawaii Press.

McLuhan, M. ([1951] 1967), *The Mechanical Bride: Folklore of Industrial Man*, 2nd ed., Boston: Beacon Press.

McMurtry, J. (2004), "Building Your Brand through Emotional Connections," *Denver Business Journal*, October 18, http://denver.bizjournals.com/denver/stories/2004/10/18/smallb2.html.

McWilliams, N. (1999), *Psychoanalytic Case Formulation*, New York: Guilford Press.

Mead, M. (1928), *Coming of Age in Samoa*, New York: Morrow.

Meerwarth, T. L., Briody, E. K., and Kulkarni, D. M. (2005), "Discovering the Rules: Folk Knowledge for Improving GM Partnerships," *Human Organization*, 64: 286–302.

Michell, P.C.N., and Sanders, N. H. (1995), "Loyalty in Agency-Client Relations: The Impact of the Organizational Context," *Journal of Advertising Research*, March/April: 9–14.

Miller, A. (1990), "You Are What You Buy," *Newsweek*, June 4: 59.

Miller, D. (1995a), *Acknowledging Consumption*, London: Routledge.

Miller, D. (1995b), "Consumption and Commodities," *Annual Review of Anthropology*, 24: 141–61.

Miller, D. (1997), *Capitalism: An Ethnographic Approach*, Oxford, UK: Berg.

Miller, D. (ed.) (2001), *Car Cultures*, Oxford, UK: Berg.

Moeran, B. (1993), "A Tournament of Value: Strategies of Presentation in Japanese Advertising," *Ethos*, 54: 73–93.

Moeran, B. (1996), *A Japanese Advertising Agency*, Honolulu: University of Hawaii Press.

Moeran, B. (1984), "Individual, Group and Seishin: Japan's Internal Cultural Debate," *Man*, 19/2: 252–66.

Moeran, B. (2005), *The Business of Ethnography: Strategic Exchanges, People and Organizations*, Oxford, UK: Berg.

Moeran, B. (2006), *Ethnography at Work*, Oxford, UK: Berg.

Moeran, B. (2009), "Constraints and Creativity: The Case of Advertising in Japan," paper presented at the meeting of the American Anthropological Association, Philadelphia.

Moeran, B. (ed.) (2010), *Advertising: Critical Readings*, Oxford, UK: Berg.

Moeran, B., and Strandgaard Pedersen, J. (2011), *Negotiating Values in the Creative Industries: Fairs, Festivals and Competitive Events*, Cambridge, UK: Cambridge University Press.

Monari, G.L. (2005), "Anthropology: Not Just for Academia," *MedAdNews*, August: 1, 28–29.

Morais, R.J. (2009a), "Business Ethnography and the Discipline of Anthropology," *Quirk's Marketing Research Review*, February: 20–22.

Morais, R.J. (2009b), "Parallel Lines of Inquiry: Psychology and Anthropology as Complementary Methods for Tapping Respondent Emotions," paper presented to the Third Annual Institute of the Pharmaceutical Marketing Research Group, Philadelphia, October 25–27.

Morais, R.J. (2009c), "Spanning the Irrational Divide," *Adweek, Brandweek and Mediaweek*, June 22: AM2.

Morais, R.J. (2010), *Refocusing Focus Groups*, Ithaca, NY: Paramount Market Publishing.

Morais, R.J., and Barnhart, J. (2007), "Interactional Physician-Patient Research: A Path to Better Medical and Marketing Outcomes," *Product Management Today*, December: 47–50.

Mullins, P. (2011), "Practicing Anthropology and the Politics of Engagement: 2010 Year in Review," *American Anthropologist*, 113/2: 235–45.

Murphy, R.M. (2005), "Getting to Know You," *Fortune Small Business*, June: 41–46.

Neff, J. (2011), "Why the Trend of Global CMO Has Reached Its Tipping Point," *Advertising Age*, June 13, http://adage.com/article/cmo-strategy/trend-global-cmo-reached-tipping-point/228145.

O'Barr, W. (1994), *Culture and the Ad*, Boulder, CO: Westview Press.

Ogilvy, D. (1963), *Confessions of an Advertising Man*, New York: Atheneum.

Ogilvy, D. (1965), "The Creative Chef," in G.A. Steiner (ed.), *The Creative Organization*, Chicago: University of Chicago Press.

Ogilvy, D. ([1983] 1985), *Ogilvy on Advertising*, New York: Vintage Books.

Oldenburg, R. (1989), *The Great Good Place*, New York: Marlowe.

O'Looney, J.A., Gylnn, S.M., Britton, B.K., and Mattocks, L.F. (1989), "Cognition and Writing: The Idea Generation Process," in J.A. Glover, R.R. Ronning, and C.R. Reynolds (eds.), *Handbook of Creativity*, New York: Plenum.

Ortner, S. (1973), "On Key Symbols," *American Anthropologist*, 75/5: 1338–46.

Packard, V. (1957), *The Hidden Persuaders*, New York: David McKay.

Pannapacker, W. (2011), "Overeducated, Underemployed: How to Fix Humanities Grad School," *Slate*, July 27, www.slate.com/id/2300107.

Parkin, D. (1978), *The Cultural Definition of Political Response*, London: Academic Press.

Paulus, P.B., and Nijstad, B.A. (2003), *Group Creativity: Innovation through Collaboration*, New York: Oxford University Press.

Perry, N. (1998), *Hyperreality and Global Culture*, London: Routledge.

Pine, J.B., and Gilmore, J.H. (1999), *The Experience Economy*, Boston: Harvard Business School Press.

Polanyi, M. (1958), *Personal Knowledge*, Chicago: University of Chicago Press.

Postrel, V. (2003), *The Substance of Style*, New York: Harper-Collins.

Pratt, M.L. (1992), *Imperial Eyes: Travel Writing and Transculturation*, New York: Routledge.

Price, P. (2007), "Unleash Emotions for Business Growth," *Advertising Age*, March 12, http://adage.com/print/115494.

Provine, R. (2000), *Laughter: A Scientific Investigation*, New York: Penguin.

Putnam, R.D. (2000), *Bowling Alone*, New York: Simon & Schuster.

Rabinow, P. (1977), *Reflections on Fieldwork in Morocco*, Berkeley: University of California Press.

Rainey, M.T. (1997), "The Planning Context," in A. Cooper (ed.), *How to Plan Advertising*, 2nd ed., London: Cassell.

Rapaille, C. (2006), *The Culture Code*, New York: Broadway Books.

Reinharz, S. (1988), *On Becoming a Social Scientist*, Piscataway, NJ: Transaction Books.

Ritacco, G. (2010), "Ethnography Goes Digital," *Quirk's Marketing Research Review*, December 18: 20.

Robinette, S., and Brand, C., with Lenz, V. (2001), *Emotion Marketing*, New York: McGraw-Hill.

Rosaldo, R. (1980), *Ilongot Headhunting, 1883–1974: A Study in Society and History*, Stanford, CA: Stanford University Press.

Rosaldo, R. (1993), "Ilongot Visiting: Social Grace and the Rhythms of Everyday Life," in S. Lavie, K. Narayan, and R. Rosaldo (eds.), *Creativity/Anthropology*, Ithaca, NY: Cornell University Press.

Rosaldo, R., Lavie, S., and Narayan, K. (1993), "Introduction: Creativity in Anthropology," in S. Lavie, K. Narayan, and R. Rosaldo (eds.), *Creativity/Anthropology*, Ithaca, NY: Cornell University Press.

Rothenberg, R. (1994), *Where the Suckers Moon: An Advertising Story*, New York: Knopf.

Sabloff, J.A. (2011), "Where Have You Gone, Margaret Mead? Anthropology and Public Intellectuals," *American Anthropologist*, 113/2: 408–16.

Sacks, D. (2010), "The Future of Advertising," *Fast Company*, November 17, www. fastcompany.com/magazine/151/mayhem-on-madison-avenue.html.

Sanders, E. (2002), "How 'Applied Ethnography' Can Improve Your NPD Research Process," *PDMA Visions*, 26/2: 8–11.

Sapir, E. (1970), *Culture, Language and Personality*, ed. D.G. Mandelbaum, Berkeley: University of California Press.

Sartre, J.-P. (1965), *The Philosophy of Jean-Paul Sartre*, ed. R. Cumming, New York: Vintage Books.

Sawyer, R.K. (2003), *Group Creativity: Music, Theater, Collaboration*, Mahwah, NJ: Erlbaum.

Sawyer, R.K. (2006), *Explaining Creativity: The Science of Human Innovation*, New York: Oxford University Press.

Sawyer, R.K. (2007), *Group Genius: The Creative Power of Collaboration*, New York: Basic Books.

Sawyer, R.K., and DeZutter, S. (2009), "Distributed Creativity: How Collective Creations Emerge From Collaboration," *Psychology of Aesthetics, Creativity and the Arts*, 3/2: 81–92.

Schmitt, B. (1999), *Experiential Marketing: How to Get Customers to Sense, Feel, Think, Act, Relate to your Company and Brands*, New York: Free Press.

Schroeder, J.E., and Salzer-Morling, M. (2006), "Introduction: The Cultural Codes of Branding," in J.E. Schroeder and M. Salzer-Morling (eds.), *Brand Culture*, London: Routledge.

Schudson, M. (1984), *Advertising: The Uneasy Persuasion*, New York: Basic Books.

Schultz, D., and Pilotta, J. (2005), "Developing the Foundation for a New Approach to Understanding How Media Works," presented at 3rd Annual ESOMAR/ARF World Audience Measurement Conference, June 13–18, Geneva.

Schultz, K. (2010), *Being Wrong: Adventures in the Margin of Error*, New York: HarperCollins.

Schwartz, T., White, G.M., and Lutz, C.A. (eds.) (1992), *New Directions in Psychological Anthropology*, Cambridge, UK: Cambridge University Press.

Schwartzman, H. (1989), *The Meeting*, New York: Plenum.

Sengir, G.H., Trotter, R.T., Briody, E.K., Kulkarni, D.M., Catlin, L.B., and Meerwarth, T.L. (2004), "Modeling Relationship Dynamics in GM's Research-Institution," *Journal of Manufacturing Technology Management*, 15/7: 541–59.

Serf, B.J. (2007), "A Day in the Life of Your Consumers," *Medical Marketing and Media*, March: 61–64.

Sherry, J.F. (1987), "Advertising as a Cultural System," in J. Umiker-Sebeok (ed.), *Marketing and Semiotics: New Directions in the Study of Signs for Sale*, Berlin: Mouton de Gruyter.

Sherry, J. F. (2003), "Foreword: A Word from Our Sponsor Anthropology," in T. de Waal Malefyt and B. Moeran (eds.), *Advertising Cultures*, Oxford, UK: Berg.

Sherry, J. F. (2005), "We Might Never Be Post-Sacred: A Tribute to Russell Belk on the Occasion of His Acceptance of the Converse Award," in A. Griffin and C. C. Otnes (eds.), *16th Paul D. Converse Symposium*, Chicago: American Marketing Association.

Sherry, J. F. (2008), "The Ethnographer's Apprentice: Trying Consumer Culture from the Outside In," *Journal of Business Ethics*, 80: 85–95.

Sherry, J. F., Borghini, S., Muñiz, A., McGrath, M. A., Diamond, N., and Kozinets, R. (2009), "Allomother as Image and Essence: Animating the American Girl Brand," in J. F. Sherry and E. Fisher (eds.), *Explorations in Consumer Culture Theory*, London: Routledge.

Shweder, R. A. (1979a), "Rethinking Culture and Personality, Part I: A Critical Examination of Two Classical Postulates," *Ethos*, 7/3: 255–78.

Shweder, R. A. (1979b), "Rethinking Culture and Personality, Part II: A Critical Examination of Two More Classical Postulates," *Ethos*, 7/4: 279–311.

Shweder, R. A. (1980), "Rethinking Culture and Personality, Part III: From Genesis and Typology to Hermeneutics and Dynamics," *Ethos*, 8/1: 60–94.

Shweder, R. A. (2003), *Why Do Men Barbecue?* Cambridge, MA: Harvard University Press.

Shweder, R. A., and LeVine, R. A. (eds.) (1984), *Culture Theory: Essays on Mind, Self, and Emotion*, Cambridge, UK: Cambridge University Press.

Singer, N. (2011), "Making Ads That Whisper to the Brain," *New York Times*, November 14: 4.

Spatz, I. (2011), "Better Drug Ads, Fewer Side Effects," *New York Times*, February 10: A25.

Spradley, J. (ed.) (1972), *Culture and Cognition*, San Francisco: Chandler.

Squires, S., and Byrne, B. (eds.) (2002), *Creating Breakthrough Ideas: The Collaboration of Anthropologists and Designers in the Product Development Industry*, Westport, CT: Bergin and Garvey.

Steel, J. (1998), *Truth, Lies and Advertising: The Art of Account Planning*, New York: John Wiley.

Stewart, K. (1996), *A Space on the Side of the Road*, Princeton, NJ: Princeton University Press.

Stewart, D., Prem Shamdasani, N., and Dennis, W. R. (2007), *Focus Groups: Theory and Practice*, Thousand Oaks: Sage Publications.

Stoller, P. (2009), *The Power of the Between*, Chicago: University of Chicago Press.

Strathern, M. (1999), *Property, Substance and Effect: Anthropological Essays on Persons and Things*, London: Athlone Press.

Suchman, L. (2007), "Anthropology as Brand: Reflections on Corporate Anthropology," paper presented at the Colloquium on Interdisciplinary and Society, Oxford University, February 24.

Sunderland, P.L., and Denny, R.M. (2003), "Psychology vs. Anthropology: Where Is Culture in Marketplace Ethnography?" in T. de Waal Malefyt and B. Moeran (eds.), *Advertising Cultures*, Oxford, UK: Berg.

Sunderland, P.L., and Denny, R.M. (2007), *Doing Anthropology in Consumer Research*, Walnut Creek, CA: Left Coast Press.

Sunderland, P., Taylor, E.G., and Denny R. (2004), "Being Mexican and American: Negotiating Ethnicity in the Practice of Market Research," *Human Organization*, 63/3: 373–80.

Synnott, A. (1991), "Puzzling over the Senses: From Plato to Marx," in D. Howes (ed.), *The Varieties of Sensory Experience: A Sourcebook in the Anthropology of the Senses*, Toronto: University of Toronto Press.

Taussig, M. (2003), *Law in a Lawless Land*, New York: W.W. Norton.

Tedlock, D., and Mannheim, B. (eds.) (1995), *The Dialogic Emergence of Culture*, Urbana and Chicago: University of Illinois Press.

Thrift, N. (2000), "Performing Cultures in the New Economy," *Annals of the Association of American Geographers*, 90/4: 674–92.

Tian, R.G., Lillis, M.P., and Van Marrewijk, A.H. (2010), *General Business Anthropology*, Toronto: North American Business Press.

TNS Media Intelligence (2006), *Industry Report*, February.

Trotter, R.T., Briody, E.K., Sengir, G.H., and Meerwarth, T.L. (2008), "The Life Cycle of Collaborative Partnerships: Evolutionary Structure in Industry-University Research Networks," *Connections*, 28/1: 40–58.

Turner, E.S. (1953), *The Shocking History of Advertising*, New York: Ballantine Books.

Turner, V.W. (1964), "Betwixt and Between: The Liminal Period in Rites de Passage," in *Proceedings of the American Ethnological Society, Symposium on New Approaches to the Study of Religion*, Washington, DC: U.S. Government Printing Office.

Turner, V.W. (1969), *The Ritual Process: Structure and Anti-structure*, New York: Aldine.

Turner, V.W. (1974), *Dramas, Fields and Metaphors: Symbolic Action in Human Society*, Ithaca, NY: Cornell University Press.

Turner, V.W. (1988), *The Anthropology of Performance*, New York: PAJ Publications.

Turow, J. (1984), *Media Industries: The Production of News and Entertainment*, New York: Longman.

Turow, J. (2006), *Niche Envy: Marketing Discrimination in the Digital Age*, Cambridge, MA: MIT Press.

Twitchell, J. (2004), *Branded Nation*, New York: Simon & Schuster.

Tyler, S.A. (ed.) (1969), *Cognitive Anthropology*, New York: Holt, Rinehart and Winston.

Underhill, P. (1999), *Why We Buy*, New York: Touchstone.

Van Gennep, A. ([1909] 1960), *The Rites of Passage*, Chicago: University of Chicago Press.

Van Maanen, J. (1988), *Tales of the Field: On Writing Ethnography*, Chicago: University of Chicago Press.

Vangkilde, K. T. (2011), "A Funky-Formal Fashion Collection: On Entering a Space Betwixt and Between and the Creativity of Uncertainty," paper presented at the Evaluative Practices of Creativity in the Creative Industry, Copenhagen, September.

Von Hippel, E. (2005), *Democratizing Innovation*, Cambridge, MA: MIT Press.

Walcoff, M. (2006), "Image Boost for an Entire Brand: Head of GM's Cadillac Division in Town for Grand Opening of Forbes Showroom," *The Record* (Kitchener-Waterloo, Ontario), May 5: C6.

Wallace, A.F.C. (1970), *Culture and Personality*, 2nd ed., New York: Random House.

Wasserman, T. (2003), "Watch and Learn," *Adweek*, November 3: 21–22.

Wasson, C. (2000), "Ethnography in the Field of Design," *Human Organization*, 59/4: 377–88.

Wax, M. L. (1987), "Some Issues and Sources on Ethics in Anthropology," in J. Cassell and S. E. Jacobs (eds.), *Handbook on Ethical Issues in Anthropology*, Washington, DC: American Anthropological Association.

Weiner, A. (1976), *Women of Value, Men of Renown: New Perspectives in Trobriand Exchange*, Austin: University of Texas Press.

Wellner, A. S. (2002), "Watch Me Now," *American Demographics*, October: S1–S5.

Whiting, J.W.M., and Child, I. L. (1953), *Child Training and Personality*, New Haven, CT: Yale University Press.

Williamson, J. (1978), *Decoding Advertising*, London: Barion Boyars.

Wilson, E. O. (1998), *Consilience: The Unity of Knowledge*, New York: Knopf.

Wilson, E. (2003), *Adorned in Dreams: Fashion and Modernity*, New Brunswick, NJ: Rutgers University Press.

Wittgenstein, L. ([1953] 2009) *Philosophical Investigations*, 4th ed., London: Wiley-Blackwell.

Young, C. E. (2000), "Creative Differences Between Copy Writers and Art Directors," *Journal of Advertising Research*, May/June: 19–26.

Young, J. W. (1946), *The Diary of an Ad Man*, original from the University of Virginia, Charlottesville, VA: Advertising Publications.

Young, J. W. ([1963] 2001), *How to Become an Advertising Man*, New York: McGraw-Hill.

Zaltman, G. (2003), *How Customers Think*, Boston: Harvard Business School Press.

Zukin, S. (2004), *Point of Purchase: How Shopping Changed American Culture*, New York: Routledge.

Zwick, D., and Cayla, J. (2011), *Inside Marketing: Practices, Ideologies, Devices*, Oxford, UK: Oxford University Press.

Index